Thinking Peace

Also by Michael Sky

Breathing
The Power of Emotion
Dancing With the Fire
Sexual Peace

Thinking Peace

How We the Peaceful
Can Wake Up, Connect,
Share Power, Get Healthy,
and End the War on Terra

Michael Sky

Copyright © 2007 by Michael Sky

All rights reserved. Manufactured in the United States of America. Except as permitted under the United States Copyright Act of 1976, no part of this publication may be reproduced or distributed in any form or by any means, or stored in a database or retrieval system, without the prior written permission of the publisher.

Library of Congress Cataloging-in-Publication Data

Sky, Michael, 1951-
Thinking Peace: How We the Peaceful can Wake Up, Connect, Share Power, Get Healthy and End the War on Terra / Michael Sky
    v. cm.
Contents: 1. The Dangerous Logic of Domination — 2. The Dominist Manifesto — 3. The Common Infection — 4. Bias, Denial and the Status Quo — 5. The End of Democracy — 6. Thinking Peace — 7. Living Peace — 8. Making Peace.

ISBN 978-1-4303-1852-1

Contents

1. **The Dangerous Logic of Domination**: The Parable of the Tribes; Viral Dominism; Pandemic

2. **The Dominist Manifesto**: Might Makes Right Makes Might; With God On One Side; Still A Man's World; Different, Therefore Less Than; The Tyranny of the Bottom Line; Competing Values; Secret Governance; The War on Terra

3. **The Common Infection**: Dominism Embodied; Gender War; Poisonous Pedagogy; The Family of Man

4. **Bias, Denial and the Status Quo**: Media Bias; Living in Denial; Political Denial

5. **The End of Democracy**: Cowboy Diplomacy; We the Silenced; Domocracy

6. **Thinking Peace**: The War on Everything; Waking Up; The Light of Awareness; The Best Disinfectant

7. **Living Peace**: Rational Defense; E Pluribus Unum; One People, Many Gods; Differently Equal; Gender Peace; For the Common Good; Humanature

8. **Making Peace**: The Cycle of Fear; Connect and Conquer; Talking Peace; The Parable Resolved

Acknowledgments

With gratitude:

to Andrew Bard Schmookler, Alice Miller, Niro Asistent, and Riane Eisler, for the core ideas;

to James Bertolino, whose poetry always turns my thinking toward peace;

to the folks at Lulu.com, for making self-publishing fun and easy;

to Anita Holladay, for her wise and incisive editing;

to an unknown 13th-century wood carver, for the cover illustration;

to Penny and Lily, just because.........

Preface

We gathered in the village green a few days after the attacks of 9/11 to offer our thoughts and prayers, to memorialize the dead, and to console the living. It's a small town, so I knew most of the people who came that day, and all of the speakers. Yet as I listened to my neighbors struggling to bring meaning to that terrible time, I felt a growing disquiet.

I was immediately put off by all the appeals to patriotic pride. Several speakers stressed that America had suffered through an evil like none the world had ever known and that the thousands who died deserved special standing in the history of human conflict. Moreover, they proclaimed that America's response had been uniquely heroic: that the rush of emergency workers into the doomed buildings was a distinctly American act, as was the very depth and manner of our mourning.

But it was not only Americans who died on 9/11 and the continuing threat of international terrorism was obviously not just America's problem. Chest-thumping proclamations of America's greatness would strike many, friends and foes alike, as aggressive assertions of American dominance, inappropriate to the moment, and generally offensive. I simply could not understand the need to wave the flag at such a time.

Even more troubling were the calls for violence. Before any of the facts were in or any attempt had been made to understand what had happened—before we knew exactly who had attacked us and why—decent Americans were calling for violent retribution. No one mentioned that such vengeance would surely cause the deaths of thousands of innocent civilians somewhere else in the world, giving the decent people of that country good reason to answer with yet more vengeance.

As I listened my disquiet turned into the awful certainty that a new, especially horrific cycle of violence had been loosed on us all.

Internationally, 9/11 had invoked an extraordinary call for solidarity. "We are all Americans!" proclaimed a French newspaper, a sentiment that was echoed worldwide. For a fleeting moment we became one planet, united in pain and grieving collectively. It seemed possible that something good would ultimately emerge from those evil acts.

But most Americans doubted overtures of global unity and spurned offers of assistance. By insisting on American exceptionalism—none have suffered as we have or acted as heroically—we insulted and belittled would-be friends. By asserting American dominance—we will respond in our way, on our terms, and without reference to the concerns of others—we split the briefly uniting nations back into separate actors. By threatening with American military power—you're with us or against us, and any suffering we inflict on others is justified beyond question—we pushed people everywhere down a path of ever-increasing violence.

The events of 9/11 had presented Americans with a clear choice: wage war or make peace. We could either set off to destroy other nations, killing thousands of non-combatants in the process, or we could join with other nations to do the hard work of making peace. Yet few considered the possibility of making peace, and most could not even imagine it. *Thinking Peace* is about that failure of imagination. Not just, "Why are we so prone to violence?" but "Why can't we even imagine living in peace?"

Because we could not imagine making peace after 9/11, America dragged the entire world into an ever-darkening morass of violence and war. While all Americans share some responsibility for decisions made and actions taken, ultimate responsibility rests with American leadership, and especially with President George W. Bush. Beginning with his first post-9/11 speech, Bush has epitomized the dangerous logic and consequences of the wage-war mentality. *Thinking Peace* tracks the first few years of the Bush administration, showing how specific policies and actions invariably increased international tensions and made the world more violence-driven and war-mad.

Yet *Thinking Peace* was not written to bash the president. Bush merely demonstrates tendencies that go to the heart of American culture. His presidency has thus provided an example-rich model for the wage-war mindset that I explore in great length.

I finished the first draft of *Thinking Peace* just before the invasion of Iraq and am writing this introduction three-and-a-half years later. In the time in between, America has endured an astonishing series of events: the whole shameful fiasco of the war on Iraq; the missing weapons of mass destruction; Abu Ghraib and other instances of American torture of its prisoners; revelation of the illegal wiretapping of American citizens; the swift-boating of John Kerry, followed by evidence of another badly-tainted election; hurricane Katrina; the suspension of habeas corpus; a series of congressional corruption scandals, flanked by a series of corporate greed scandals; the continuing inaction on the threat of global climate change and other environmental issues; and, really, too many more to list.

Everything that has happened since the invasion of Iraq has confirmed the main points of *Thinking Peace*. As long as America maintains a militaristic, unilateralist, wage-war approach toward international conflicts, the world will suffer through increasing violence and unending war. Mr. Bush's "global war on terror" has only made us a more terror-stricken planet. The more America wages its war for national security, the more international insecurity it causes.

I should mention that *Thinking Peace* does not provide a solution to the war in Iraq. While the book describes several key steps for shifting as individuals, groups, and nations from waging war to making peace, they are for the most part actions best taken before conflict erupts into violence. It is disingenuous in the extreme to demand in the midst of an all-out war that those who opposed the war in the first place now demonstrate how to make peace. For wars rarely end in peace; rather, they end when one side runs out of the bodies, arms, money, and will required to continue fighting.

The way to make peace in Iraq was to let the pre-war sanctions and inspections run their course. Had we opted for genuine negotiations with Saddam Hussein, as opposed to name-calling and vilification, we could have avoided violence altogether and spared Iraq the horrors of invasion and civil war. There will not be another opportunity for real peace in Iraq until the occupation forces have departed and the Iraqi people are free to decide matters with their own best interests in mind.

Likewise, we will never win the global war on terror as long as we insist on thinking of it as a war. Waging war against terrorists only creates more terrorism in the world. Anti-terror military campaigns always terrorize innocent civilians, and of those who survive such onslaughts some will always feel justified in seeking vengeance.

Five years after 9/11, a gunman with a 20-year grudge walked into a one-room Amish schoolhouse and systematically executed five young girls before taking his own life. As the Amish prepared to bury their dead, they invited the wife and parents of the gunman to attend the services. Americans were astonished by their actions, but to the Amish it was a simple matter: only through such forgiveness could the living hope to move forward in peace. Anything less than such forgiveness and, especially, any thoughts toward violent retribution would insure more heartbreaking loss and suffering in the future.

We end the cycle of violence by refusing to engage in violence. This requires a radical change of mind from thinking war to thinking peace. As thinking peace becomes our prevailing worldview, then we naturally start living more peacefully. When enough of us have learned to live in peace, then the long-overdue work of making a peaceful world can begin.

Michael Sky | February 2007

Part One

The War on Terra

Was there ever any domination which did not
appear natural to those who possessed it?

—John Stuart Mill

Terrorism is the war of the poor,
and war is the terrorism of the rich.

—Peter Ustinov

One

The Dangerous Logic of Domination

The terrible thing is that once you stray from absolute nonviolence you open the door for the most shocking abuses.
—Howard Zinn[1]

    The terrorist attacks of September 11, 2001 shook America to its core and pushed its people into two distinct camps. Some pleaded the cause of nonviolence, asking that we look to the motives of the attackers, that we examine the prior actions of America that may have fed such motives, that we soberly pursue peaceful communication, negotiation, and reconciliation, while using minimal force to bring the guilty parties to justice. As has proven the case throughout history, only a small percentage of Americans advocated for such peacemaking.

    The vast majority looked to their leaders to respond with overwhelming force. Their arguments ran the gamut from gaining vengeance and retribution, to displaying strength and acting with pride, to deterring future terrorists, to waging a worldwide crusade against evil. The country swiftly flared into war fever, with flags and ribbons flying everywhere. Good people struggled to sound righteous and reasonable as they spoke of the need to bomb third-world countries, even at the sure cost of innocent lives. More moderate voices were ignored, marginalized, and accused of hating their country.

    In a speech before the full U.S. Congress in which President George W. Bush announced a "new war on terrorism," he made clear that America intended to force its solution with little regard for what others thought or wanted. He defined the causes of the conflict solely on American terms and without any reference to American culpability in events leading up to the attacks of 9/11. He issued ultimatums to the rest of the world: "If you do not stand with us in this fight then you stand against us." After reading a list of demands to the people of Afghanistan, he warned, "We will not negotiate."

This last, coming from a man who had already pulled his country out of several international treaties, was said with great pride. We will not negotiate, because we have no need to negotiate, no need for talk, no need to listen to the opinions of others, let alone any grievances. Only the weak and defeated call for negotiation. Deriving power from the bully pulpit, Bush strutted America's position as global bully. He drew a schoolyard line in the sand and spit in the faces of any who dared to disagree.

For most Americans, the President's speech struck all the right notes. He had seized the moment, stood tall, rallied the troops, and inspired national pride. Most importantly, he had made the case for swift and overwhelming force as the country prepared to answer its enemies.

Few Americans considered peacemaking responses. According to the prevailing mindset, negotiating with the terrorists would have dishonored those murdered on 9/11. Changing America's behavior in any way that might suit the terrorists would have given credence to their actions and invited more of the same. Conducting an examination of the past, with an eye toward specific actions that may have caused other people to feel such anti-American hostility, seemed the worst of treason, as if it would absolve the terrorists while pointing the finger of blame at Americans. Meaningful deterrence demanded that America strike back first and talk later. Righteousness, justice, and the American way required an eye for an eye—we must do unto them as they did unto us and before they do it again.

America responded to violence the way powerful countries always do. In meeting violence with a call for even greater violence, America followed a pattern of geopolitical relationship that has driven our world for thousands of years. As the most powerful party in its conflict with a small band of religious fanatics, America moved to coerce, force, compel, and demand its way, to exert and strengthen its domination of all opposition at home and abroad. "We will not negotiate," the President declared; America would define the issues, decide upon the best course of action, and then inflict her infinite justice, at whatever the costs.

I will be using the term "dominism" to cover this whole pattern of relationship. Deriving from the Latin *dominari* (to rule) and *dominus* (Lord), dominism refers to a way of resolving social conflicts according to which party can best force matters to its advantage. Like "racist" or "sexist," "dominist" serves as both noun and adjective to describe dominism-driven individuals and behaviors. Dominists use their powers to force weaker groups and individuals into submission. In a dominist system, people make decisions and resolve conflicts not through democratic, moral, just, cooperative, or reasonable principles; rather, the dominant parties in a dominist system make all critical decisions according to self-serving criteria and then force others to comply.

In her groundbreaking book, *The Chalice and the Blade*, Riane Eisler introduced and has since written extensively about what she calls "the dominator model." She explains that beyond "conventional classifications—religious versus secular, tribal versus industrial, right versus left, capitalist versus communist—are two underlying ways of structuring relations," that she refers to as domination and partnership. "They're actually two opposite poles, with a continuum in between. At one end of this continuum is the dominator society. Dominator societies have existed throughout history and have the same basic plan, whether it's Attila's Huns, Hitler's Germany or the Taliban's Afghanistan. These societies consist of rigid top-down rankings, of "superiors" over "inferiors," men over women, adults over children, "in-groups" over "out-groups"—rankings backed up by force and the threat of force in homes, in society, and between societies in chronic wars."[2]

This model closely corresponds to the definitions of power used by ecofeminist and writer Starhawk. Starhawk writes of "power-over," the power to dominate and control others; "power-from-within," the force of our own personal abilities and potentials; and "power-with," the influence we wield among equals. For our purposes, power-over describes the essential dynamic of dominist relationship, while power-from-within and power-with together give the full sense of partnership, cooperation, and what I shall refer to as thinking, living, and making peace.

All people wield certain forms and degrees of power manifesting as physical, mental, and creative strengths; personal wealth; legal, religious and political standing in the community; and access to and control of weapons and warriors. We act either as dominists or peacemakers depending on how we use our powers. We either join with others in the pursuit of common goals and the nonviolent resolution of conflicts or we exert our powers over others, using as much force as necessary in order to dominate events to our advantage.

Both sides in the current war on terrorism act from the same dominist underpinnings. The terrorists and the anti-terror fighters all believe that by inflicting sufficient terror they can force their enemies into submission. The attacks on America and the ensuing "new war" unfolded from the beginning as a classic dominist struggle with both sides resorting to as much violence as deemed necessary to achieve their goals.

All dominist systems begin with the threat and use of force. The force can range from the extreme violence of murder and war, to the moderated violence of slavery, rape, homeland destruction, and property plunder, to the more civilized tactics of monotheism, sexism, racism, crony capitalism, targeted law enforcement, partisan politics, and various societal sanctions. The best dominist systems use as little force as possible to keep the underlings in line. Yet however velvet the glove, successful dominist systems always resort to terrorizing violence when necessary. All dominism ultimately derives from violence and inevitably involves the infliction of some degree of fear, ranging to terror, upon one person or group by another. Whenever the dominant party in a relationship uses violence or just the threat of violence to coerce behavior, the submissive or losing party has been terrorized.

When an employer makes clear the ability to fire any employee who does not follow orders, that softly-communicated threat conceals a big stick of potential terror: loss of livelihood, loss of self-esteem, loss of home, of family, and of life itself. When a man makes

The Dangerous Logic of Domination

clear his capacity to use his superior size and strength to force his way with a woman, he injects an undertone of dominist terror into all of their interactions. When a parent makes clear that a spanking will follow any childish act of disobedience, the whole family gets twisted into a terror-infected, dominist system. Though much of the dominism of modern culture has a civilized veneer, the reality of coercive force and violence always looms beneath the surface.

Dominism has been the prevailing mode of human social intercourse for thousands of years. It appeared first in early conquering tribes and has since defined the conduct of organized groups through times of empire-builders, crusaders, imperialists, inquisitors, conquistadors, colonialists, dictators, tsars, führers, and a thousand petty tyrants. Scanning human history, we see the heavy hand of the dominist in all times and places directing the course of events. The exigencies, demands, and abuses of dominism have come to color every aspect of human relationship and have shaped our world so thoroughly as to make violent struggle seem natural and inevitable. We consider it human nature that the strong resort to some degree of force whenever necessary in order to dominate the weak. Law of the jungle, we say. Might makes right, dog eats dog, to the victor belongs the spoils. Survival of the fittest.

This last bit of social Darwinism provides all the intellectual cover that modern dominists ever need. In the dominist worldview, people find themselves locked in a forever struggle over finite resources and only the fit—the strongest, the smartest, the richest, the most capable of forcing their way on others—will survive, indeed, should survive. The weak, the ignorant, the poor, and the passive deserve failure. Their passing only improves the gene pool. The meek should neither inherit nor bequeath.

Thus, in any conflict, the most dominant have every right, in fact, should feel compelled to pursue their best interests, at whatever the costs to others and with as much force and inflicting as much terror as necessary. Secular dominists see this as an eat-or-be-eaten fact of life and Law of Nature, beyond question or debate. Religious dominists hear God's own voice whispering in their ears, assuring them that God is on their side, that they are doing God's work, and that any harm to others merely fulfills God's will. Dominists of all persuasions consider too much reflection on these matters as distracting and potentially weakening.

The Parable of the Tribes

Imagine a group of tribes living within reach of one another. If all choose the way of peace, then all may live in peace. But what if all but one chooses peace?

—**Andrew Bard Schmookler**[3]

The Parable of the Tribes is both the title of a book and an elegant theory of social evolution offered by Andrew Bard Schmookler. Schmookler focuses on the seeming inevitability of coercive power in human affairs. He defines power as "the capacity to achieve one's will against the will of another. The exercise of power thus infringes upon the exercise of choice, for to be the object of another's power is to have his choice substituted for one's own."[4]

Schmookler suggests that coercive power became an issue in human relations when the activities of differing groups began to encroach upon one another. Steady increases in human population eventually brought individual societies, or tribes, into contact. Natural conflict arose over mutual needs and desires for land and resources. "As the expanding capacities of human societies created an overlap in the range of their grasp and desire, the intersocietal struggle for power arose."[5] Some societies, exercising their freedom of choice, began to infringe upon the free will of other societies. The society that could best "infringe upon" or dominate others tended toward more certain survival.

Schmookler's question, "What if all but one choose peace?," is the crux of the Parable of the Tribes. If, in the pursuit of conflicting desires, one society resorts to coercive domination, then every other society of necessity gets driven into dominist patterns of relationship. A peaceful society, under attack, faces three choices—to fight back, successfully or not; to retreat to new territories; or to surrender to

The Dangerous Logic of Domination

either eradication or assimilation into the dominator's culture. (We will explore a fourth choice, the ways of peacemaking, in the second half of this book). However, "in every one of these outcomes the ways of power are spread throughout the system."[6]

The inevitable spread of power-over dynamics appears most obviously in the choice to fight back. Once a society decides on a course of warfare it undergoes a series of predictable changes. Social resources shift from the common welfare to the stockpiling of weapons and building of armaments. Boys and men start training in the ways of making war at the expense of other avocations, studies, and labors. Because of their natural advantages in size, strength, and testosterone, and their freedom from pregnancy, childbirth, and early childcare, men-as-a-group take dominance over women-as-a-group in positions of leadership and resource allocation. Laws and social mores become militarized, as the everyday conduct of the people bows to the demands of preparing for war, even in times of relative peace. Religious texts and sermons turn to angry and vengeful deities who give holy justification to crusades and jihads. Eventually, the legends, stories, songs, art, myths, histories, and dreams of a people all take on the harsher tones and harder beats of human aggression.

This shift to dominist culture occurs for both winners and losers at war. Once touched by the social contamination of organized violence, the ways of dominism take over like a chronic, systemic infection. For some societies, dominism rages with acute intensity, leading to dictatorships, police states, pogroms, populace "cleansings," and a terrible history of social controls from the Spanish Inquisition to Mao's Cultural Revolution to the Taliban's twisted *fatwahs*. Other societies, such as America, manage to institutionalize and consecrate enough individual freedoms and civil rights to somewhat mitigate the worst of dominism, at least during times of peace and prosperity.

The second option for a society facing attack—to retreat to new territories—worked as a viable response in early human history. As long as a tribe was not overly attached to its present home, had few important possessions, and could still find suitable, unpopulated lands to emigrate to, then retreating from an aggressor allowed for the survival of culture unaffected by dominism. However, with the shift from gatherer-hunter tribes to land-based agrarian societies that had significant holdings and meaningful investments in place, retreating societies became but sorry and submissive refugees. Even if they could find unpopulated land, the magnitude of their loss inflicted the chronic curse of dominism upon them.

Moreover, as our world has become more crowded, refugees rarely find unpopulated lands. If, on the one hand, a retreating culture has happened upon a peaceful and/or less militarily advanced culture, then the refugees have turned dominist and colonized the "new" territories. In every such case of colonization, the resulting society has begun with and grown from deep dominist roots. When, on the other hand, the retreating culture has arrived at a strong, dominist culture, then the refugees have bargained for the best assimilation into the dominant culture that they could manage. Invariably, they have remained a submissive underclass for several generations at best, and in some cases permanently. In every outcome, then, retreat eventually leads a people to dominism.

Yet if both fighting back and running away either destroy or fundamentally alter a once peaceful culture, submission in the face of dominism does no better. Throughout history, societies that have met aggression passively have been overrun, looted, dismantled, enslaved, colonized, renamed, reformed, absorbed, and assimilated. Societies that merely turn the other cheek face some form of failure ranging from utter destruction, to living under an occupier, to assimilation into dominist culture. Should a passive group manage to maintain its unique identity and even survive to throw off its occupier in the future, it will nonetheless undergo the same inevitable shifting toward culture-wide dominism as if it had fought back from the start. The self-perpetuating power-over of dominism overwhelms any passive society it encounters and ultimately turns all social institutions toward abusive, power-over dynamics.

The Second World War proved the utter futility of mere pacifism. First, the allied appeasement of Hitler opened the way for the Nazi blitzkrieg of much of Europe and thus allowed a localized dominist outbreak to explode into a planet-threatening terror. Even worse, the almost uniformly passive response of the world in the face of the Holocaust made it possible for the Nazis to slaughter millions of people with few casualties of their own. We now call World War II a "good war" because we can easily see the righteousness of the Allied cause and the clear necessity (in that case) of fighting back.

What I have called "mere pacifism"—in contrast to the active and relatively forceful peacemaking that we will explore later—has proven similarly futile throughout history. In the short term, pacifists lay their bodies down like doormats, opening the way for dominists to greater conquest. Terror-driven dominists will not trifle over the finely spun arguments and radiant lives of even the most noble pacifists, but will simply flick the sword and have done with them, and then go on to trample yet more undefended people.

Lovers of peace cannot avoid this hard truth: dominism spreads like fire in a bone-dry forest and to struggle against it usually means to become consumed by it. Schmookler calls this "the dangerous logic of power." When people resolve conflicts according to which party has the greater capacity for aggressive force, then logically and invariably the world reduces to power-over dynamics rooted in violence. We cannot escape this dangerous logic by fighting back, by running away, or by passively submitting. Once the dominist's means and methods enter into the human equation, all human relations slide into dominism, the rule of force, violence, and terror.

Viral Dominism

One aggressive and potent actor upon the scene can impose on each of the others the necessity of gaining power to protect itself, or the inevitability of becoming absorbed into the power of another. Thus, because power acts as a contaminant, it is also in such a system a necessity.

—**Andrew Bard Schmookler**[7]

We have to understand that terrorism is fundamentally a "meme"—a kind of "virus of the mind," a set of beliefs and attitudes that spreads from person to person. One way to squelch terrorism is to kill or arrest the people whose brains are infected with the meme, and the Bush administration has done some of that effectively. But some forms of killing and arresting—especially the kinds that get us bad publicity—do so much to spread the meme that our enterprise suffers a net loss.

—**Robert Wright**[8]

We often refer to the sort of fanatics who perpetrated the crimes of 9/11 as "true believers." The term recognizes the fact that such individuals hold absolute and unwavering beliefs about life that compel their extreme behavior. Suicide bombers typically believe that their violence fulfills God's will; that it guarantees them blessings in the afterlife; that it brings joy and honor to their family and friends; that it addresses the crimes that they and their loved ones have suffered at the hands of others; that all nonviolent means of conflict resolution have been exhausted; and that their terrorizing actions offer the best and only way to serve God, family, culture, and the soul's cry for justice.

Rather than just dismiss these people as evil miscreants we would do better to appreciate the creative power of beliefs (for good and evil) and to explore ways to alter the beliefs in ourselves and others that so inexorably feed into cycles of violence. While responding to terrorism with overwhelming military force may temporarily stem the flow of bomb-wielding zealots, in the long run it increases their numbers by fanning the fires of fanatical belief. The more furious the fight against terrorism, the more surely and widely the formative beliefs of the terrorists spread. Only by revealing the underlying systems of belief on both sides of any conflict can we ever hope to reach a mutual understanding, much less work toward genuine resolution.

Like the software in a personal computer—lines and lines of digitized thought that tell the computer what it can and cannot do and how to do it—an individual's beliefs comprise a constellation of declarative thoughts that largely determine the limits and possibilities of life and the way most everything works, including the body, other people, nature, and God. To the extent that one believes in Santa Claus, or in this morning's weather report, or that sugar rots your teeth, or that Italians all belong to the Mafia, or that girls can't do arithmetic, or that Jesus was born of a virgin, or that God rewards suicide bombers, one becomes programmed to a specific worldview and lifestyle. That most beliefs actually fail to describe the true nature of things matters little; whatever the beliefs, and especially those most tenaciously held, they create a self-contained and, to the believer, logically consistent world.

Just as different software can make a computer function in totally different ways, each of us thinks, feels, and behaves according to the beliefs encoded within; we only ever change how we think, feel, or behave by altering our beliefs—in essence by rewriting our software. However, precisely because beliefs play such a central, omnipresent, and controlling role in our existence, it can prove difficult to change them.

Our beliefs form an all-encompassing psychoemotional lens through which we perceive reality and respond to events. While we deride optimists for looking at the world through rose-colored glasses, in fact we all look out at the world through glasses colored by cherished beliefs. We tend to see the world we most believe in (believing is seeing) and to experience other people acting as we believe they will act. Try though we may, we cannot separate reality and the nature of things from our beliefs about "the truth." Whatever *is* true, we have so colored it with our personal beliefs as to render it undecipherable.

Scientists have long struggled to overcome this dilemma by structuring investigative techniques, such as double-blind experiments, that rule out human beliefs and biases so that truth can emerge. Yet the findings of quantum physics strongly suggest that the mere act of observation changes the observed, that experimenter's bias seeps into all experiments, and that human consciousness plays a key role in the creation of objective reality. Our inner world to some degree influences manifestation in the outer world; much of that influence stems from our personal belief systems.

The creative power of beliefs begins with this perceptual bias—we see what we believe we will see—and then extends into our actions. We naturally respond to people and events based largely on our perceptions. If we believe Muslims side with the terrorists, then we will find ourselves reacting defensively around anyone who looks (to us) Middle Eastern. If we believe black men in expensive cars most likely got there by dealing drugs, then we will stop, harass, and arrest such drivers in disproportionate numbers. If we believe that life constitutes an unending competitive struggle for survival, then we will distrust those who behave cooperatively. If we believe that a particular set of writings contains the one and only word of God, then we will brand as evil anyone who thinks otherwise. If we believe that profitable industry takes precedence over environmental concerns, then we will fail to see all signs and warnings of impending ecological disasters. If we believe that superior force offers the only viable solution to violence, then our reading of history will always validate that might makes right and we will study war rather than peace.

We perceive the world according to our preconceived beliefs and then respond to people and events according to what we have perceived. Our actions follow our perceptions, which derive from our systems of belief.

The world, in turn, responds to us, as circumstances unfold in reaction to our actions, giving us feedback on what we believe. Typically, our experiential feedback seems to validate and strengthen our causal beliefs. I say "seems" because all experiential feedback filters through our belief-colored perceptual system. Even when our actions lead to horrible consequences—when life in effect tells us to seriously consider changing course—we tend to only perceive "evidence" that supports our position. We may continue on in the most foolish ways because our beliefs, perceptions, and responses remain hopelessly stuck in a counterproductive behavioral cycle.

This cycle—beliefs into perceptions into actions into experience into reconfirmed beliefs—explains how people can adhere so rigidly to failed and destructive worldviews and lifestyles. Like fish swimming in polluted water, we barely notice the causal force of belief, much less that it causes such trouble. This also explains why people tend to grow conservative with age, as the broad and freewheeling beliefs of youth gradually calcify from a lifetime of belief-confirming experience.

Both sides in the current terror war hold calcified beliefs about themselves and their opponents that virtually guarantee that things will get much worse before they ever get better. Every new suicide bomber confirms the utter evil of the terrorist cause; every innocent person killed by the superior firepower of anti-terrorist armies confirms the terrible injustice of dominist power. Like a macabre firing squad in which everyone demands both a blindfold and a gun, more carnage surely lies ahead for our world, with fresh legions of true believers marching into the fray.

Yet, for all the creative/destructive power of one's personal beliefs, they become infinitely more potent, and so much more dangerous, when invested with strong emotional energy. Emotionally charged beliefs have the capacity to spread—like social contaminants—from person to person and from group to group. The vital energy of human emotion turns a merely personal belief into a contagious psychoemotional toxin that can proliferate without bounds, inflicting the same poison upon countless others.

Thus, I may harbor the belief that people of other races have distinct genetic inferiorities. I may cultivate this belief through a lifetime of selective study and will likely gather belief-confirming experiences with time. Such racist beliefs will surely limit my world and cause me to act poorly toward those of other races. Still, to the extent that my beliefs lack passion, then the causal effects of those beliefs may never extend beyond my personal experience; close friends and family may never even glimpse the reality of my racism.

If, however, I have at some point in my life experienced a terrible trauma that I perceived as caused by one or more of *them*—if my sister was raped, or my village overrun, or my livelihood taken, or my sense of self painfully undermined—then I may carry a lifelong seething hatred toward, or disgust for, or fear of all people of that race (or religion, ethnic group, class, gender, or nationality). The unresolved emotional energy will intensify and empower my racist beliefs, making them so much more self-constricting and, even worse, turning them into dangerous social contagions. I will become a toxic carrier for the social contaminant of racism, spreading my vile beliefs to other vulnerable people.

Any belief invested with strong emotional energy can turn into a self-replicating and proliferating pathological force that we can call a "social virus." Just as a biological virus consists of fundamental information about living processes enfolded within the most rudimentary of material forms (simple proteins), and a computer virus consists of fundamental information about digital processes enfolded within the form of a disk or electronic transmission, a social virus consists of fundamental beliefs about reality enfolded within a force-field of psychoemotional energy. Just as biological and computer viruses use their unique forms to move about the world and to find, enter into, and infect vulnerable hosts, a social virus uses its body of psychoemotional energy to travel between people and to spread toxic information. And just as biological and computer viruses have the capacity to cause a wide range of pathologies in those they invade, social viruses, by altering the belief systems of infected individuals, can utterly transform lives, invariably for the worse.

I see the "dominism virus" as the oldest and most pernicious of social viruses. I believe the virus came into existence in early human history as individuals and tribes resorted to coercive force to resolve conflicts. It gathered strength from the intense currents of emotional energy that characterize any struggle for domination. An individual confronted with dominism typically experiences some combination of fear, anger, hate, shame, and terror; the powerful energies of such emotions provide both vital form and means of locomotion for spreading dominism. The dominism virus has propagated since its origins into a global pandemic infecting the full scope of human existence.

When one country (or individual) invades, attacks or in any way forcefully coerces another country (or individual), a whole matrix of beliefs about the nature of the world and human relationship gets "transmitted" through the coercive act. The man who forces himself sexually upon a woman psychoemotionally contaminates her with ideas of shame, sin, inadequacy, helplessness, and weakness. When the wealthy use their financial power to manipulate and control events to their advantage they simultaneously spread a set of economic "truths" that celebrate their overclass standing while denigrating the innate weaknesses of the underclass. Parents who physically or verbally abuse their children pass on the most viral of poisons from old bodies to young bodies, teaching: "This is the nature of human relationship."

Any individual or group forced to react to another's coercive violence or abuse as a matter of course becomes conditioned to dominist relationship: a bundle or field of information about the world enters into and intertwines with personal beliefs, opinions, attitudes, philosophies, dreams, expectations, and patterns of behavior. Such poisonous information ultimately seeps into the deepest sense of self, thus affecting and infecting all future relationships.

As viral dominism spreads, its misinformation encodes at the vital core of the human organism; it becomes virtual human nature. Dominism-infected families, organizations, and governments, through their continual transmission of dominist beliefs, naturally serve to reinforce the virus's internal grip. If we seem so inevitably bound by the dangerous logic of dominism, how could we not? Dominism has for millennia been carved into the marrow of all human bodies and into the primary commandments for all our relationships.

We can no more avoid the dominism virus than we can a common flu virus. Nor, however, must we manifest the aberrant sickness of dominist relationship any more than we must become sick with flu. But to free our bodies and societies of viral dominism, we must greatly expand human awareness about the creative power of beliefs, about childhood conditioning, and about the numerous dominist patterns of relationship that define and control our societies.

Pandemic

They would like us to be so lost in hysteria that we can't think straight. They would like us to be so terrified, so anxious, so belligerent, that we lose perspective and make rash and destructive decisions. If we stay within the bubble of our fear, then the bin Ladens of the world will have won.

—**John Robbins**[9]

An eye for an eye will only make the whole world blind.

—**Mahatma Gandhi**

On November 4, 1995, at a mass rally held under the slogan "Yes to Peace, No to Violence," Israeli Prime Minister Yitzhak Rabin was assassinated by a Jewish true believer. Rabin had been elected on the pledge that he would make peace with the Palestinians; had participated in an historic Rose Garden meeting with Palestinian leader Yasir Arafat, for which he won the Nobel Peace Prize; and had taken several key steps in the design and implementation of a viable plan for peace. His assassination effectively halted the peace process and ushered in a new, more deadly round of suicide bombings and military reprisals. Moreover, both the Israelis and the Palestinians grew increasingly unyielding toward any hopes for a peaceful resolution of their conflict.

Like a huge stone thrown into still waters, the Rabin assassination caused waves of dominism-infected thought and emotion to ripple outward in all directions. In the Middle East and throughout the world, those who had even a modest stake in that conflict felt more or less affected as waves of viral dominism reached their psychic shores. Most dealt with the experience quietly and on their own terms. Some found themselves roused into strong and toxic emotional states; for days they projected their feelings of anger, terror, and anguish into everyone they met. Still others were so powerfully disturbed by the contaminating waves of dominism that they moved into action—they lashed out with some form of answering violence—setting yet more waves of viral dominism rippling outward, causing yet more individuals to react with violence.

The Dangerous Logic of Domination

If the Rabin assassination dropped a huge stone into our shared psychoemotional energies, the abominations of 9/11 struck our world like a radioactive meteor. Waves of the most poisonous of beliefs exploded outward in all directions and flooded the planet with human evil. All of the fear, pain, and psychopathic loathing that seethed within the al Qaeda true believers rushed out—furiously multiplying—like a toxic tsunami, like a vile and viral sludge that engulfed and overwhelmed, that choked and stifled, that invaded and infected and utterly contaminated men, women, and children worldwide.

All dominism derives from the capacity to inflict violence and abuse; all violence and abuse produces viral waves—fields of psychoemotionally-charged belief that saturate and then emanate out from the site of a violation. The more violent the act of dominism, the more surely and deeply the viral waves will infect. Yet even the most benign and gently expressed dominism still contains the threat of force, still frightens and abuses, and thus still produces soft but nonetheless coercing viral waves.

These rippling outward waves of psychoemotional energy—these *force fields*—serve as the vectors for the spreading contamination of the dominism virus. The virus rides the waves of anger, hatred, fear, and terror that violence and abuse produces the way a malaria germ rides a mosquito or a flu virus rides a sneeze. Strong human emotion provides both the body for the dominism virus and the tangible means or vector for its spread.

The Parable of the Tribes describes the gross mechanics of social contamination by coercive force. The waves of viral dominism that coercive force produces cause the actual spreading of dominist infection to human individuals. Thus, as marauding Huns approach a peaceful village, the tribe of that village moves into fight, flight, or surrender, with the inevitable consequences outlined above. At the same time, as each man, woman, and child of the tribe experiences the invading waves of viral terror, they become infected with dominism and undergo some degree of psychoemotional change. Each person succumbs, more or less, to the dangerous logic of dominist beliefs.

Violence so clearly illustrates the connection between the personal and the political. The dominating, power-over, and ever-violent acts of tribes and nations invade the individual—as belief, as emotional energy, as coercive will—to contaminate heart and soul and essential human nature. Such malformed and diseased individuals in turn form the body politic and perform the violent and abusive actions that define a tribe or nation's character, purpose, and means. The personal and political cycle one into the other, violence into further violence, dominism into greater dominism.

While we can most easily sense the contaminating waves of viral dominism projecting from wars, bombings, and assassinations, all acts of dominism produce more or less infectious force fields. Whenever someone forcefully coerces you, a critical aspect of the interaction involves the aggressive projection of their will, in the form of dominating thoughts and oppressive emotional energies. You experience these waves of aggressive will as vibrational input that invades, intimidates, coerces, and ultimately infects. Whether you react by fighting back, or running away, or simply giving in, the experience leaves its mark inside. It changes you. It alters your beliefs and perceptions. It programs future behavior.

Imagine a preverbal child facing the wrath of an enraged parent. Without physically touching, the psychoemotional wave of the parent's anger blows through the child, like the shock wave of an exploding bomb, and leaves scattered dominism, like maiming shrapnel. Though the child cannot understand the heated invective rushing from the parent's face, the meaning—you will submit!—comes clear enough. The child gets the force-or-be-forced facts of life. And if the parent adds corporal abuse to the message, then the dangerous lesson gets twisted that much deeper into the child's body and psyche.

All forms of dominism reduce to the capacity to overpower another, with as much force as deemed necessary; consequently, dominism always projects some degree of terrorizing psychoemotional energies and causes some degree of social contamination. This pertains to the domination of children by their parents, women by men, the weak by the strong, the poor by the rich, the out-group by the in-group, and the minority by the majority. It pertains to the domination of the primitive by the industrialist and of the pacifist by the soldier. It pertains to the domination of one species over another and to the domination of nature by humans. The terrorizing effects of viral dominism pertain to virtually every aspect of modern life.

Two

The Dominist Manifesto

We have a choice: either to change the way we live, which is unacceptable; or to change the way that they live. And we chose the latter.

—Donald Rumsfeld, Secretary of Defense[1]

The "war on terrorism" is violent and punitive. The war will be won by those who are able to exact the higher price in lives and resources, by those who are able to instill the greater fear. In short, the victor in a violent war on terrorism will be the party that is most adept at inflicting terror.

—Lee Griffith[2]

Three months after the terrorist attacks on America, and two months into the war on terrorism and the bombing of Afghanistan, a small group of Pakistani terrorists assaulted the Indian parliament, killing several people. The incident had the predictable effect of pushing two long antagonistic nations to the brink of war. It seemed eerily like 9/11 all over again, with one huge added terror: since the last time they warred, India and Pakistan had both added nuclear weapons to their arsenals.

As troops mounted along the Indian-Pakistani border, America faced a conundrum. On the one hand, Pakistan's cooperation was critical in the assault on Afghanistan and the continuing search for al-Qaeda cells and leaders; Pakistani President Pervez Musharraf had taken a perilous position in joining the American war and the prospect of a radical uprising in his country loomed large. On the other hand, India clearly had suffered a terrorist attack, at the very heart of its democracy, and thus had every right to follow America's lead: to brand Pakistan as a nation harboring terrorists; to demand Pakistan's immediate and non-negotiable compliance in eliminating future threats; and, as the militarily dominant of the two nations, to threaten mass destruction and massive civilian casualties if Pakistan failed to fall in line.

As if the danger of a nuclear meltdown in Central Asia did not frighten enough, this same scenario was simultaneously unfolding in several other global hotspots. The Israelis ran out of patience with the Palestinian uprising and decided they would no longer deal with Yasir Arafat; instead, Israeli antiterrorist rhetoric and threats began to mirror America's in tone and effect. Russian President Putin framed his nation's continuing war in Chechnya as a terrorist crisis requiring antiterrorist action. The Chinese started referring to their dissident Muslim populations as terrorists, as did the Spanish the Basque separatists, and the Nepalese a small group of Marxist insurgents.

In response to all of these festering threats, President Bush could only issue platitudes about the need to show restraint and peacefully work out differences. He seemed unaware of the contradictions and outright hypocrisies of his position. Or perhaps he grasped the situation perfectly: one set of rules for America, another for everyone else, and darn those annoying consequences.

What began as an American-directed morality play, pitting the darkest evil against the purest good, had mutated into a murky mess of realpolitik and tangled truth. As all the king's men embarked on this new crusade against terrorism, it became clear that some old scores were getting settled. Moreover, in every case the "terrorists" had similar grievances: they had suffered humiliating defeats and abuses; they had lost loved ones, land, and resources; they felt forced to live in debilitating circumstances; and they believed that they had exhausted all non-violent means to resolving their grievances. They all lived as subjugated people in dominist systems and felt rightly compelled to attack the systems, however misguided, futile, and inhumane their efforts.

Ever since President Ronald Reagan defied the U.S. Congress and the United Nations with his secret support of the Nicaraguan *contras* against their popular government, the line between terrorists and "freedom fighters" has been hopelessly blurred. Few so-called terrorists get to the point of waging violence without having experienced dominist-inflicted abuse and suffering. Few so-called freedom fighters can lay claim to blameless pasts or lily-white intentions. If we assume for all people the inalienable rights of self-defense and the pursuit of personal and political freedoms, then, try though we may, we simply cannot define terrorism—and thereby justify antiterror actions—based solely on the apparent righteousness, or lack thereof, of a combatant's cause.

Grasping for a better definition of terrorism, the new crusaders point to the utter depravity of terrorist tactics. Only terrorists, they say, target civilian populations. Indeed, the argument goes, unlike civilized nations, terrorists aim to demoralize an enemy by terrorizing its women and children. Civilized nations openly declare war and then conduct it according to a high code of ethics that forbids the intentional targeting of civilians; terrorists break all such rules, commit unpardonable sins, and deserve neither consideration nor quarter from good people.

In the wake of 9/11, this argument easily won the support of some nine out of ten Americans, along with strong majorities of Canadians, Australians, and Europeans. It presents such a stark and terrible picture—*they* intentionally murder innocents; *we* never would—that for months after 9/11 any attempts to question or even slightly moderate this viewpoint got branded as the worst of treason, as a vile insult against all victims of terrorism, as consorting with evil itself.

Most Americans believe strongly in this fiction of the perfect moral compass. Yet, without even cracking a history book, a painful litany comes to mind: the Indian wars, Sherman's march, Dresden, Hiroshima, Nagasaki, Tokyo, Vietnam, Nicaragua,

Panama, Baghdad. When America goes to war, we *always* kill civilians. We can try to cover it with terms like "collateral damage" or with the claim that our smart, new precision bombing kills so many fewer civilians. We can ignore the monumental suffering of innocents that occurs when we intentionally destroy a country's vital infrastructure and ecology, as we did in Viet Nam, Iraq, and Afghanistan. We can likewise ignore, though the rest of the world will not, the disquieting truth that in more than two hundred years, America has lost a mere handful of civilians in war compared to the yearly tallies of so many other peoples. Indeed, it only took a few months for the "smart" bombs in Afghanistan to kill more civilians than the terrorists killed on 9/11; given that Afghanistan has a fraction of the overall population of America, we can only conclude that its people suffered far more.

The horrible events of 9/11 that so catalyzed America—that struck us as so extraordinary and life-altering, that created such a moment in our history—occur with such frequency as to seem commonplace to many of the world's oppressed. Moreover, in too many instances America sold the weapons or supported the generals or manipulated the politics that led to the horrors. So "they target civilians" fails as an argument; since all organized violence inevitably kills civilians, America, the current master of war, kills far too many innocents, and certainly far more than the small bands of fanatics we call terrorists.

At this point we fall back on moral reasoning: Regrettably, some civilians do suffer from our attacks, but we act in a just cause, while the enemy does not, and besides, they started it. We justify our actions by claiming *a priori* the justice of our actions. We simply ignore the circular reasoning and suspend, and perhaps even forbid, any further discussion. Case closed and off with their heads.

So-called terrorists and antiterror warriors all follow the same militaristic thinking: they believe that by inflicting sufficient quantities of suffering they can influence the choices and actions of others. Any group—nation, tribe, or al-Qaeda cell—that commits itself to organized violence as the primary solution to intergroup conflict of necessity embarks upon a path of inflicting terror. Militarism always terrorizes, and the most dominant militaries terrorize most effectively. Moreover, militarism always spreads dominist poison, which leads to some measure of militaristic response among those it terrorizes—a response that, from the perspective of the terrorized, seems patriotic, courageous, and utterly justified. And so the cycle of terror and violence, of vengeance and revenge, self-perpetuates endlessly.

Contrary to Bush-speak, terrorists do not arrive on Earth as the devil's spawn; rather, they grow inevitably from previous acts of dominism. In their adherence to terrorizing tactics as the best way to control other people, George W. Bush and Osama bin Laden can lay equal claim to the title of preeminent world terrorist. When militaries move from "strong defense in the face of clear and present danger" to "offensive, punishing, coercive force to dominate others" they cross over into the terrorist camp and their violent acts do not eradicate but rather feed future terror.

The dangerous logic of militarism dictates the mean and hostile nightmare world of modern times. As long as nations—and especially the most dominant—consider organized violence a legitimate response to real and perceived injustices, then we can expect no respite from ever-escalating terrorism. We will never move beyond dominism into a world of lasting peace unless we resolve the cycle of militaristic action and reaction forever and for all.

Militarism represents only one of several beliefs and behavioral patterns that mark the dominist worldview and lifestyle. Beginning with the "survive at any costs" imperative invoked by the Parable of the Tribes, viral dominism has grown through time and human experience into a complex matrix of coercive belief and behavior. In the past few millennia, dominism has spread into virtually every facet of human affairs and has developed a set of overlapping and mutually-affirming thoughts and emotions that, taken together, amount to a near impenetrable worldview.

Might Makes Right Makes Might

But by diplomacy we mean invariably ultimatums for peace backed by the threat of war. It is always understood that we stand ready to kill those with whom we are "peacefully" negotiating.

—**Wendell Berry**[3]

The U.S. does not want to establish the principle that it has to defer to some higher authority before carrying out the use of violence. It's a very natural position....If a state is powerful enough, it wants to establish the principle that it can act without authorization.

—**Noam Chomsky**[4]

Several months before 9/11, the Bush administration pulled out of negotiations over the Kyoto Agreement, an international attempt to address global climate change. Before his first year in office was over, Bush would also repudiate international treaties that limited the testing of nuclear weapons; that limited the production of chemical and biological weapons; that called for an end to the production and use of landmines; and that proposed an International Court for the trial of war criminals. In every case, the president justified his actions with the same terse explanation: the treaty does not serve America's best interests.

Even with the onset of the war on terrorism and the pressing need for international cooperation, Bush made clear that America would act as manager of the team rather than member of a coalition. You're with us or against us, he told the world, and if you're with us, then listen up while we give you your marching orders. Nor would this war require the input or services of the United Nations, an international body that Bush largely ignored; despite its successful peacekeeping mission in Bosnia, the UN would not be called in to help make the peace in Afghanistan, and would only be consulted with the greatest of reluctance before the invasion of Iraq.

In his staunch rejection of genuine, peer-to-peer partnerships with other nations, the President echoed a unilateralist position that has long been a fundamental tenet of dominism. Unilateralist nations conduct their foreign affairs separately and seek minimal consultation and involvement with other nations, including their allies. Though all nations have unilateralist tendencies, as a rule unilateralism only works for dominant nations who, by virtue of their superior strength, can force their ways upon others. Weaker nations, by contrast, only act unilaterally at their peril; they have more to gain by forming active alliances with others and by pursuing the peaceful resolution of conflicts, though not all nations have the wisdom to see this.

To some extent, dominists take unilateralist positions simply because they can. Why bother with the opinions of others when they have no power to resist you? This sums up the means, method, and rationale of the bully: do whatever you must to prove to others that they cannot stop you. Such bullying plays a part in all unilateralism.

Yet the underpinnings of unilateralism run even deeper: dominists come to believe that because they have superior power (as measured in armies, weapons, resources, or money) they also have superior intelligence, morality, ethics, vision, and leadership. Survival of the fittest morphs into survival of the wise, the worthy, the blessed, and the pure. The dominant nation sees itself as the best of all nations and as a beacon in all ways to the rest of the world—the head of the family, chairman of the board, dean of students, bulwark against evil, and keeper of the grail.

Moreover, having established its superiority in all things that matter, the dominist feels compelled to pursue only ends that add to its powers. So runs the argument against cooperation and multilateralism: if, in the effort to resolve conflicts, we must seriously engage with differing viewpoints and agendas, then we will almost certainly make decisions and take actions that oppose "our best interests," as defined by the dominant group within a nation. Since we sincerely believe that achieving our best interests serves the best interests of the rest of world, then the right course of action, always, lay in the unilateral pursuit of our agenda.

    Dominists see their superior strengths and achievements as indication of their innate superiority as people and institutions. Their might makes them right. Then they use the mantle of rightness, backed up with the threat of force, to manipulate circumstances to increase their strengths and achievements. Their might makes right makes further might. They have no need for the input of others, nor inclination to undermine this pernicious logic of power by taking their eyes off the prize of "our best interests." For dominists, unilateralism brings the symmetry and order of a tightly run ship; multilateralism invokes the chaos of children running loose with knives.

    Seen in this light, Bush's unilateralism made perfect sense. Despite the monumental threats posed by global climate change, and the near-universal consensus of scientists at home and abroad pleading for the kinds of actions proposed at Kyoto, Bush and his supporters simply could not see beyond the short-term threats to American corporations. Since addressing environmental concerns seemed to undermine their best interests, the President felt duty-bound to save his world by ignoring all things environmental. More insidiously, by refusing to take certain critical steps—such as taxing gasoline to lower consumption—America became, at least temporarily, stronger compared to the rest of the world.

    Similarly, though the treaties restricting nuclear weapons brought thirty years of steady progress toward the elimination of these horrible weapons; though the Russians had made commitments and taken steps to drastically reduce their nuclear arsenals; and though the treaties created standards that all but a few rogue nations followed, the treaties did not serve the best interests of the American defense industry. So Bush unilaterally announced the repudiation of the treaties. No need for negotiations with the Russians. No inclination for international discussions. While this matter obviously concerns all of the world's people, the opinions of all but a handful of wealthy Americans could not matter less.

Nowhere does the foolishness of American unilateralism become more apparent than in its dealings with the United Nations. The UN has long represented the world's best hope for peace in our times as it gathers nations together to talk conflicts through in an atmosphere of mutual respect and careful listening. Yet American unilateralists, especially those on the political right, have worked fanatically to undermine the UN. Their chief complaint: that any decisions of the United Nations that disagree with our best interests amount to attempts to usurp American sovereignty. The most dominant nation in history simply will not—does not have to—stoop to multilateralism.

With God On One Side

We should invade their countries, kill their leaders and convert them to Christianity. **—Ann Coulter**[5]

If your brother or son or daughter or wife or friend suggests serving other gods, you must kill him, your hand must be the first raised in putting him to death....If the inhabitants of a town that once served the Lord your God, now serve other gods, you must kill all the inhabitants of that town. **—Deuteronomy 13:6, 15**

Just two days after 9/11, the Reverend Jerry Falwell and Christian Coalition founder Pat Robertson had a televised chat in which they blamed the terrorist attacks on America's failures as a Christian nation and suggested that God was punishing America for its flirtations with heathens, feminists, and the ACLU. Though a brief hullabaloo followed reports of their conversation, it quickly passed. Few spoke out against them, and both men continued to enjoy widespread respect and to find prominent perches from which to crow their tired nonsense.

Leaving aside the sick notion of a God who would slaughter innocents to get a whole nation to change its ways—God the Almighty Terrorist—someone needs to take both of these so-called religious men for a good, long look in the mirror. For just their sort of religious fundamentalism appears as the common ingredient in so many acts of terrorism: the Islamic fundamentalists who attacked America heard the very same God issuing commandments in their ears as do the Falwells and Robertsons of Christian fundamentalism, as did the Jewish murderer of Yitzhak Rabin and other militants of Jewish fundamentalism. Indeed, if the God-fearing and -obeying adherents of these three old-time religions would just stop fighting among themselves, the world would at once become dramatically more peaceful.

One of the more hypocritical post-9/11 discussions focused on the notion that Islam has essentially violent tendencies, deriving from its sacred text, the Koran. The Christians and Jews who make such claims have the historic grasp of infants and the self-reflection of stones. For the Koran only mirrors the many examples of, justifications for, and exhortations to violence spread throughout the Old Testament of the Bible. The fact that the Old Testament serves as a basic text for Jews, Christians, and many Muslims suggests that if we really want to get to the roots of fundamentalist violence, maybe we should start in Genesis.

Beginning with the expulsion from Eden, and on through the murder of Abel, the Flood, the destruction of Sodom, the razing of Babel, the torments of Job, the slaying of Jezebel and massacre of her followers, and the countless scriptural justifications of rape and exhortations to torture, the Old Testament describes a terrible world, filled with wicked and abusive people, ruled by an angry, jealous, vengeful God. And while we can blame much of this horrid history of human suffering on bad people making bad choices, the bulk of it stems from the stern ultimatums of God—"But ye shall destroy their altars, break their images and cut down their groves, for thou shalt worship no other god, for the Lord whose name is jealous is a jealous God." (Exodus 34:13-

14)—along with the constant "natural" disasters this Dominus Deus, this God the Dominator, inflicts as punishments.

But God the Dominator does not stop with the subordination of his minions; he goes on to dictate the total domination of everything and everyone on earth by those who obey his laws. He divinely curses nature in Genesis and then gives his followers dominion over all plants and animals. We search the Bible in vain for the simple love of nature that so inspires the Upanishads, the Tao Te Ching, and the mythologies and oral histories of many Native American and other indigenous cultures. It follows directly from the Bible that Judeo-Christian-Islamic culture has grown into an ecological blight upon the entire planet.

Yet of all of God the Dominator's actions and commands, none has so effectively terrorized this world as his First Commandment. "I am the one and only God," he insists. With this single proclamation, the genocide of entire races, the rape and conquest of whole civilizations, the violent eradication of pantheistic religions, the burning of temples, holy texts, and sacred groves, the torture and murder of witches and pagans, the brutal conversion of "ignorant savages," and an endless saga of crusades, jihads, and holy wars all thunder into terrible and unrelenting parade. "Thou shall have no other Gods before me," he commands, thereby giving his blessing to any abuse inflicted in the service of his universal domination. As his followers adamantly point out, God leaves no uncertainty in his first commandment, no room for negotiations, and no doubts about the fate of unbelievers: you're either with him or against him and if you're against him, then it's to hell with you and extra hosannas for those who send you on your way.

Only one God, only one way: once one makes that choice, so many other choices become dictated, commanded, preordained. For the real fanatics—the suicide bombers and cross-wielding crusaders—all free will, conscience, and personal morals get subjugated to this dangerous logic of monotheism.

Only my God, only my way: monotheists apply the Parable of the Tribes to the religious impulse by forcing everyone they encounter to either fight (thus betraying the peace and good will of one's religion); to flee (thus abandoning the holy earth from which most non-monotheistic religions derive); or to convert (thus becoming righteous recruits in God the Dominator's army).

Wherever and whenever monotheists encounter "other-believers," this same tableau of forced conversion occurs. While individuals may freely choose the new god and religious practices, for the invaded culture as a whole, and for its established religion(s), the conversion process follows classic dominist principles: with as little force as possible, but as much force as required, everyone will set aside their blasphemies and come to the One and Only God. For those who do not gracefully accept being "saved," then it's flag-draped crosses and onward Christian soldiers. Monotheists brook no opposition because God commands them not to and because, according to his dictates, all other-believers are bound for eternal damnation. Monotheists sincerely believe that they serve others by delivering the word of God and changing infidels into believers. So runs the dangerous logic of monotheism: we dominate you for your own good; to not dominate you would constitute the worst of failings.

Monotheism functions as the fundamental of all fundamentalisms. From the rigid belief in God the Dominator flows an equally rigid adherence to His teachings as revealed in specific writings. While in truth a great deal of editing and all-too-personal selectivity determines which of a body of writing actually represent God's word and (of those writings) exactly how to interpret His meanings in present terms, fundamentalists have no use for such considerations. They glorify the supposed perfection of "the world as God intended" and "the way it used to be." They see themselves as divinely chosen to pull the sinning masses back into line. Anyone who does not conform to the writings of a bunch of long-dead Middle Eastern men must repent, convert, or suffer extreme sanction. Monotheism leaves neither middle ground nor gray area; whatever does not strictly conform gets terrorized into submission.

As a nation founded by men and women who were themselves fleeing from monotheistic oppression, America has labored from its beginnings to tolerate all gods, religions, and spiritual practices. By separating church and state, the Founders hoped to avoid the overwhelming coercion that occurs when those two institutions agree in dominist thrust. Two centuries later it seems clear that, despite its brave and enlightened birth, America has developed into an ardently Judeo-Christian, monotheistic nation in all of its politics and most of its community life. While other-believers feel safer and have greater freedom in America than most other countries, Buddhists do not run for office, Taoists do not push their opinions from regular seats among the TV punditry, and sports teams do not gather in circles to perform Wiccan rituals. To the contrary, virtually all legal and political proceedings, as well as most elementary school days, begin at the very least with an invocation of "one nation under God." To the fundamentalists, this does not go nearly far enough; they constantly cavil about America's failings as a monotheist nation and, with utter gall, portray monotheists as victims of even the slightest accommodations to the views or feelings of other-believers.

All aggressive religious states tend toward monotheism because it provides the ultimate cover for the State-sanctioned violence of war. Nothing creates masses of willing martyrs, ready to storm the bulwarks of evil, better than the wide-spread and deeply-engrained belief that God himself commands the army, directs the battle, and lifts the dying straight to heaven. Any personal fears, realpolitik ambiguities, or nagging moral nuances fade before the bright and shining image of God bestowing his exclusive blessings upon the troops. True, the other side usually thinks the same, but that's the genius of monotheism: they're wrong! Praise the Lord and pass the ammunition.

Still A Man's World

I finally understood that men, who own all laws—since they make, interpret, and enforce them—will never manipulate their legal systems in a way that threatens their privilege.

—**Sonia Johnson**[6]

In the mid-1990s, when the Taliban began to take over Afghanistan, the world's feminists raised a hue and cry about the resulting mistreatment of Afghani women. America paid no attention to these outcries and actually tried to develop the Taliban as a good and useful ally. Yet when American bombing brought the collapse of the Taliban, and the status of women in Afghanistan began to moderate ever so slightly for the better, American leaders quickly positioned themselves as ardent defenders of women's rights.

It made for good PR spin: Sir George and his knights went off to slay the dragon and rescue the damsels in distress. In truth, the plight of Afghanistan's women served as but a useful pawn in the political strategizing of the moment. If Bush and company really cared about the systemic oppression of Afghani women, then they would have had to show similar concern toward ending the oppressive conditions of women worldwide, including in America, and especially in such countries as Saudi Arabia, Pakistan, and Kuwait. But no such feminist revolution occurred; as we collectively moved on from the war in Afghanistan, women's issues disappeared back into the shadows of neglect and denial. We should never expect dominists to willingly work for women's liberation because the subjugation of women stands side-by-side with militarism, unilateralism, and monotheism as a first tenet of dominism.

For Western and Middle Eastern cultures, the subjugation of women begins in Genesis with "God the Father." The father or male principle appears throughout the Bible as the active, initiating force and sustaining presence for all aspects of the human experience. We find little reference to a mother or female principle, anywhere in the Old Testament, which does not even have a word for "Goddess." The New Testament does have the Virgin Mary, but she acts as a mere mortal in the company of the divine Father and Son. Clearly, the men who wrote the Bible made certain to establish God as masculine. Though they tell us that God created us in his likeness, in fact quite the opposite occurred.

Having determined God's gender, the first few pages of Genesis go on to cast woman as a subordinate—a mere afterthought—to man. God creates Eve from Adam's rib as his "helpmeet" and to keep him from his loneliness. She then engineers the big booboo of listening to the smooth-talking snake. For her sin, God damns all of humankind, makes childbearing forever painful, and deems that a woman's desire should turn only to her husband and ruler.

This biblical story has profoundly affected all of the Jews, Christians, and Moslems who have ever read the Old Testament and considered it the word of God, as well as all of the other people of the world who have found themselves under the domination of one of these three Old Testament religions. In the first few pages of the Bible, the nature of woman as subordinate to man gets divinely cast and forever justified. Remember, she asked for it.

The travail of women, through both the Old and New Testaments, makes such a sorry tale that one wonders how so many can think of the Bible as "the greatest story ever told" or, for that matter, as a holy book. The very people who so revere the Bible would quickly denounce as pornography any book written today that contained so much rape, pillage, murder, bondage, and child abuse. Yet because God himself demands the constant violence and violation in the Bible, his believers deem it sanctified. Brutality in the name of God the Dominator becomes righteous, even holy, because he commands it.

Any religion that so posits the father/man as a power over the mother/woman invariably becomes a system of domination, of ranking and judging, and of ordained abuse by men against women. This in turn gives credence, and the blessings of God, to the many precepts of dominist culture: only men can serve as priests; only husbands can own property and only sons can inherit; female sexuality brings suffering and sin into the world; and, man rules over woman and has dominion over nature.

Men rule the world; women serve as helpmeets. In the next chapter, we will explore in greater depth the biological and social explanations for why and how such sexism naturally arises in any dominist culture. For now, understand that however much a nation might strive to create balanced and equitable gender relations, so long as that nation's underpinnings derive from Old Testament doctrine, the very idea of women's liberation will strike many as utter nonsense, if not terrible blasphemy.

To the fundamentalist, women's real liberation comes in serving the roles defined for them 2,000 years ago in the Bible. The many coveted freedoms of modern women—to take part in all levels of society, including as political and religious leaders; to follow their passions and skills to whatever work most excites them; to receive payments for their efforts equal to the payments men receive for like efforts; to have sovereignty over their bodies; to genuinely cooperate with men in matters of sex, reproduction, and raising children—all of these cherished liberations run starkly counter to biblical doctrine. A nation led by religious fundamentalists can only see women as divinely ordained to be second-class citizens.

As in the case of monotheism, biblical sexism derives from the absolute, non-negotiable, and unambiguous word of God. Women who stray from the fundamentalists' rigid proscriptions get punished according to their cultures. The Taliban called such women harlots and stoned them to death in public squares. In America, we call them shrill, aggressive feminists and marginalize them with legal chicanery, media spin, and glass ceilings. Or we shrug as Falwell, Robertson and their ilk denounce uppity women from public pulpits and inspire fanatics to attack women's health clinics. Or we simply take for granted that, even in modern America—leader of the free world and bastion of civilization—violence against women occurs with soul-sapping regularity.

Like militarism, unilateralism, and monotheism, sexism virally spreads in dominist culture. The more widely-accepted the dominist version of men's and women's God-given roles, the less that individual men and women will ever see beyond their proscribed realities, and the more likely that most people (sinners aside) will come to confirm God the Father's supposed plan. So runs the dangerous logic of sexism: because God ordained from the beginning that women should not tarry with things such as reading, writing, and thinking deeply, men wrote the books that for thousands of years have been used to keep women from pursuing literacy and education; because God ordained from the beginning that only men should serve as political and religious leaders, women never had a voice in developing the political and religious systems that oppress them so; most tragically, because God ordained from the beginning that the differences between men and women led naturally to non-negotiable roles and standing in life, individual freedom and untold human potential has withered on the vine of sexist predetermination.

Different, Therefore Less Than

Look carefully at the face of the enemy. The lips are curled downward. The eyes are fanatical and far away....Nothing suggests that this man ever laughs, is torn by doubts, or shaken by tears. He feels no tenderness or pain. Clearly he is unlike us.

—**Sam Keen**[7]

When George W. Bush talks about the war on terrorism, he always casts it as a battle between good and evil. He branded the 9/11 perpetrators as "evildoers" in his first speech on the matter and in his 2002 State of the Union address he used the word "evil" five times and introduced a classic of Bush-speak: the "axis of evil." As a self-proclaimed born-again Christian with deep ties to fundamentalist doctrine, it certainly makes sense that Bush would perceive events through a biblical prism. Yet, for all his holy posturing, his words have more to do with politics than theology; like all war leaders, he has learned to characterize the enemy in ways that will inspire his people to the bloodletting hatred that success in war requires. If such characterizations require that you lie about the enemy, turning ordinary people into vessels of absolute evil, then lie you must.

As a far more accomplished war leader, Winston Churchill, observed, "truth is the first casualty of war." When dominist cultures come into contact with peaceful cultures, truth always gets tortured as the prelude to aggression. Rather than honestly reaching for the fruits of peace and partnership, the aggressors proffer a litany of war-inducing lies. "They threaten our survival," declare the dominists. "We must have their land and food. We cannot trust them to cooperate. We stand for good, but they stand for evil. God demands their ruination. They are evildoers, but we act at God's behest in a just and righteous cause. We cannot avoid this war, so in the name of all that is good, we must prevail, at whatever the costs."

One linchpin lie holds the whole dishonest business of war in place: difference means inequality. Under the spell of this lie, one people looks across the divide at another, notices obvious differences, and turns those differences into proof of the others' inequality and subhuman status. Because they do not look, sound, or act like us, they deserve mistreatment, enslavement, displacement, and death. "Differently human" gets twisted into "weaker," "poorer," "dumber," or "less evolved." The myriad shades and colorings of diverse cultures become the grounds and justifications for the actions of the thief, soldier, empire-builder, missionary, colonizer, industrialist, and predatory capitalist: "They are different. They are less than us. If those subhumans get in the way, dispose of them."

Any differences we see in our adversaries stand as evidence of their inferiority, wickedness, and unworthiness, and we do well in ridding the world of them and their kind. This millennium-old lie has been told with perfect sincerity by the winners in every war that humans have ever fought: Their differences make them less than us and—the crux of the matter—their pain, hardship, and death do not count for as much as ours. They do not bleed as we bleed, nor cry as we cry, nor love their families as we love ours; we do the world a favor by eliminating such vermin.

This xenophobia—this visceral dread and loathing of *them*—may have served early humans well as they negotiated a world of infinite unknowns. And throughout history, though some have surely known better, most people have lived in such ignorance and superstition as to easily give in to xenophobic fears. In America, the demonization of other races, religions, creeds, nations, and political systems prevails as a simple fact of life. The xenophobic disregard and disdain that Americans once felt for Injuns, transferred easily to niggers, to wetbacks, to Krauts, to Japs, to Wops, to commies, to Arabs. In times of peace, these ill feelings toward *them* may settle into mild dislike and vague distrust; but once the war drums start thumping and the hatemongers start spewing their different-and-less-than screed, the American people have always marched off, brains properly holstered, bound to eradicate evil once again.

Of course, no one calls it xenophobia. We prefer terms like "manifest destiny" and "American exceptionalism," terms that allow us to feel pride in our dominist aggressions while we ignore the inevitable wake of collateral damage that follows us everywhere. We Americans fancy our nation as a "benevolent hegemon"; we conquer people for their own good. We stand as the one true beacon of democracy throughout the world—isn't that why they hate us so?—and, regrettably, we often have to thwart the democratic impulse in those who just don't seem ready for it yet. Democracy's not easy, we tell the "developing" world, like parents telling children they're too young to drive.

True, America helped rebuild Germany and Japan after conquering them, and at least tried to do the same for Afghanistan and Iraq. But such aid always happens on America's terms and to the distinct advantage of key American industries, beginning with arms manufacturers. As our penchant for unilateralism ever demonstrates, we have no interest in creating real partnerships with former foes or faithful allies; rather, we act as we need to act—sometimes benevolently, sometimes harshly—to further our domination of nations and events.

As the world's only superpower, America's xenophobic tendencies naturally have wider visibility and effect. Yet, just as all nations have more or less succumbed to dominist infection, people everywhere display varying degrees of xenophobia. The visceral distrust of *them* underlies a wide range of all-too-normal but ultimately pathological human behaviors. Xenophobia can manifest as a deep-seated fear and hatred of those who merely look different (racism, antisemitism), or those of different sexual orientation (homophopia), or those from different economic backgrounds (classism), or those from other nations (patriotism, nationalism), or even those from other schools, fraternities, or sports teams (boosterism, provincialism, parochialism). For each of these common human tendencies we can find countless examples of people treating other people abysmally, simply because of their differences.

The dangerous logic of xenophobia meshes neatly with the dominist drives toward militarism, unilateralism, monotheism, and sexism. Dominists crave monocultures in which all diversity has been weeded out, all deviants have been assimilated, and everyone marches to the same conformist tunes. One God, one color, one language, one history, one ideology, one culture—one world ordered in service of the best interests of those giving the orders. Those who stand outside of the established order, by definition threaten it, and thus invite their own ruin. It was us or them, the dominists proclaim, and who can argue with that?

The Tyranny of the Bottom Line

Our business and political class owes us better than this....If ever they were going to put patriotism over profits, if ever they were going to practice the magnanimity of winners, this was the moment. To hide now behind the flag while ripping off a country in crisis fatally (fatally!) separates them from the common course of American life.

—**Bill Moyers**[8]

An infectious greed seemed to grip much of our business community.

—**Alan Greenspan**[9]

The American economy took a terrible downspin in the immediate aftermath of 9/11. Wall Street closed and all stock market activities paused for an unprecedented five business days. With the nation facing billions of dollars in repair bills, and even more for homeland security and the war against terrorism, and with the airline and insurance industries both reeling, many Americans, including those in the financial community, fretted over an economic collapse. They especially worried about a widespread sell-off of stocks when the markets reopened.

As reopening day approached, a groundswell of support arose for the idea of not selling any of one's stocks. The Internet hummed with impassioned pleas for everyone to hold onto their stocks, at least for the first few weeks, to give the markets time to stabilize and to reestablish the all-important aura of confidence. Well-meaning investors pitched the whole notion as an act of patriotism: each of us can and should do this one thing, should make this sacrifice for the greater good, should demonstrate to the whole world the infinite power of Americans acting as one nation, indivisible.

Sorry, no deal. The market dropped precipitously when it reopened on September 18, and continued losing ground for several days. Both individual and institutional investors sold rather frantically. The American economy eventually slipped into a recession, and things would get much worse in the months to come.

What happened? Though the impulse toward a patriotic *esprit de corps* undoubtedly tugged at most investors, an even stronger force pulled them in the opposite direction: they simply could not intentionally lose money. In the final analysis, investors had to take the steps that would tend to enhance their individual and corporate financial positions. They had to follow their own best chances for profit; before their service to the greater good came their service to the bottom line.

I should say right now that I have no quarrel with capitalism per se, or with the notion that one should make a reasonable profit for valued work. Problems arise, however, when we place the concrete realities of material gain and loss—the bottom line—ahead of less tangible realities, such as friends and family, service to one's community, the health of the environment, and vital matters of ethics, morality, love, commonwealth, and spirituality. Whatever the overarching economic system, to the extent that people must value, attend to, and take direction primarily from the world of money and things, their lives grow narcissistic and greedy. They move in tinier orbits, with limited range of curiosity, perception, imagination, and creativity. When whole nations become overly materialistic, they in effect place a price tag on everything; decisions come down to what will help or hurt the economy—especially, the pocketbooks of those making the decisions. Concerns that do not conform to some measure of profit-loss accounting fall off the table of discussion and out of public awareness.

This reveals another key principle of dominism: command over and control of the material world leads to greater powers of domination. Those who control the flow and use of natural resources; who control the labors of other people; who control the production and marketing of valued goods and services; who control the development, manufacture, and distribution of weapons; who control the creation and flow of information; who control the necessary supports for scientific and technological progress; and who control the movements of and access to capital, naturally and inevitably gather power, and thus greater riches, to themselves. This simultaneous accretion of power and wealth dictates that small groups of dominist elites (the overclass) come to feel self-evidently entitled to lord over far larger numbers of the poor and dispossessed (the underclass). The rich get richer, the poor get poorer, and the gap between rich and poor—citizens and nations—invariably grows larger.

All such dominance of the material world ultimately reduces to one's ability to pay for it. As the modern "golden rule" puts it: those who have the gold, rule. Money has become the one true measure of power as well as the most straightforward and socially acceptable means for exerting said power. In a dominist world, the full range of human experience gets subjugated to the exigencies of finance. The most basic rights to food, shelter, healthcare, and education become mere line items in government budgets; the rich and overfed quarrel over whether they can afford to fund such things. The self-serving concerns of a single corporate CEO can sidetrack such patently reasonable ideas as species and wilderness protection, universal childcare, or the development of alternative energy sources. Demonstrably foolish and failing programs—like the War on Drugs or the space-based defense initiative—can go on squandering public resources for decades as long as they enhance the bottom lines of the power elite.

Modern America reigns as the all-time champion of bottom-line materialism run amok. From its origins and nearly two centuries as a slave-based economy, through a tear-soaked trail of broken treaties with its indigenous peoples, and on through the modern era of robber barons, rapacious monopolizers, resource plunderers, labor exploiters, inside traders, market manipulators, and corporate raiders, the captains of American industry have always been willing to do—have felt it their most solemn duty to do—whatever it takes, however amoral, unethical, or illegal, to increase profits and power. Every day brings new evidence of a pathologically sick economic system: the obscene gains of failed CEOs, who cash in their lucrative stock options even as they cashier thousands of longtime employees; a campaign finance system that requires politicians to spend more time influence peddling than governing; the plight of local communities who watch vital industries skip town in pursuit of cheap labor and weak environmental standards; the money-stoked, full-steam-ahead marketing of genetically-modified crops, cloning, and nanotechnologies despite a host of troubling, unanswered questions; the industrial polluters and chemical purveyors, the megamall builders and paradise pavers, the old-growth loggers, oil drillers, stripminers, and factory farmers—all doing their jobs, just making their livings, while destroying whatever gets in the way of their God-given rights to turn a profit.

The Enron collapse in the fall of 2001 neatly demonstrated just about everything that can go wrong with bottom-line materialism. The largest bankruptcy in American history, and the series of related business scandals that followed, became a counter-balancing passion play to the War on Terrorism. In the end, we learned that when corporate executives, board members, financial auditors, and government regulators all have a stake in a company's bottom line then—surprise!—no one can be counted on to tell the truth or do the right thing. When bottom-line, paper profits become the top-of-the-mind, all-encompassing, prevailing corporate priorities, no one can afford to follow socially responsible, much less sound, business practices. When "I got mine" becomes the driving force and primary mantra in a culture, few will worry over the needs of others, bother with ethical concerns, or even notice the boundaries of common human decency.

Of course, America paid $500 billion to learn those same lessons just fifteen years earlier via the Savings and Loans fiasco. For that matter, business scandals of all stripes and sizes, from the epic to the crass and ordinary, have littered the American landscape from the beginning. It doesn't take a hard-boiled cynic to assume that the high-stakes shenanigans, ponzi schemes, and creative accounting practices that brought down Enron still pass for business-as-usual in too many corporate boardrooms. Though the wingtip crowd will make obligatory motions toward better understanding "what went wrong" and will pass a new law here and a regulation there, nothing substantive will change; especially, no changes will occur that might actually inhibit the profit-seeking prime directive of corporate culture. No amount of government regulation or industry self-audit and oversight can overcome the basic formula that drives bottom-line materialism: money increases power increases domination increases money.

"Greed is good," proclaimed Norman Gecko, the archetypal successful businessman in the movie *Wall Street*. Though Americans may cringe at the sentiment, we never actually refute it. Bottom-line materialism makes us greedy, which makes us money, which makes us good Americans.

The dangerous logic of bottom-line materialism dictates that every player—individual, small business, or large corporation—lives or dies according to its ability to keep income greater than expenses. This tyranny of the bottom line demands that non-material concerns have low priority in the day-to-day business of life. All of us must do what we must do to survive, to get ahead in the game, to stay on top. While many (indeed, most) try to run their lives and businesses without abandoning ethical, moral, or spiritual principles, and while some (far fewer) actually manage to balance great material success with non-material ideals, the greatest successes and largest corporations invariably follow, embody, and reflect the fundamental tenets of me-first, whatever-it-takes dominism.

An old story tells of a scorpion who, needing to cross a river, enlisted the aid of a turtle. "Let me climb on your back so you can carry me across," said the scorpion. The turtle protested, "But you will sting me and not only will I die, you will drown." The scorpion replied, "Nonsense, why would I do such a foolish thing?" So the turtle assented. Halfway across the river, the scorpion stung the turtle. As they both sank beneath the water, the turtle cried, "Why did you do that?" to which the scorpion replied: "I'm a scorpion."

As surely as a scorpion must sting, a bottom-line materialist must do whatever it takes to turn a profit. Greed is good, because greed increases profits. Increasing profits means increasing power means—bottom line—everything in dominist culture.

Competing Values

Virtue consisted in winning....Life was hierarchical and whatever happened was right. There were the strong, who deserved to win and always did win, and there were the weak, who deserved to lose and always did lose, everlastingly.

—**George Orwell**[10]

The trouble does not lie simply with the individual, nor can a single individual prevent it in his own isolated case. The trouble arises from the generally received philosophy of life, according to which life is a contest, a competition, in which respect is to be accorded to the victor. This view leads to an undue cultivation of the will at the expense of the senses and the intellect.

—**Bertrand Russell**[11]

A competitive culture endures by tearing people down.

—**Jules Henry**[12]

The year of America's War on Terrorism also brought the Winter Olympics to Salt Lake City. Before the games even began, a tawdry financial scandal undermined Salt Lake's selection as the host city, multiple allegations arose concerning public investments going into the pockets of private individuals, and a chorus of foreign voices protested excessive American jingoism at what fancies itself as a nation-transcending event. As the games wore on, several controversies erupted over dubious judging, Russia and South Korea threatened to quit and go home angry, and the usual bevy of doping scandals led to some withdrawn medals and questioned records.

Some games. In fact, like most sports from Little League baseball to the World Series, the Olympics have far more to do with fighting than playing. Though some individuals always stand out with their childlike love of play and the sheer joy they find in overcoming adversity, pushing beyond limits, and setting new standards of excellence, for too many athletes and fans it all comes down not to how you play the game, but whether you win or lose. Only one racer can finish first, only one team can win a championship, only one Olympian gets the gold: everyone else loses, falls short, disappoints, lets down, fails. In the end, everyone asks, "Who won?" and that's who we reward and remember. For the losers, the end comes like sudden death—cold, final, and heavy with regret.

Granted, many not only see no problem with this description of sports, they believe that the win-or-lose challenge provides the motivation, rationale, and ultimate thrill of any athletic contest. Athletes aspire to and achieve greatness, the argument goes, *because* of their deep drive to compete. One athlete on his or her own can only go so far, so fast; when two or more vie against each other, then all go further and faster. Competition, we're told, makes the mediocre great and the great, even better; without the hovering threat of loss, no one would rise to the challenge, would make the good fight, or would ever reach the top.

In dominist America, this pro-competition credo extends beyond sports to color virtually all aspects of life. It most obviously pertains in the business community, where competition looms as an omnipresent, vital force that—supposedly—keeps the engines of society well tuned and powering on. As early as kindergarten we see the introduction of win-lose learning experiences and pedagogic techniques that stress one student's success over another's failure. Primary and secondary education present a never-ending series of scores, tests, bees, contests, challenges, evaluations, tournaments, and final exams that grade and rank students from top of the class or team to bottom. We say this prepares students for the real world and, indeed, various competitions typically pursue one through life, determining where one works and what one gets paid and whether or not one gets funding for projects, or gets elected, or gets the girl, the promotion, the grant, the scoop, the recognition, or the best parking space. Our legal system assumes an adversarial relationship between any two parties in conflict and imagines that with advocates on both sides competing fiercely to win the case, truth and justice will somehow emerge. Similarly, our majority-rule political system divides people into two ever-bickering sides on every issue, as if the nasty business of competing for votes could actually render good public policy.

It will come as a surprise to most Americans to hear that a large body of scientific research[13] has demonstrated that all of the supposed benefits of competition amount to little more than shop-worn myths. Competition does not make athletes, workers, students, artists, lawyers, or politicians perform better. To the contrary, the evidence shows that the stresses of competition undermine the performances of most people, including winners. Being more competitive does not make businesses any more innovative, efficient, or productive. Rather, the structural demands of constant competition, including the aforementioned interpersonal stresses, deplete and misdirect human and natural resources that would otherwise go into products and services. Competition does not improve one's chances of surviving conditions of scarcity. The resources allocated toward grabbing and protecting a bigger piece of a limited pie ultimately cost more than the apparent prize. Competition neither reflects nor properly prepares one for the "real world." Instead, early exposure to competitive means and values can utterly destroy real human ways of cooperation, sharing, compassion, tolerance, and service to a greater good.

Even without the voluminous research on this subject, the many problems that competition brings to individuals, businesses, and nations appear with stark clarity to those willing to see. For every professional athlete gushing on about the joys of the competitive spirit, thousands of young people quit team sports, sickened and frustrated and determined to forever avoid all competition. The billionaire CEO crowing about the wonders of free market competition neatly overlooks the myriad bankruptcies, lawsuits, scandals, layoffs, polluted environments, unsafe products, dangerous work conditions, and everyday corporate misdeeds that pass for business-as-usual in any competitive system. The educators who prescribe yet more standardized testing for already troubled schools simply ignore the many signs—learning disabilities, attention deficit disorders, alcohol and drug abuse, truancy, cheating, violence—that point to grade-stressed children who have long lost their natural joy for learning.

Faced with such evidence, defenders of competition will resort to their fail-safe argument: Competition is basic human nature. To the competitor, the whole natural world functions as one big game of King of the Mountain. All living creatures necessarily compete—critter against critter, species against species—to meet their basic needs and to successfully reproduce. Survival of the fittest becomes the ultimate game; humans, as part of nature, must compete, and must do all that they can to survive, to live well, and to pass on genes.

This dog-eat-dog caricature of nature finds little validation within the scientific community. Since early in the 20th century, naturalists have been pointing to common and at times remarkable examples of cooperation throughout the plant and animal kingdoms. In any biosystem, we find a lush profusion of living beings, from microscopic bacterium to large, complex mammals and everything in between, which display an astonishing degree of interconnection as every creature in some way relates to every other creature. What the competitive see as a tooth and claw war for survival, to the cooperative-minded appears as the continuing cycle of all living systems: give and take, eat and be eaten, live and die.

Species disappear not because the sorry losers failed to compete, but because they failed to adapt to a changing environment. The historical record shows as many tough and nasty predator species gone extinct as "uncompetitive" weaklings. Survival of the fittest means that those who can best fit in will survive, and fitting in requires giving and taking in balance with the surrounding ecology. In periods when the environment remains stable, all species tend to thrive as they in essence cooperate to sustain the balance of life. When the environment becomes unstable—due to extreme conditions (weather, earthquake, fire, flood), the invasion of new species, or the actions of humans—then only those species that can adapt to new patterns of cooperation live on.

To our detriment, we mistakenly project human patterns of competition onto nature, proclaiming, "Competition is natural!" We utterly fail to see, much less appreciate, the dynamic interconnection and cooperation that governs the natural world. Most tragically, we fail to embody the essential, humane, and ever natural spirit of peaceful cooperation that should likewise govern the human world.

Competition diminishes people by directing their most creative juices toward the odious task of defeating others. When this becomes the predominant definition of a life, then whither love, compassion, empathy, sharing, play, wholeness, and simple human kindness? When we make the goal of beating others our top priority, we naturally have less focus on and commitment of energy and resources to the task at hand, much less to the interpersonal and psychoemotional consequences of our actions. Nice guys finish last, while the winners typically leave a trail of stepped-on toes and elbowed ribs in their wake.

American dominists show zero tolerance for anti-competitive views and dismiss all such talk as the nattering lamentations of the weak, the lost, and the envious. Competition, they never tire of shouting, has made America great, while cooperation has long been discredited as the foolish standard of communism, socialism, and '60s counterculturalism. Our leaders do everything they can to turn governance into a cutthroat competition for money and votes, then cast aspersions upon the evils of "big government" and taxation that might allow for the cooperative funding of essential goods and services. The culture makes icons out of millionaire rogues and thieves, while woefully underfunding, and basically ignoring, such noncompetitive professionals as nurses, teachers, police, firefighters, EMTs, and childcare workers. Having established competition as the state religion, America consigns losers to a purgatory of restricted access, marginal rights, under-funded opportunities, and outright disenfranchisement.

Like the other basic tenets of dominism, competition eliminates contrary viewpoints and values. As the Parable of the Tribes predicts, within any system if just one individual or group becomes competitive, then all must eventually compete or perish. Wherever the competitive ethos rules, cooperation becomes less viable. The dangerous logic of competition allows no other way; from insects to human beings to mono-God Himself, everything contends with everything else in a winners-take-all game of life. Only losers have cause to complain and no one listens to losers.

Secret Governance

I believe there are more instances of the abridgment of the freedom of the people by gradual and silent encroachments of those in power than by violent and sudden usurpations.

—**James Madison**[14]

The 7,000 pages of the Pentagon Papers prove that nothing our leaders said should have been taken at face value. It's naive and even irresponsible for a grownup today to get her or his information about foreign policy and war and peace exclusively from the administration in power. It's essential to have other sources of information, to check those against one's own common sense, and to form your own judgment as to whether we ought to go to or persist in war.

—**Daniel Ellsberg**[15]

If we live in a world filled with evildoers and cutthroat competitors where the mass of humanity stands against us rather than with us, and if constant interpersonal struggle, violence, and war so define the human condition, then common sense dictates that we approach most relationships from a protective veil of suspicion and secrecy. As a necessary function of growing up dominist, we come to view others—even family members, but especially strangers, foreigners, and those we perceive as fundamentally different—as potential threats to our happiness. Everyone more or less becomes "the other side" in the great and petty wars that fill our days. Just as we learn to never show our hand in a game of cards, so we learn, in the dominist game of life, to keep our innermost thoughts and feelings securely to ourselves.

The more dominist a relationship becomes, the more essential the need for secrecy between parties. For two or more people engaged in a struggle for dominance, each person's "inside" information has the potential to become, in the opposition's hands, a weakening force or fatal blow. The need to keep one's secrets to oneself, combined with the quest to discover the secrets of others, can cast a distrustful subtext on the most innocent of relationships.

Any group, organization, or social enterprise made up of such secrecy-inflicted individuals develops an information hierarchy based on access to inside information. We can picture this as a large circle defining the group, with a series of concentric sub-circles within, defining deepening levels of information access. All members of a group become classified according to level of access, a classification which relates to power and money. The closer one moves to the inner circle of a group, the more one learns of the group's deepest secrets. Group function comes to depend on the members of each sub-circle keeping secrets from those outside the sub-circle, while the whole group keeps most everything secret from absolute outsiders. Naturally, everybody learns to distrust most everyone else, distrust well earned as most everyone else tries to uncover everybody's deepest secrets.

Secrecy, in such an organization, functions like a form of currency. Success, power, and wealth obtain to the one that can gather the most secrets and keep them most securely. Businesses jealously guard their research, designs, formulas, and plans, even as they ferret out the inside information of their competitors. Governments develop great and complex webs of data classification; the more dominist the government, the more assiduously it hides information from other governments, from its civilian population, and within the government, one agency from another. Athletes hide their game plans and strategies, as journalists hide developing stories, politicians hide personal agendas and dirty laundry, financial analysts hide insider tips, religious authorities hide the shameful behavior of subordinates, manufacturers hide product flaws, and environmental polluters hide incriminating data. Lawyers, by law, hide every word, document, or communication that comes their way. Likewise, the military hides everything it can and considers the willing breach of its classified information the worst form of treason.

While we may raise a great ruckus over specific secrets as they come to light, we rarely question the personal and professional impulse to hold secrets in the first place. Rather, like all things dominist, we tend to accept chronic suspicion and the cult of secrecy as just human nature and the way things work.

When, however, the most dominant government in history takes the practice of secrecy far beyond the limits of common sense and basic decency and when, in its craving to keep things hidden, it casually violates a host of ethical and moral standards, and when it connives to conceal especially odious, even criminal, circumstances, then we can certainly hope for a widespread awakening to the dangers of secret governance. Enter the George W. Bush administration.

One of the first acts of the new President was to counter a Freedom of Information law that would have released documents from the Reagan and Bush Sr. administrations. This was followed by a series of still-secret meetings led by Vice President Dick Cheney at which executives from the oil and energy industries helped to craft the nation's energy policies. After 9/11 came the USA Patriot Act, a collection of laws and fiats that, among other things, closed formerly open immigration hearings and led to the secret arrest and detainment of hundreds of individuals. As the War on Terror progressed it spawned the standard trappings of the Security State: increasing government surveillance of the People, decreasing transparency of government activities, and authoritative assurances throughout that it was all for the nation's own good.

Yet, conversely, for more than a year the Bush administration resisted the sort of independent congressional investigation into 9/11 that had followed many similar, though far less serious, events in American history. The administration seemed bent on engaging in the classic blunder of presidential cover-up. Little tidbits that managed to leak to the press—showing data overlooked and warnings ignored—only added to the sense that someone had something to hide. When Bush finally did appoint an investigative commission, he named master secret-monger Henry Kissinger to lead the effort. Though Kissinger would eventually withdraw from the commission (he was unwilling disclose personal secrets), his brief association with it and the fact that Bush would even consider him for the job left the whole enterprise tainted.

With the passage of the Homeland Security Act in October 2002 the Bush administration's quest for absolute control of the nation's secrets turned utterly Orwellian (a word that, after just two years of Bush and company, had grown in use a millionfold). The bill authorized the new Total Information Awareness office to snoop into every aspect of American life—from grocery purchases to internet traffic, to every airplane taken and motel room rented, to medical prescriptions, housing sales, video rentals, and tax statements—and then to correlate the data with individual fingerprints and social security numbers. In an action sure to arouse Big Brother watchers and conspiracy theorists, the office was given the logo of an all-seeing eye scrutinizing the planet from atop a giant pyramid with the motto *scientia est potentia*—knowledge is power.

The pernicious logic of secrecy dictates that knowledge/power accrues to those who best control the flow of and access to information. The Bush administration contended that the knowledge gained from its invasion of the public's privacy and suspension of civil rights was needed to make the nation powerful enough to win the war on terrorism. They had to know the People's secrets, even as they kept government secrets from the public. By expanding its knowledge of everyone who may in any way stand against it, the administration would increase its powers, promote its survival, and prevail against hordes of evildoers. Simultaneously, by concealing its own secrets from all outsiders, it would undermine the powers of potential enemies. That all this was, according to Bush, driven by the exigencies of a perpetual war, meant that Americans should grow accustomed to living with suspicion, paranoia, and the cult of secrecy.

The War on Terra

The "control of nature" is a phrase conceived in arrogance, born of the Neanderthal age of biology and philosophy.... It is our alarming misfortune that so primitive a science has armed itself with the most modern and terrible weapons.

—**Rachel Carson**[16]

No sane person seeks a world divided between billions of excluded people living in absolute deprivation and a tiny elite guarding their wealth and luxury behind fortress walls. No one rejoices at the prospect of life in a world of collapsing social and ecological systems. Yet we continue to place human civilization and even the survival of our species at risk mainly to allow a million or so people to accumulate money beyond any conceivable need.

—**David C. Korten**[17]

One final arrow in the dominist quiver demands our attention: To the extent that an individual, group, or nation turns dominist, it inevitably turns against the environment. Wherever dominists go, they terrorize the local ecology by depleting natural resources, generating excessive wastes, spewing toxins into the earth, air, and water, and eliminating plant and animal species. To the planet, dominist humans behave like out-of-control cancer cells, multiplying beyond the bounds of balance and reason, while destroying the host in the process.

The fact that their lifestyles prove so detrimental to the environment causes little concern to dominists. "Since humans are superior to plants and animals," they reason, "human needs matter more than the needs of other species, which matter not at all." The Bible makes clear that nature exists to serve humanity; God commands that man shall "have dominion over the fish of the sea, and over the fowl of the air, and over every living thing that moveth upon the Earth." The modern gods of mammon concur: any degradation of the Earth, including the wholesale elimination of other species and entire ecosystems, makes good sense if it supports the best interests of and turns a profit for the dominist elite.

Such antienvironmentalism flows ineluctably from each of the aforementioned dominist principles. Militarism, for example, causes unfathomable damage to nature. Contending armies have been setting the enemy's fields and forests afire, killing their livestock, poisoning their wells and streams, and salting their earth since the beginning of organized warfare. America, the reigning prince of war, has blanketed the Japanese cities of Hiroshima and Nagasaki with nuclear radiation, has defoliated Vietnam with the extreme toxin Agent Orange, has similarly poisoned the marijuana- and coca-producing landscapes of several nations, has used uranium-tipped bombs in Iraq (twice) and Bosnia, and has rained tons and tons of destruction on too many biosystems to mention. Just practicing and preparing for war takes a horrible toll in wasted and misdirected natural resources. Moreover, in modern times especially, the destruction goes on long after the fighting stops, from scattered land mines and unexploded bombs, and long-persisting toxins, and flora and fauna that may take generations to recover. War is hell, especially, because it leaves the environment hellish.

The militant dominists who perpetrate these crimes do so without a trace of hesitation or thought given to the ecological consequences of their actions. While they have learned to at least pay lip service to the problem of civilian casualties—those nagging collateral damages—damage to nature still goes unacknowledged. Worse, those who try to raise environmental concerns during war get branded as fools and sissies; standing for the environment always means standing against the dominists.

We likewise see strong currents of unilateralism in the antienvironmental worldview. The more pressing ecological concerns transcend boundaries between peoples and nations. One nation acting alone cannot hope to address such issues as ocean and air pollution, ozone depletion, species extinction, or climate change; people everywhere contribute in large or small measure to these problems and genuine solutions demand that all people come together and work cooperatively. Yet one superpower acting unilaterally can throw a tar-ball of self-interest into the best laid plans of expert panels and global conferences. As America repeatedly demonstrates, when might makes right, it also makes any contrary or discomfiting science wrong, especially that coming from do-gooder environmentalists.

The dominist principles of monotheism, materialism, competition, and sexism also tend toward environmental ruin. I have already mentioned some of the antienvironmental antecedents found in the Bible. While people of various religions have at times behaved destructively toward the local ecology, monotheists have by far done the most serious damage, in part because their theologies focus adherents more on heaven than on a deep and abiding love of nature. Likewise, while other economic systems, most notably communism, have taken terrible tolls on the environment, the competitive, bottom-line materialist greed of 20th century America has brought the entire planet to the brink of ecological disaster on multiple fronts. Wherever sexist, male-dominating culture takes root, Mother Nature suffers as badly as the women do. Conversely, the most gender-balanced societies today, such as Sweden and Norway—have the world's most environmentally progressive and enlightened attitudes and practices.

Antienvironmentalism especially reeks of xenophobia. The xenophobe's fear and hatred of others logically extends to wild and unruly Nature. Xenophobes attack Nature's otherness with evangelistic zeal, aiming to cage, tame, domesticate, or eliminate all creatures that give offense. Nothing rankles the xenophobic dominist more than the profuse, teeming diversity of Nature. He will raze a forest to plant the straight and ordered rows of a woodlot, will bulldoze mountains to lay the straight and ordered asphalt of an interstate, will dam, dredge, and redirect rivers to create straight and ordered industrial waterways.

Dominists suffer such a profound disconnection from alien Nature that they barely feel the tragic consequences of their behavior. While the whole planet slips into a chaotic stew of global climate change, with people everywhere crying out for enlightened leadership, with scientists everywhere crying out for immediate action, members of the dominist overclass plunder-blunder on, utterly incognizant of the terrors they perpetrate. They rigidly view others—human, plant, and animal—as separate, different, and probably evil, and perforce fail to understand the self-inflicted wounds of their xenophobic attacks.

The twisted logic of antienvironmentalism leads us down a hard path of ever-increasing peril: Those who do not experience connection with the environment will come to fear and hate it, will thus abuse it, will thereby turn it unsuitable for healthy human habitation, and will therefore experience increasing disconnection, fear, and hatred. Moreover, while dominism has always cast an antienvironmental pall upon the world, the past century and a half of industrial dominism has resulted in threats of planet-sized dimension. For all the dangers of global militarism, antienvironmentalism poses the most serious of challenges to sustainable human culture.

This examination of antienvironmentalism reveals a critical key in our understanding of dominism. Like threads in a finished tapestry, or like strands of viral DNA, each of these basic tenets of dominism—militarism, unilateralism, monotheism, sexism, xenophobia, materialism, competition, secrecy, and antienvironmentalism—connects to, feeds upon, interacts with, and reinforces the others. Militarists tend to behave unilaterally, to take absolute religious and philosophical beliefs, and to create sexist, materialistic, competitive, secretive societies. Xenophobes fervently militate against other races, religions, ethnic groups, economic systems, species, and the opposite sex. Materialistic societies develop strong militaries, fixed gender roles, highly competitive culture, and an errant disregard of the environment. We never see just one of these behavioral patterns in isolation; rather, they tend to manifest, in varying degrees, as essential elements of a whole worldview and lifestyle.

While an individual will embody certain of these tenets more than others, and may bypass some entirely—the soldier who loves nature, the male CEO who treats women as full equals, the ardent monotheist who preaches non-violence and antiracism—the more dominist a person or group becomes, the more powerfully they will manifest the full pattern of dominist thought and behavior. Since the dangerous logic of dominism dictates constant viral expansion, dominist individuals and groups invariably grow more militaristic, unilateralist, monotheistic, sexist, xenophobic, materialistic, competitive, secretive, and antienvironmental with time and experience. Once infected with any aspect of viral dominism, one eventually succumbs to the whole disease.

Three

The Common Infection

But if violence is "just" in one instance as determined by the state, why might it not also be "just" in another instance, as determined by an individual? How can a society that justifies capital punishment and warfare prevent its justifications from being extended to assassination and terrorism? If a government perceives that some causes are so important as to justify the killing of children, how can it hope to prevent the contagion of its logic spreading to its citizens—or to its citizens' children?

—Wendell Berry[1]

The events of September 11th, 2001 prompted a great rush of change throughout the world. It had an immediate impact on the workings of governments, as all reacted with some combination of dominism-driven fight, flight, and surrender. Geopolitical structures and dynamics tilted perilously, with unlikely alliances forming here, and international treaties collapsing there, and every nation struggling to adapt to the exigencies of the newest world war. The global economy teetered on the brink of collapse for several months, while world markets went through periods of chaos and rates of unemployment increased everywhere.

The changes spawned by 9/11, and by the anthrax scares that followed, swept through every crevice and corner of American culture. Most businesses underwent some degree of reexamination and alteration. Airports and airlines, the U.S. Postal Service, and the insurance industry all moved to quickly adapt to the stark realities of terror America. A whole new government agency came into existence with the brief to do absolutely whatever it takes to guarantee homeland security. A country that had for years been moving away from "big government" suddenly discovered a groundswell of demand for increasing federal budgets and expanding the scope of public health services, law enforcement agencies, safety inspectors, product regulators, and everything military.

All of these changes cost huge amounts of public and private monies, and thus overrode the economic assumptions, forecasts, plans, programs, and policies that existed before 9/11. Along with this drastic shock to the American economy, most civil rights—the whole culture of American freedom—squirmed beneath the stiffening thumb of security-driven government. We saw patriotic censorship of the media as several journalists lost their jobs for questioning the nation's leadership. The head of CNN demanded of his reporters that they only show and tell news that supported America's war in Afghanistan. The Congress passed legislation, with near unanimity, that gave a host of restrictive new powers to law enforcement, expanding the government's ability to eavesdrop, to search and seize, to imprison without trial, and to deport without due process. The FBI pushed for the right to use torture when necessary, the CIA for permission to assassinate foreign leaders. Racial profiling as a law enforcement tactic suddenly gained the approval of many formerly squeamish liberals, including a large percentage of African-Americans.

As the nation's institutions twisted and turned to the new post-9/11 reality, we the people also changed. The "it will never happen here" confidence that had graced the American people through all the gruesome violence of the 20th century crumbled with the collapse of the twin towers and further dwindled with every new report of anthrax. Americans rushed out in droves to purchase more guns and to tighten security systems, as if either offered adequate protection from the threats at hand. We became, in many ways, a shell-shocked people, a whole nation suffering from post-traumatic stress and feeling vulnerable to dire but unseen threats. As our tension levels increased and persisted, physical, mental, and emotional health declined. People of all ages reported difficulty sleeping, addiction counselors saw a national trend of increasing substance and alcohol abuse, and doctors and emergency rooms strained to provide optimal care to all while dealing with fears of anthrax, antibiotic misuse, the onset of flu season, and a whole nation reeling with stress-induced symptoms.

In the immediate aftermath of 9/11, America did experience some positive responses, as people came together in one great national embrace, with heart-thumping praise for the many acts of heroism, with prayers for the dead and assistance for the suffering, with a patriotic fervor to stand behind our leaders and to act with unambiguous unity, and, especially, with a near-universal need to see God's presence in all that had happened and all that must arise from such tragedy. Yet within weeks the awesome sense of being connected began to unravel. The bipartisan pledges and actions of our leaders went first, as parochial interests, rigid ideologies, and plain old pig-at-the-public-trough greed drove most members of the ruling class back into their me-first corners. The warm honeymoon for the American people also came to a harsh end as myriad forms of religious intolerance, social injustice, and interpersonal bigotry once again gripped the American psyche. For too many Americans, such traits only worsened with 9/11.

In essence, America experienced and eventually succumbed to a dominist plague of immense scope and destructive force. If the nation's first response felt strong, healthy, and bittersweet good, it only mirrored the body's first response to a new infection, as the immune system mobilizes to meet the challenge and all of the body's innate strengths and healing powers come into action. But just as an especially tenacious virus can overwhelm the immune response of even the healthiest of bodies, so the extraordinary force of the viral wave unleashed by 9/11 expanded the load and sheer power of the dominism virus throughout American society and ultimately overwhelmed America's best.

America had always been dominism-infected, as indeed the world has been for thousands of years. As always happens during times of war, the degree of contamination greatly increased, as did the severity of symptoms. The more dominist tendencies of the culture gained succor from the fresh infection, becoming ever more coercive and forceful, while forms of otherwise latent dominism flared into new social pathologies.

Dominism Embodied

And so I walk the streets, aware of the pervasive ugliness of the people ... the lines of hurt and anxiety and greed around their eyes and mouths, the imbalance of their walk, the deformation of their bodies. Oh no, it is not genetic. Civilization has twisted and scarred those bodies as surely as it has damaged and tortured the face of the planet.

—**George Leonard**[2]

Spreading dominism begins with the contamination of individual minds and bodies. The dominism virus travels as coercive beliefs enfolded within matrices of vital emotional energy. As the virus invades and proliferates within a person, it plants some variation of dominist thoughts that grow, quickly or slowly, from infectious ideas into central and compelling beliefs about oneself and the world. "It's kill or be killed, win or lose, succeed or fail," a person thinks. "I must exert my power over them before they exert their power over me." To the dominism-infected mind, competition makes more sense than cooperation, physically controlling a situation makes more sense than talking things through, and gaining security through aggressive threats makes more sense than developing trust and common ground.

The dominist worldview rests upon the ancient and toxic belief in unending struggle for limited resources. To the dominist, life consists of a series of zero-sum competitions. There can only exist so much land, food, work, money, fame, political power, friendship, love, or room in heaven: there's them that gets and them that don't, and however tawdry or shameful the process of getting may get, it always beats losing. Even the sorriest losers in the struggle for dominance tend to judge themselves guilty of failure, rather than question the overarching system. Everybody wants to win.

The more dominism-infected one's mental processes, the more one sees a world of power hierarchies, with winners on top and losers on the bottom and everyone driven by chronic patterns of fight, flight, and surrender. The dominist mind sees conflict everywhere. Other people represent threats to one's current position or opportunities to move up. Dominist thinking turns the most mundane of activities—driving on the highway, picking a line at the supermarket, dressing for work—into stressful, win-lose competitions.

Naturally, dominism produces many more losers than winners. In a perverse way, this provides comfort to the losers, since misery does love company, and the fact that so many others share one's awful lot makes it easier to accept, easier to think "it's just the way life is." For the winners, the fact that so few manage to reach the top proves their own worthiness and that they deserve their rewards. To the extent that the losers envy and wish to emulate the winners, they validate and support the whole system. To the extent that the winners fear losing their privileged positions, they feel justified in doing whatever it takes to sustain dominance.

Once infected with the dangerous logic of domination, our minds become trapped in unending cycles of self-destroying prophecy. Like rats in a sadist's maze, our thoughts run back and forth, forever covering the same old ground and coming to the same old end: dominate or submit, win or lose, do unto others before they do unto you, survive at any and all costs. Dominism-infected minds can only see a dominist world and can only think of dominist responses to all that happens in that world.

Viral dominism also sinks deeply into our emotional energies and changes the way we feel about ourselves and about others. As the virus proliferates within a person, it expands the charge and force—the coercive power—of difficult emotional energies. Feelings such as fear, anger, shame, grief, depression, guilt, and terror grow stronger, taking on ever more power and overwhelming one's more positive and productive thoughts and emotions.

Emotional contamination begins with the demands of fight, flight, and surrender. Viral dominism triggers within the individual some mix and measure of emotional response to the ancient quandary of coercive force. One feels driven from within—emotionally compelled—to fight back, run away, or passively submit. Ironically, the more coercive an external force, the more coercive the feelings aroused within. The more dominated we feel by events, the more self-dominating our emotional energies become.

Coercive emotional energies have the power to completely overtake a person or group and to render reasoned responses to a situation as ineffective or even unimaginable. Panic attacks, nervous breakdowns, stage fright, stress-induced illness, and a myriad of compulsive, obsessive, and addictive behaviors all point to some degree of emotional overwhelm—of times when emotions dominate and drive human behavior. Likewise, instances of mass hysteria, market panics, and war fever show the power of coercive emotional energies to command even large populations.

Call it the dangerous illogic of negative emotion. One fears that unpleasant feelings will get worse, or rages about having lost control, or feels depressed about how depressed one has become, or feels ashamed of one's shame. At such times, an emotional response to negative emotions frustratingly feeds the original negativity, setting in motion an ever-intensifying loop of negative feedback.

I have written at length elsewhere[3] about ways to resolve this emotional conundrum and to turn human emotion into a creative and transformational force. Suffice it to say that unless we actively and intentionally *use* our feelings then we tend to become contaminated and lessened by them. All emotions consist of creative energies that either give power or overpower, depending on whether we use the energy or struggle against it.

Most people never learn the healthy and creative use of emotional energy. They feel dominated by emotional energies, as difficult emotions self-perpetuate into ever more difficult feelings and eventual overwhelm. Or they manage some degree of dominance of their emotions: they control their feelings by suppressing any movement of emotional energies and stifling their whole emotional experience.

Unfortunately, while collapsing into emotional overwhelm puts one at the effect of debilitating feelings, dominating oneself into a state of stifled and unmoving emotional suppression does no better. The more we suppress the difficult feelings, the less able we become to feel anything at all. We may indeed successfully control our emotions, but at such a cost. We run the risk of becoming the living dead, stone-hearted and unfeeling, one of a great tribe of insensate humans that has throughout history inflicted endless harm upon others.

Moreover, as numerous medical researchers have demonstrated, suppressed emotional energies—our unresolved stresses and tensions—cause a wide variety of physical and mental problems. A healthy body and mind depends upon the free movement of vital energies. The more we suppress our emotions, the more stuck and stifled our vital energies become, and the more vulnerable we become to various pathologies.

When we succumb to viral dominism we turn into, as mind and body, both victims and carriers of this most ancient disease. We all harbor the dominism virus, just as we all manifest some degree of dominist thought and behavior, ranging from the mildly chronic to the dangerously acute. Moreover, we, the dominism-twisted and -scarred, form the relationships, populate the groups and institutions, and perform the very actions that create and define human nature and experience.

Gender War

Wealth engendered the need for defense, and by the time the men were through protecting the women, they would be talking about protecting their women.

—**William Irwin Thompson**[4]

Most men—even most men who believe in principle that this "right" is unfounded—cling hard to their right to rule the world. And most women—including many who are ashamed of the feeling—feel deep down a certain willingness to let them go on ruling it.

—**Dorothy Dinnerstein**[5]

Because so much of human relationship derives from the toxic demands of viral dominism; because dominist thought turns differences between people into hierarchical rankings; and because humans have been infected with dominism for so long as to consider it normal, natural, and "just the way we are," the most insidious and undermining effects of dominism occur in the primary relationship between man and woman. We have already examined the sexism that derives from fundamentalist religious beliefs; now we must explore the biological and social roots of viral sexism.

From the time that people first found themselves having to deal with threats of violence, the natural differences between women and men mutated into reasons why each gender should confine itself to specific, non-negotiable roles in life and positions in the community. Since men-as-a-group have always had bigger and stronger bodies—more capable of fighting, of reacting to attack, and of inflicting harm—they naturally took charge of all things having to do with warfare, weapons, and fortifications. They became the defenders of society and the agents of all aggressive activities. Moreover, because the exigencies of actual and threatened violence trump all other needs, a host of further powers accrued to man-the-warrior: men took over governance of the group, determined collective priorities, directed the acquisition and allocation of essential resources, and, in most cases, took control of the group's spiritual life. Simultaneously, men-as-a-group also took charge of the family: patrilineal descent became the rule, as did male control of finances, childrearing, and sexual relations.

Since women-as-a-group have always been potentially or actually pregnant, birthing, nursing, and mothering young children, they naturally took charge of all things related to that vital yet confining stage of life. In peaceful societies the woman's role as progenitor of the race tended to draw other powers to her, leading to instances of matriarchal rule and matrilineal descent in early human culture, as well as women in key roles as healers, teachers, and priestesses. But the coming of violence would change all that. In a dominism-driven society, the demands of mothering, and especially the late term of pregnancy, become major liabilities. The woman can do little to aid in the common fight, nor can she move quickly in times of flight; indeed, she and her brood require special assistance and protection from man, making his job that much harder.

Thus there arose a rigid dominist mindset: women and men display fundamentally different designs and capabilities so, for the good of society, each should stick to what they do best. Women should confine themselves to hearth and home, manage issues of female fertility, pregnancy, and birth, take care of the little ones, and handle various domestic needs of men so that they can better handle their worldly duties. Men should husband all things, from hearth and home (where they wisely delegate to the women and children certain manageable tasks), to the workings of society, to interactions with other cultures, to relations with the cosmos and divinity. Men should take charge of life, women should submit unto their husbands, and God will rain His blessings on the whole deal.

The more dominist a culture, the more sensible this arrangement would become. Man would seem destined and designed—genetically "hard-wired"—to serve not only as warrior and protector, but as king, priest, hero, philosopher, scientist, artist, explorer, inventor, teacher, doctor, boss, provider, head of the family, and all-round expert. Woman would seem differently designed, somewhat flawed, but nonetheless perfectly suited for sex, babies, motherhood, and providing welcome assistance to man—nurse to doctor, secretary to boss, handmaiden to hero, prostitute to soldier/worker, and wife to husband.

With time this gender arrangement has settled deeply into the human psyche. Any mental, physical, emotional, or spiritual differences between men and women—even the slightest differences, even imagined differences—became proof for the dominist's pudding. Men-as-a-group became the dominant gender by genetic design, practical consequence, divine fiat, common sense, and simple observation; women-as-a-group became the weaker sex, the second-class citizen, the spare rib and helpmeet. The more dominist a society, the more it would view gender inequality and fixed roles as basic human nature and God's own plan and the less it would tolerate any deviances from this "natural order."

Yet we have to ask: were this sociosexual arrangement truly natural, would it require such unfathomable violence to maintain? As modern feminists have painstakingly catalogued, living as the submissive gender in a dominist world has been an unrelenting experience of beatings, rapes, burnings, veilings, foot-bindings, genital mutilations, enslavements, infanticides, witch hunts, intimidations, molestations, harassments, disenfranchisements, disempowerments, and, through it all, unending and dehumanizing subordinations to men. So mundane and ordinary has it all seemed, that only in the late 20th century—again, thanks to the courageous scholarship and political actions of the feminist movement—have terms and concepts such as "wife battering," "date rape," "glass ceiling," "sexual harassment," and "domestic violence" entered the common lexicon. After thousands of years of suffering, we have only just begun to bring light to this darkest aspect of the human experience.

Consider, for example, the practice of patrilineal descent, a simple and nearly universal legality that gives financial and political power to husbands, sons, and brothers. Consider the profound impact of this system on generations of female bodies and souls: the lifelong feelings of poor self-esteem from growing up as the "wrong" sex; the anatomical effects of forever lowering one's gaze in the presence of men, of cutting off one's voice, or of stooping lest one seem too tall; the utter malnourishment from getting less food, less encouragement, and less education than spouses and brothers; the deep-seated, visceral anxieties from having no control over money and property, nor any rights to take such control; and the degraded sexuality of one who has been forced into submission.

Or consider war. Histories of warfare always recount the experiences of the kings, princes, knights, and soldiers, sometimes with brief asides to the inevitable civilian casualties. Only at the dawning of the 21st century have we begun to acknowledge that a prime weapon of most every conquering army in human history has been the rape and humiliation of the loser's women and girls. Every great empire, from the Romans to the Americans, has derived much of its dominance from the violent subjugation of women.

Yet, as terrorizing as dominist culture has been for women-as-a-group, men-as-a-group have fared no better. Men have been equally brutalized by the ways and means of domination. The young boy, bred and conditioned for warfare, loses most of the vibrant, tingling joy of life before the battles ever begin. If he does not die—another young, male body for the ever-hungry war machine—he will likely suffer some degree of physical or psychoemotional maiming. To the extent that organized violence has been a primary preoccupation of dominist culture, men have paid with dehumanizing training, dreadful deeds forever remembered, and inevitable suffering, win or lose.

When men are not marching off to war—for the good of country and family and usually with the approval of the women in their lives—they march their bodies off to work, for the very same reasons and with equal encouragement. "Making a living" defines a man, and as the bodies of miners, lumberjacks, truck-drivers, and white-collar workers all painfully proclaim, the muscle-wrenching, bone-weary reality of work can make a slow but steady dying out of every day. While men take great pride in their working lives—the healthy sweat of honest labor, the rough and calloused hands of a man's job, the strong but aching muscles of a good day's work, and the weary satisfaction of providing for one's family—too much of a man's labor occurs at the dominating demands of bosses, bankers, and bill collectors.

And how do men really feel about their primary duties as protectors and providers? A fair enough question, but one rarely answered. Basic to a man's training as cannon fodder and/or cog in the wheel comes a profound loss of somato-emotional feeling. The little boy learns to rein in his emotions, to suppress his tears, to never show any weak or womanly loss of control over his internal experience. Emotions provide no value for the warrior/worker, so he chokes them off instead. Sadly, such denial of feeling means nothing less than slow suicide and, tragically, such living-dead men perfectly populate violence-driven and dominism-bound societies.

Naturally, the sexual experience of those at constant war with all bodily feelings and sensations raises something of a quandary. Sex can provide a great healing balm for men, if it brings them home to the simple pleasures of physical embodiment and intimate connection with another. Sex more often becomes an ordeal, an unfulfilled aching, an empty, driven conquest, or a brief, explosive moment of something so sweet, but so quickly gone again. No wonder that men, conditioned from early childhood for the lifelong competitions of war and work, so compulsively turn sex into yet another competition against other men. Nor that men, inculcated from early childhood with the normality of violence, so often and so easily cross over the line from making love with women to waging war against them.

For all their perks and powers as the dominant gender, men-as-a-group suffer as miserably in dominist culture as women-as-a-group. Though men hold many advantages over women, and though women experience terrible abuses at the hands of men, in truth everybody loses under dominism, for everybody becomes differently though equally demeaned, lessened, and abused. Both genders breathe the same foul air; nobody reaches his or her full human potential.

Remember, dominism produces many more losers than winners, so most individual men find themselves under the domination of somebody. Conversely, most individual women become the dominators of somebody else. Wealthy women dominate the poor of both genders, just as educated women dominate the uneducated, beautiful women dominate the unattractive, white women (in America) dominate people of color, and women everywhere dominate their children. Dominist culture creates a number of overlapping and interacting power-hierarchies and pecking orders; an individual will find him or herself at the top of one and at the bottom of another and will shift beliefs, perceptions, and behaviors accordingly. In modern America, poor, uneducated black women face the bleakest of prospects, which helps to explain the high birthrates and widespread single motherhood among such women—within their own little families they hold real power.

Some women may protest that we trivialize the enormous suffering that women have sustained, so much at the hands of men, by suggesting that the suffering of men has been equally grave. Consider, however, that in most of the world women outlive men despite the violence and inequities women everywhere endure. The organized abuse of dominism has done both genders incalculable harm.

On the other hand, some men may protest that we cannot stress enough the extent to which women have been partners in so much of dominist culture: in the socio-sexual conditioning of sons and daughters; in the glorification and lustful encouragement of warriors, soldiers, outlaws, and bad boys; in joining in the mythologizing of the "good provider" while coming to expect that men effectively manage the external world; and in often finding pleasure in sexual submission. At the very least, the modern man, fed up with being blamed for all of the world's sins, will gripe that women must admit to some self-serving complicity in the varied abuses of dominism.

All such complaints, from men and women both, utterly miss the point. The flesh-and-blood reality of both genders tells an equally sad story of dominist-driven suffering. The weight of countless generations of viral dominism has changed what it means and how it feels to live as woman and man and has degraded the nature and experience of all human relationship. We must concern ourselves not with assigning blame but with understanding the fundamental pain of all human beings so that we may finally begin to heal and thereby discover the ways of thinking, living, and making peace.

Poisonous Pedagogy

Almost everywhere we find the effort . . . to rid ourselves as quickly as possible of the child within us—i.e., the weak, helpless, dependent creature—in order to become an independent, competent adult deserving of respect. When we reencounter this creature in our children, we persecute it with the same measures once used on ourselves.

—**Alice Miller**[6]

At some point after every act of terrorism, we learn all about the perpetrator. We discover, typically, a young man driven by dark and unforgiving inner demons. The family, friends, and neighbors of the young man all swear that he was once a normal and in every way ordinary little boy. He was not, they assure us, born rotten; somehow, in the passing from toddler to young man, something went terribly wrong. What happened, then, to turn the little boy into the cruel monster?

The Common Infection

We have thus far been exploring the effects of organized violence in both creating and spreading viral dominism. We have seen that the dominating actions of groups, tribes, and nations invariably force other groups, tribes, and nations into like actions and that the resulting infection eventually reaches to the very heart of human nature and the relationship between men and women. Now we come to the saddest of all facts of life: dominism-bound men and women naturally raise dominism-infected children. The family serves as host, incubator, and prime vector for viral dominism.

All of the world's terrorists, aggressors, tyrants, and oppressors, male and female, past and present, share one trait: they grew up in dominist families. The Spanish inquisitor, torturing pagans, witches, midwives, and other nonbelievers, was himself the end product of a dominism-infected family system. He had been conditioned from birth by his primary caregivers to accept the dominist's ideology and the angry dictates of a dominating God. As with the young in any abusively dominating culture, he himself had been abusively dominated as a basic part of his early upbringing. By the time he rose to church-based power, he was a festering plague of dominist abuse, obsessed with putting to the stake any semblance of peaceful reality.

When, several hundred years later, an American president pulverizes a tiny third-world nation to show the costs of arousing America's wrath, he too acts as the product of a dominism-infected family system that conditioned him to the colonizer's values, the warmonger's means, and the fundamentalist's high moral ground. He too was bred for dominist reality from the beginning—first through interaction with his parents, and later within the dominist systems of preppie clubs, the military, and government service. By the time he struggled to the position of commander-in-chief, he could not even think of peace, much less live it.

We do not come into life genetically programmed for dominism, nor do we easily take up the bit of human cruelty. We must undergo conditioning to such behavior by those already so conditioned. We suffer contamination from those already infected. The most powerful of the conditioning happens to us as children, within the confines of our primary family systems.

Much of this conditioning perfectly reflects dominist reality. Parents beat their little boys to make them tough enough to survive, and command them not to cry when hurt, and berate them with the necessity of winning at competitive games. Little girls may suffer through years of sexual abuse, and stern prohibitions from specific "male" activities, and demands that they obediently serve their fathers, brothers, and mothers. In many cultures and families, learning to become a dominant male or submissive female is the whole point of growing up.

At the same time, children experience equally forceful but mostly unconscious conditioning. Observation of adults, especially parents, communicates to a child the "true nature" of human relationship. If father uses physical size and strength to dominate mother, or if mother mostly dominates within the domestic sphere while father proves the final authority in important matters ("Wait until your father gets home!"), then son and daughter take on eons of sociosexual programming before they learn to speak. The sins of the father and mother contaminate the son and daughter. People locked in dominism-infected patterns of behavior can only communicate the same to their children.

The most significant of childhood conditioning occurs within the relationship between parent (or other caregiver) and child. To the extent that this primary relationship expresses dominist beliefs and behaviors, the child becomes conditioned for a lifetime of such relationships. A child dominated by his or her parents—physically, emotionally, or psychologically—suffers infection with dominist relationship and will forever have difficulty approaching others in the spirit of peace and partnership. When the child grows to have his or her own children, the cycle repeats.

"But," countless generations of parents might fairly ask, "isn't it correct to dominate one's child? Shouldn't parents make rules and set limits? Spare the rod and spoil the child! Don't children need firm guidance and discipline? Don't parents have a duty to teach good manners and to help the child properly meet society's expectations? Don't the child's spontaneity and free expression need to be reined in, controlled, and left behind? And don't parents do it all, especially the hard parts, for the child's own good?"

Psychoanalyst Alice Miller has shown, much to the contrary, that such child-rearing attitudes and practices, however common and accepted, produce a "poisonous pedagogy" from which most children never recover, to society's great detriment. "I now believe," she writes, "that there is a universal psychological phenomenon involved here that must be brought to light: namely, the way the adult exercises power over the child, a use of power that can go undetected and unpunished like no other. There is a whole gamut of ingenious measures applied 'for the child's own good' which are difficult for a child to comprehend and which for that very reason often have devastating impacts later in life."[7]

As Miller describes the actual practice of poisonous pedagogy, it all sounds so normal: "An enormous amount can be done to a child in the first two years: he or she can be molded, dominated, taught good habits, scolded, and punished—without any repercussions for the person raising the child and without the child taking revenge. The child will overcome the serious consequences of the injustice he has suffered only if he succeeds in defending himself, i.e., if he is allowed to express his pain and anger. If he is prevented from reacting in his own way because the parents cannot tolerate his reactions (crying, sadness, rage) and forbid them by means of looks or other pedagogical methods, then the child will learn to be silent. This silence is a sign of the effectiveness of the pedagogical principles applied, but at the same time it is a danger signal pointing to future pathological development."⁸ The adult so thoroughly dominates that the child's spontaneous and essential emotional responses atrophy; with time, the child stops expressing any difficult feelings and, indeed, may stop feeling altogether.

Miller stresses throughout her writings the utter insanity of a culture that casually accepts such practices as good child-rearing: "It is unlikely that someone could proclaim 'truths' that are counter to physical laws for very long (for example, that it is healthy for children to run around in bathing suits in winter and in fur coats in summer) without appearing ridiculous. But it is perfectly normal to speak of the necessity of striking and humiliating children and robbing them of their autonomy, at the same time using such high-sounding words as chastising, upbringing, and guiding onto the right path."⁹ The unquestioned assumption, simply put: We must dominate children "for their own good."

Every generation of parents feels practically compelled, socially sanctioned, and divinely justified in dominating their children, doing whatever it takes and using whatever force necessary to turn them into proper adults. It rarely occurs to approach one's children as equal partners in life and in their own development.

Instead, parents dutifully pass on the dominism virus. The dangerous logic of dominist relationship passing from parent to child puts the poison in any pedagogy. However well intended an adult's exercising of power over a child may seem, it teaches power-over dominism nonetheless. When parents act as masters of their children—forcing children into dominist relationship—they send another generation of dominism-infected people into the world.

In effect, every family reenacts the Parable of the Tribes. When members of a family with conflicting desires use coercive, power-maximizing dynamics to resolve the conflict, then waves of viral dominism touch the whole family. The dominating poison of one person in the family spreads throughout the system, forcing all the others to believe, perceive, feel, and act in dominist ways.

Some of Alice Miller's most provocative work has examined the childhoods of the famous and infamous and then showed the connections between the poisonous pedagogy they received as children and the adults they later became. For instance, though it hardly absolves him of his actions, Miller relates that his father beat Adolph Hitler throughout his childhood, that young Adolph witnessed on many occasions the violent abuse of his mother, and that he was treated literally like a dog—a subhuman animal. In his own words, from Mein Kampf: "At the age of six the pitiable little boy suspects the existence of things which can fill even an adult with nothing but horror. . . . All the other things that the little fellow hears at home do not tend to increase his respect for his dear fellow men."[10]

Similarly, the Romanian dictator Nicolae Ceausescu grew up in dire poverty and was, with his nine brothers and sisters, regularly beaten by his alcoholic father. He took to torturing animals as a child and was in jail by the time he was a teenager. Again, this does not absolve him of his horrible crimes, but it certainly does help us to understand him, or at least to sense the internal pains and horrors that drove him to inflict such pain upon others. Dominism-abused, he grew into a violently abusive dominist; dominism-infected, he became a plague upon his society.

The current crop of Islamic terrorists all share similar stories. They grew up in strict fundamentalist families and cultures that instilled key dominist values from an early age—including rigid sexism, monotheism, and deep feelings of historic grievances and the need for revenge. Throughout their childhoods they heard of the greatness of jihad, of holy war, and they came to believe that suicidal martyrdom in the service of jihad would guarantee eternal rewards to them and their families. All that was needed to turn these boys from merely angry to maddened fanatics was the dominism-inflicting and -initiating experience of acts of violence done unto them or their families. The Middle East, alas, never stops generating such experiences.

Some will argue that however real viral dominism and however commonplace poisonous pedagogy, few children grow into Adolph Hitlers or suicide bombers. While most people may grow up in dominism-infected families, few become violently abusive adults. We cannot blame our parenting or society, the argument goes: the individual must take ultimate responsibility for how she or he turns out. If one person can manage to live through an abusive childhood without becoming abusive to others, then all can and should do the same. The sins and crimes of an individual must remain the failures of that individual alone; we compound failure by blaming the parents or society and we engage in the most futile of bleeding-heart liberalism by struggling to understand humanity's worst. Evil is as evil does, and we should only concern ourselves with the prompt and resolute elimination of all evildoers.

I have several responses to this argument. First, understanding that I became dominism-infected by my parental conditioning does not mean that I blame my parents for my present behavior. I still act as a free agent, responsible for my own actions. Knowing the unique thrust of my childhood conditioning can only help me to greater freedom. Moreover, I realize that my parents underwent conditioning by their parents too, who had parents also, who had parents also. . . . We cast no blame, but consciously name, as a first step toward ending, the common mistakes of toxic childrearing.

Second, while all abused children do not grow into Hitlers, the evidence strongly suggests that all Hitlers suffered terrible abuses as children. Rather than ignoring the effects of poisonous pedagogy because some manage to overcome it, we should work toward ending it altogether. Why beat, humiliate, humble, shame, dominate, or abuse any child unless we have to? *We never have to.* Only time and experience will tell if history can create a Hitler, a serial killer, a bully, or a suicide bomber without the help of toxic parenting and dominism-infected social conditioning. For all our perpetual yearning for solutions to the problems of this world, how monumentally foolish not to try something as simple as greeting the present generation of children with love, respect, honesty, and gentle protection.

Third, the fact that most children do not grow into violently abusive adults does not mean that they have avoided the serious infections of viral dominism. Murder, rape and torture only mark the far extremes of a broad spectrum of pathological behaviors that have their roots in poisonous pedagogy and dominism. From the more personal problems of substance abuse, addictions, eating disorders, workaholism, low self-esteem, phobias, suicidal tendencies, and nightmares to the greater problems of racism, sexism, bigotry, political and religious totalitarianism, and greed, the psychoemotional poisons of childhood render us all as damaged and tragically limited adults who can only create damaged and tragically limited societies.

Finally, the experiences of those who have survived the harshest of childhood abuse without becoming horribly pathological adults provide important insights into overcoming viral dominism. According to Miller: "If mistreated children are not to become criminals or mentally ill, it is essential that at least once in their life they come in contact with a person who knows without any doubt that the environment, not the helpless, battered child, is at fault."[11] Every child needs to experience treatment as a genuine equal by at least one other person—a true ally, an adult who listens, hears, and respects the child's feelings while offering honest and noncoercive support.

Since 9/11, any attempt to understand the terrorists or their motives has been cast in the most sour of terms. Would-be "understanders" have been accused of treason, of America-bashing, of coddling criminals, and of obstructing the prosecution of just wars. The American people seem too terrified to undertake a consideration of root causes and personal motivations. Refusing to examine one's own childhood conditioning renders one incapable of comprehending or feeling any compassion for the conditioning of others. Lacking such understanding and compassion, we condition the next generation of children to viral dominism and virtually assure new and ever more terrible acts of terrorism.

And so the Parable of the Tribes repeats with every new generation of girls and boys. This constitutes the worst damage ever done to human beings. The child conditioned to viral dominism and abuse takes on patterns of body and relationship that continuously dictate a dominism-infected and abusive world. Once a child bows to the overwhelming force of poisonous pedagogy, the child suffers deep and festering wounds of body and psyche. That we can take such damage in children for granted merely indicates our own deeply wounded bodies and psyches.

Any real transformation of our world must involve a significant change in how we raise our children. When we resolve the Parable of the Tribes as it plays out in the family, we will reverse, once and for all, the dangerous logic of viral dominism. Until we manifest peace and partnership with our most intimate family members, we cannot expect our world to really change. The personal becomes the political. Unless we become conscious of and move beyond the common poisons of our family systems, we will hardly notice, much less overcome, the collective poisons of our societies.

Four

Bias, Denial, and the Status Quo

"We knew that something unpleasant was afoot, but on the other hand there was a great deal that was pleasant. That was what we wanted to see. We didn't want to walk around the whole day filled with remorse because of what others did, others we didn't have anything to do with....What was decisive was the utter indifference, the callousness with which we as a people in general easily came to terms with it and accepted it."

—**German citizen reflecting on the rise of Nazism.**[1]

I first heard about the events of 9/11 on the morning news from National Public Radio. The second of the World Trade Towers had just been struck. A few minutes later, the first tower collapsed. The announcer struggled to describe the horror as it happened, his voice cracking with obvious anguish and lapsing into long silences.

At some point, I felt that I myself had been struck by a huge explosive force, felt that something precious was collapsing, breaking up, and burning within me, felt the horrible suffering of a thousand murdered souls and of the tsunami waves of grief rushing out from every stolen life. I could feel in that moment powerful effects stirring within me, as if my radio has just dosed me with the most potent of drugs. I could sense millions of Americans sharing in the same sickening hurt and I thought to myself: A dominist plague upon our people, upon all people, upon our planet.

9/11 instantly became one of those media-mediated events that have come to define the modern era. We sat at our radios, televisions, and online connections for hours on end, hungrily taking in every morsel of news and opinion, while hearing and seeing certain sounds and images repeatedly. The media carried all of the terror, pain, and heartbreaking realities of "ground zero" to people everywhere. Moreover, the media amplified the force and effect of the whole event, especially the emanating viral waves.

One irony to the attacks of 9/11 came with the anthrax scare that followed. While Americans got sucked into the terror of infectious spores spreading via the daily mail, they missed the far more pernicious and destructive transmission of infectious beliefs through radios, televisions, and computers. Only a few people actually died from anthrax while hundreds of millions became pathologically sickened with media-spread dominism.

As surely as dominism spreads from any act of violence or abuse, it spreads that much more surely, and widely, when carried by modern media. In the past, the physical distances that separated different populations somewhat isolated one from another and provided a sort of quarantine from infectious beliefs and social viruses. It took the active and abusive invasion of another's body or social space to spread the dominism virus. One individual's behavior coercively infected a second individual, who spread it to a third, and so it went, spreading inexorably, but in a way and at a pace that left the individual with some measure of free response.

The advent and growing sophistication of communication media has made the spreading of dominism much more rapid, far-reaching, and difficult to resist. The violence of 9/11 caused waves of viral dominism to explode outward from the sites of the violations to pathologically contaminate all of the people who worked or lived near the attacks, and all who rushed in to offer aid, and then all of the close relations of all of those people. Simultaneously, the media amplified the local horror and broadcast it worldwide. It was as if millions and millions of people plugged themselves into intravenous bags dripping with plague; by 9/12, nineteen dominism-infected fanatics had spread their soul-sick worldview and terrorizing behavior to people worldwide.

Modern media, and television especially, has the ability to communicate both the data of an event—the who, what, where and when—and the emotional charge of those most immediately affected. Television, radio, the internet, and, to a lesser extent, print media, thus serve as ideal vectors for widespread transmission of the emotion-wrapped beliefs of dominism. The media powerfully communicates this most communicable of diseases with every broadcast of an emotionally charged act of dominism. Although the media *could* serve as a primary channel for spreading healthy beliefs and fostering positive social evolution, in chronically dominist societies the media generally works to tighten the grip of dominism.

Thus, while Americans had known for decades that African-Americans did not always receive fair treatment from the police, the amateur video showing Rodney King being kicked by officers as he lay helpless on the ground, broadcast to the whole nation and repeated endlessly, caused a huge rise in dominism-infected action and reaction. Though many hoped that the airing of such an event would shine the light of truth on U.S. race relations and lead to real improvements, the sheer impact of spreading dominism overwhelmed all such expectations.

Most Americans had similar hopes during the dramatic days that followed the Presidential election fiasco of 2000. One might have expected that, with the thousands of journalists and reporters and television cameras that flooded Florida, a clear picture and true tally of the votes would emerge. Instead, the story devolved into a classic high-stakes blood sport. Americans came away not with a clear annunciation of the facts, but with a soap-operatic tragedy tale of two men locked in a winner takes all battle for domination. The country slowly got behind Bush not because he garnered the most votes, but because, as framed and amplified by the media, he most assiduously followed the rules of whatever-it-takes dominism. Gore acted like the tribe that says, "O.K., let's all sit down and talk this through" even as the Huns invade. In the end, the ugly saga left the nation more dominism-infected than enlightened, more committed to dominist beliefs and practices than to cooperation and peacemaking. Predictably, it led to no substantive changes in American electoral practices, as the 2004 elections painfully demonstrated.

Mainstream media coverage of America's war on terrorism followed the same pattern. Some labored to lay out cogent analyses of such pertinent issues as the all-too-human causes of terrorist actions; the role of Saudi Arabia in the attacks of 9/11; the significance of the Palestinian crisis and America's bias toward Israel in all Middle Eastern affairs; the many ways in which other nations perceive American actions as terrorism; and the degree to which American culture, business, government, and foreign affairs all bend before the gods of cheap oil. For the most part, however, the media served up State-filtered information wrapped in the emotional imperative of "my country right or wrong" patriotism. Contrary voices discovered that even when they found an outlet for their opinions, any questioning of American history, present leadership, or anti-terror tactics aroused huge waves of anger and accusations of anti-American treason. Going against the emotional tides of the time proved difficult, even dangerous.

Modern media has become the ultimate two-edged sword. On the one hand, it can help people to overcome dominism by illuminating human possibilities, by educating in the ways and means of cooperation and peacemaking, by spreading the thoughts and feelings of loving relationship, and by fostering positive social evolution. Various media have long helped to bring literacy to impoverished societies, to speak truth to power, and to deliver hope and life-saving tools to the oppressed and embattled. Most recently, we have witnessed the irrepressible force of the Internet spreading the social virus of democracy to long-repressive cultures. The truth *can* set us free; when wielded properly, the media serves as both primary defense against dominism and as a positive force leading the way to something better.

On the other hand, so much of modern media utterly fails in this regard and only works to make viral dominism more omnipresent. Two key problems undermine the media's role in society and turn it from potential savior to prime disease vector. First, institutional and personal biases of media organizations and their agents cause them to routinely predigest, censor, and spin the information they deliver. Second, almost everyone—media makers and consumers—engages in some degree of unconscious denial that prevents them from separating the truth from the false and misleading.

Media Bias

George Bush is the president, he makes the decisions, and, you know, as just one American, he wants me to line up, just tell me where."

—**Dan Rather, CBS News**[2]

In short, we have a situation rife with conflicts of interest. The handful of organizations that supply most people with their news have major commercial interests that inevitably tempt them to slant their coverage, and more generally to be deferential to the ruling party.

—**Paul Krugman**[3]

For any polarized issue in America, both sides will typically complain about media bias. Even the most bland and impersonal recitation of facts tends to offend somebody and leads to charges of prejudicial reporting. Moreover, when media representatives go beyond delivering just the facts and begin providing overviews, drawing conclusions, or, as happens so aggressively now on talk radio and pundit TV, staking out highly emotional positions, then bias in the media can get unabashedly blatant.

Though everyone proclaims the virtue of pure objectivity in reporting, in practice, media bias occurs as naturally and inevitably as the perceptual biases in our personal lives. All of the reporters, photographers, analysts, commentators, editors, news anchors, publishers and station owners involved in the production of media content individually experience the world through uniquely personal perceptual filters and respond to events accordingly. Journalists can no more deliver perfectly neutral and balanced reporting than they can purge themselves of their personal histories. Just as physicists have learned that the mere act of observing a quantum experiment affects the outcome, we must accept that reporters inject themselves—their thoughts, feelings, perceptions, and beliefs—into unfolding events and thereby bias any reporting.

Such bias occurs at every stage of media production and consumption: the core values and bottom-line demands of media corporations, publishers, and station owners; the allocation of news-gathering resources and the assigning of stories; reporters' observation of events and subsequent writing; editorial shaping, amending, and censoring of content; the manner and placement of content, including promotion or lack thereof; the availability of specific content in the marketplace; and, the final consumption of content through the perceptual filters of readers, listeners, and viewers. By the time a news item wends its way through the production process to show up in the morning paper or evening newscast it has at best been subtly smudged, as if various handlers left their ink-stained fingerprints. At worst, it has been smeared beyond recognition.

To the extent that the media industry reflects specific demographics, then the perceptual habits of individuals grow into system-wide biases toward specific positions. For most of American history, news people came out of what we would now think of as a liberal arts education and a lower-to-middle class background. Media bias therefore tended toward liberal/progressive sensibilities on political, economic, and social issues. Studies have shown that in presidential elections since the

1960s a large majority of reporters voted Democratic, which lends credence to right-wing complaints of liberal bias in the press. Just as Hollywood has always leaned to the left, since most of the people drawn to theater and the arts also tend toward liberal arts education and lower-to-middle class backgrounds, the media industry has long been rooted in what we now think of as liberal values and has naturally slanted its output leftward.

However, a sea change has occurred in the institutional structures of American media that has profoundly altered all aspects of mass communication. First, we have seen a steady consolidation of media ownership into the control of but a few huge corporations. Where America once had thousands of independent family-owned newspapers, it now has only dozens. Similar consolidation has occurred in radio, and though television seems to have trended in the opposite direction—the three big networks have spawned a proliferation of cable channels—overall market share still belongs to a half dozen corporations. Even on the Internet, a large percentage of the traffic passes through a handful of corporate-owned sites. This steady consolidation of mass media has left a corporate sheen on all media content. Stories that in any way reflect poorly on the parent company rarely show up in the daily news; conversely, many so-called news items amount to little more than advertisements for the corporation's products or services.

Simultaneous with this corporatization of media has been the vertical integration of products and services within the corporation, combined with corporate ownership of many non-media businesses and interests. AOL-Time-Warner, for example, now owns newspapers, news magazines, radio stations, television stations, cable channels, Hollywood production companies, Internet sites, and several politicians. So when they produce a movie (filled with "product placements" of their own merchandise), it receives positive reviews in all of their media outlets, gets a guaranteed showing in all of their movie theaters, and may even appear in their news outlets, cleverly disguised as a "hard news" item. While merely annoying in regard to entertainment products, this coalescing of media interests turns utterly perverse when it comes to important issues. When media corporations have significant stakes in specific decisions or outcomes then the whole notion of an independent press becomes naïve and antiquated. Whether or not we see hard-hitting, fact-filled reports on such matters as global warming or federal tax policy or high-level shenanigans in the financial industry has less to do with what the American people want or need than with how such reporting will affect any of the dozens of businesses that make up a modern media empire. Whatever does not serve the mega-corporation does not make it into print or on the air. Anyone who thinks otherwise needs to wake up and smell the bias.

Finally, in the past few decades we have seen a steady rise in the net worth of media owners (all millionaires, if not billionaires), as well as in the income of major media personalities—lead reporters, news anchors, syndicated columnists, and television pundits. In a country with an ever-increasing gap between rich and poor, most of the people who produce the news lead comfy lives in the land of the rich. Thus, though 45 million Americans do not have health insurance, the key people involved in reporting on such a critical issue all have terrific insurance, thank you, so we should not expect the sort of gripping journalism that might actually move our elected representatives—all nicely insured also—into real reforms. Nor should we expect this portfolioed crowd to deliver disturbing reports on the stock market in general or specifically on any of the companies they've invested in, even when said companies factor into major events of the day. The Fourth Estate in America has truly become an estate, peopled with overclass scribes who give their full attention to the trials, travails, and titillating scandals of the royals, with but occasional and condescending nods to the not very interesting problems of the serfs.

Taken together, these changes in the media have shifted the bias of the system towards the service of its own interests—identical to those of the dominist elite of American society. Where once we could rely on the press to counterbalance the dominating force of the ruling class, to speak truth to the powerful, and even to yank the most egregious of knaves down from their perches, our modern media has become at best marginalized and at worst fraudulent. On key issues—Social Security reform, the federal estate tax, the war on drugs, energy policy, climate change, genetically modified foods, global arms sales, campaign finance reform, universal health- and child-care, to name a few—the media have failed miserably to adequately frame the debates, much less encourage answers. An ever-shrinking chorus of dissenting voices gets dismissed with a sneering "oh, them again," while mainstream reporting dutifully toes the bottom lines of those paying the bills.

Despite this dominist takeover of modern media, conscientious journalists still do strive to produce fair and balanced content. Yet even the best efforts can go awry. It has become standard practice in reporting on contentious issues to "balance" statements from those on one side of an issue with statements from the other side. But the weight given to such statements, as measured in column inches or on-air time, rarely reflects actual percentages of the represented populations and may skirt all questions of speaker credibility. Thus, as happens regularly in reporting on environmental issues, we end up with a single paid expert speaking at the paid behest of a large corporation "balancing" the views of an international coalition of Nobel scientists. Or, as typically occurs in political reporting, one party's position statement gets "balanced" with the other party's statement, as if both statements automatically have equal relevance and represent equal populations of Americans.

Even worse, such attempts at balancing the news have the pernicious effect of grossly oversimplifying issues. Everything gets reduced to the pro argument neatly balanced by the anti. You're for legalizing drugs or for jailing all users, for raising taxes or for lowering them, for protecting the environment or for giving free rein to industry, for providing a social safety net or for eliminating social security. You're either with the terrorists or you're against them. Nuanced opinions and complex arguments wind up on the cutting room floor. In the easily balanced world of black and white, all shades of gray get edited out. As a society, we have become unable to even discuss certain issues with any real depth, much less with minds open to new information or innovative solutions. Which, again, neatly serves the dominist overclass of American culture.

I have already mentioned the failure of the media during the 2000 presidential post-election fiasco, but that whole election cycle demonstrated the dangers of a dominist-owned and -directed press. Rather than delivering a frank and thorough discussion of each candidate's thoughts on important issues—the kind of national conversation that might actually lead to substantive change—the media functioned as but a scandal-mongering, sound-bite-proffering, fluff-and-puff-slathering swarm of sycophants. A contingent of the press actually booed at one of Al Gore's speeches. These hardly fair and not at all balanced reporters went on to saddle Gore with a number of trivial "events" as evidence of his dishonesty—for instance, his supposed claims that he invented the Internet, that his romance with his wife Tipper inspired the movie *Love Story*, or that he first discovered the toxic waste problems at Love Canal. No amount of deconstructing of these falsehoods by Gore's defenders could undo the damage done; most of the defenses did not even make it into print or on the air. Given the closeness of the final vote, corporate media's incessant attacks on Gore's character surely nudged the nation to Bush's side.

Of course, some will say that I have just displayed my own bias and proven my initial point—that both sides in any contentious issue always decry the media bias. Bush supporters certainly had their own legitimate complaints about the coverage of their candidate. We'll leave it for future historians to resolve the question of "Who got spun worst?" We *can* say that the mainstream media's coverage of both sides slanted toward the values, interests, and goals of corporate America and the dominist elite. America has degenerated into "the best democracy that money can buy." The rich and powerful, with the aid of their vast media empires, do all of the buying long before the votes ever get counted (or not).

Later we will explore ways to return the media to the service of truth, justice, and positive social change. For now, we had best accept that, like everything else in our world, modern media has succumbed to the pathological demands of viral dominism. All the news that fits the dominist worldview, they print.

Why, however, do we buy it? While everyone knows that you cannot believe everything you read in the papers or online or see on TV, we go on believing it anyway. As powerful as media corporations have become, their real power to influence people and circumstances derives from the fact that most of us live so deeply in denial that we can no longer see through the psychoemotional fog of our own misperceptions, much less the murky blur of media bias.

Living in Denial

Each member shares the mythology of the family trance. Each unconsciously agrees to share a certain focus and a certain denial. The denial constitutes the family system's "vital lies."

—**John Bradshaw**[4]

Once an administration believes that it can get away with insisting that black is white and up is down—and everything in this administration's history suggests that it believes just that—it's hard to see where the process stops. A habit of ignoring inconvenient reality, and presuming that the docile media will go along, soon infects all aspects of policy. —**Paul Krugman**[5]

If Thomas Jefferson were to walk into a modern twelve-step meeting and tell his story—"My name is Tom. I am a leader of the greatest social experiment in the history of mankind and, uh, well, I'm also a lifelong owner of slaves,"—everyone in the room would start shaking their heads, thinking the same thing: "Denial. Major league denial, Tom."

"Denial" is an unconscious psychoemotional mechanism that protects the status quo in our lives by obscuring the truth. It serves as a form of ego-protection, a matrix of mental and emotional forces that operates below the surface of conscious awareness to shield and defend one's sense of self. An individual, family, organization, or nation lives "in denial" when it unconsciously suppresses certain truths, memories, or insights that would prompt the need for serious change if brought to conscious perception and reflection. Like an obscuring veil, denial dims the mind whenever we engage in behaviors or relationships that violate our most heartfelt human sensibilities.

We may live in denial about our spouse's infidelity and thus fail to notice inconsistent behavior (obvious to everyone else) that, if fully experienced, could lead to divorce. We may live in denial about addictive behaviors because fully experiencing the truth might threaten the foundations of our lifestyle and relationships. Or we may live in denial about early childhood: we cannot remember extremely traumatic or formative events because fully experiencing the truth could upset our family structures and whole sense of self. In such cases, the psychoemotional mechanism of denial functions below conscious awareness to suppress key thoughts, feelings, images, and memories and thereby spare us the more challenging work of facing truth and undergoing change.

Denial differs from deliberate lying. When we deliberately lie, we consciously protect ourselves and accept the costs of our dishonesty as necessary. When we live in denial, we unconsciously protect the status quo in our lives and remain largely unaware of the costs to others and ourselves. For instance, an alcoholic may engage in much deliberate lying (hiding bottles, sneaking drinks, using breath mints) to protect a lifestyle that he or she considers necessary. At the same time, the alcoholic and family members may all live mired in unconscious patterns of denial as each suppresses certain truths—old wounds, communication breakdowns, failing relationships, financial pressures—that would threaten the existing family stability if brought to conscious awareness.

Lying and denying differ primarily in the scope and intensity of one's awareness. Liars know that they lie and tend to recognize the costs of their dishonesty. Those in denial have little awareness of their problem behavior or of its consequences.

Since denial serves to protect the status quo, and since the status quo in human affairs has for so long consisted of dominism-infected relationship, the human capacity for denial stands as a crucial determinant in the establishment and continuing existence of dominist culture. If people could not engage in denial—if we felt acutely conscious of the whole truth at every moment in our lives—then the ugliness, shame, foul odor, and unending abuse of dominist relationship would force us into either mass suicide or constant revolutionary strife. Instead, the mechanism of denial has allowed the human race to sink into a psychic swamp of collective amnesia bordering on outright insanity—a perfect state of consciousness for the inhumane ways and means of dominism.

Denial helps to answer a crucial question: "Why would reasonable people continue to sustain the patently abusive relationships of dominism?" In whatever way viral dominism first entered into human affairs, and however it spread from tribe to tribe, all of the men and women it touched engaged in some measure of denial as the simple human truths of peace, cooperation, and partnership relationship went into decline. Every act of dominist abuse, from the dawn of recorded history to the present moment, has simultaneously invoked the mechanisms of denial within both the abuser and the abused. Everyone involved in a dominist system must deny the true nature of reality if they want to go on living with the status quo and effectively survive in a dominism-infected world.

Thomas Jefferson could not have written the Declaration of Independence if he had not also remained largely unconscious of the constant abuse he inflicted in his daily affairs. We can say that he should have known better and that he must have seen that he himself was keeping his slaves from their "unalienable rights of life, liberty and the pursuit of happiness." However, given the powerful and unconscious nature of denial, he most likely had but a vaguely disturbing sense of the contradictions in his life along with a set of sincere and oft-repeated beliefs for those moments when the truth encroached upon his conscious awareness.

Moreover, his family and culture supported Jefferson in his denial. Though some plantation owners did in fact free their slaves while Jefferson did not, the prevailing mindset of his time and place counseled—as it always will—that he maintain the status quo. For Jefferson, the status quo included an aristocratic lifestyle plagued by chronic indebtedness that made giving up slavery an incomprehensible notion, tantamount to suicide. *He simply could not think of it.* Nor would his mind dwell overly on the awful, antidemocratic abuses of slavery; rather, he lapsed into the requisite denial to prevent the truth from undermining his status quo.

All members of a dominist system necessarily and unconsciously engage in denial as a fundamental fact of dominist life. When abusive patterns of domination touch and infect an individual's reality, she or he must suppress the feelings of pain, along with any sense of a better, kinder, more honest, and more loving way of life.

I cannot overly stress the unconscious nature of denial. Denial has its roots in earliest childhood and earliest civilization, and, for this reason it proves difficult for any but the most determined to recognize their denial-bound realities, much less to initiate change. As Alice Miller writes, "It is the tragedy of well-raised people that they are unaware as adults of what was done to them and what they do themselves if they were not allowed to be aware as children."[6] Conditioned to unawareness and denial as children, we grow into essentially unaware adults lacking the very feelings, perceptions, and acumen necessary to understand the depth and enormity of our dilemma.

Denial begins as a childhood survival mechanism. Faced with conflicting and untenable feelings and situations—"I want to live/I am born to violence and separation"; "I love my father/my father abuses me"; "I love my mother/my mother is an embarrassing alcoholic"; "I feel wonderful pleasure in my body/my body is mistreated and abandoned"—the child screens from conscious perception and reflection those truths that feel most threatening. The child acknowledges all the love and nurturance present in the family while suppressing any dysfunctional behavior from conscious awareness. The child holds to the best that the family system offers—the status quo—and denies the abuses, contradictions, and lies. Sadly, the child eventually loses her or his own easy innocence and innate capacity for loving, pleasurable, peaceful relationship.

The child must do this to survive. To live with the constant awareness of unloving or abusive caregivers, or of a family on the verge of breaking apart, or of shamefully degraded bodily sensations, presents an unbearable burden. Nobody can reasonably live and securely grow among such harrowing disparities and uncertainties. So the child denies as much of the truth as possible while focusing upon, and sometimes inventing, more loving and stable truths. The child fashions a worldview with beliefs, attitudes, opinions, desires, emotions, dreams, and memories to fit the world that he or she has landed in. Whatever does not fit, the child denies.

Given the more or less abusive conditioning that children receive in even the best of families, their capacity for denial functions as a mercy and a saving grace. How else could they survive their initiations into violence? How else could they survive the lack of genuine bonding and the inevitable fall from innocence that passes for a normal childhood? How else could they go on living, separated from the elementary partnership with mother and father, with life, with the world, that every child deserves? Denial serves as a shield, a balm, and a way of making sense of a terribly mixed-up world. Denial acts as a movement of the child's vast and creative intelligence; ironically so, since denial ultimately inhibits intelligence.

We can safely say that all children engage in some measure of denial as a function of growing up, though the more dominist the family system and surrounding culture, the more the need for denial and protection. To the extent that families present dysfunctional environments, children deny the dysfunction as much as they can. They do this to survive, to carry on, and to make the best of what life offers. While this serves as an effective short-term strategy for dealing with harsh realities and represents the best that children can do, denial in the long term greatly diminishes them as human beings.

From the beginning, denial causes an awful waste of a person's vital energies. The difference between a child delighting in the body's natural feelings of warm, tingling pleasure and a child desperately suppressing all feelings amounts to a depletion of sexual and creative energies. The difference between a child alive with eager, eye-sparkling intelligence and a child trying hard not to see or hear the truth manifests as a degradation of innate potential.

It takes vital energy to suppress the truth, and the more painful the reasons for doing so, the more effort it requires. It requires continuing energy to sustain such denial and keep the truth far from conscious awareness. However compelling the immediate need for denial, the child pays for denial with essential life force for the rest of his or her life. To the extent that, as adults, we sustain the denials of childhood, we engage in a form of slow suicide; the truth denied by the child becomes the sickening lie of the adult.

Denial also makes us ignorant. Our denial of reality means that we more or less withdraw from certain aspects of the world and thus cut off key sources of information. The child who unconsciously suppresses certain truths relinquishes a significant degree of native intelligence. The child cannot withdraw from specific family dysfunctions without withdrawing in some measure from other dimensions of reality. Nor can the child diminish awareness of certain abuses without also becoming less aware of life in general.

Furthermore, the blinders that we erect in childhood to screen out family abuses and dysfunctions do not go away; rather, they persist through time, rendering us unable to fully comprehend our world. The more urgently we deny reality as children, the more we miss seeing as adults. The web of denial, once specific to a given situation, becomes a general shield from all truth. Our short-term protection of unconsciousness becomes a long-term lack of consciousness. We become ignorant.

We become too ignorant to resolve the gross contradiction of owning slaves while preaching equality; too ignorant to see that we reactively inflict the same abuses on our children that we ourselves received when growing up; too ignorant to pierce the veil of media bias; too ignorant to comprehend the insanity of killing in God's name; to ignorant to insist that women and men must coexist as equal partners; and, too ignorant to perceive and understand the self-inflicted nature and continuing costs of denial. Having unconsciously withdrawn from the truth during childhood, we never reach our full intellectual capacities.

It has become something of a cliché to say that we use but a small portion of our brains. Certainly, many indicators point to untapped reserves of human potential. So much of our latent potential gets stifled by this mechanism of denial. Moreover, the tenacious strength with which viral dominism holds our world derives from the common and collective denial of countless generations of girls and boys grown into denial-bound women and men. Our self-imposed submission to denial gives dominism an ideal medium in which to thrive.

Political Denial

In our age of slaughter, madness threatens every thinking person. To dwell on the absurdity of a culture that congratulates itself on its "progress" while carrying out geocide is to risk hearing your mind go spronnnng *while spending the rest of your days gnawing the bark off trees.*

—**Brian Swimme**[7]

The paradox is this: the less we think about these things—the less we confront the ways in which our public policies enrich the powerful but endanger the rest of us—the likelier it is that such policies will kill us. It's enough to make you sick.

—**Geov Parrish**[8]

It is difficult to get a man to understand something when his salary depends on his not understanding it.

—**Upton Sinclair**[9]

The personal denial of Everychild naturally grows into the political denial of every dominist religion, organization, corporation, or government. All dominist systems rely on mechanisms of political denial that originate in and reflect the denials of ordinary childhood. Just as whatever capacity we have to reach our full individual potential demands that we first recognize and overcome our deep-seated denials, so does the task of transforming global dominism demand that we recognize and eliminate the ubiquitous denials of our political systems.

System-wide political denial arises, like childhood denial, as a necessary mechanism for the protection of the status quo. Status quo for a child resides in her or his developing ego, the stability of the family, and regular access to life's necessities. Status quo for a political system resides in the positions, perks, and powers of the ruling elite, the stability of the system's operational ways and means, and regular access to the very necessities that give the system its reason for being.

Status quo for an organized religion resides in its priesthood, its creeds and doctrines, and its promise of certain salvation for its followers. Status quo for a corporation resides in its high-level management, its financial and legal structures, and its ability to consistently turn a profit for its shareholders. Status quo for a government resides in its most powerful politicians, its laws and enforcements, and its continuing delivery of such necessities as food, shelter, employment, education, and health care to its populace.

The people who make up a dominist system tend to deny any information or experience that does not effectively serve or protect the system's status quo. Since the People already live deep in personal denial, they easily deny the contradictions, lies, and abuses in their political lives. In fact, the denial within dysfunctional families leads directly into the denial of dysfunctional political systems. Just as the child's denial of family dysfunctions serves to support those very dysfunctions, so the adult's denial of political dysfunctions serves to keep the system in place, whatever its failings.

Moreover, any dominist system develops mechanisms of political denial above and beyond the personal and habitual denials of its individual members. The system's governing documents and laws, its key institutions, and its operational ways and means all support the status quo, however dishonest or abusive. The system initially derives from dominism-infected human beings; then its structural parameters actively and forcefully spread the infection.

A simple choice of words in a governing document—such as "All men are created equal" or "I am the one and only God"—can hold a system-wide dysfunction in place for generations. Many of the written laws of civilized culture literally translate personal denials into political forces, such as a law that forbids contraception, a law that permits citizens to bear arms for the primary purpose of shooting one another, or a law that allows the state to execute the powerless. The core structures of any system, such as the male-only priesthood, or electoral practices that favor the wealthy, or the lack of personal accountability within corporations, can demand unyielding denials of the worst of abuses. And the basic operational ways and means of a system, such as accounting practices that ignore costs to the environment, or culturally-sanctioned mores of racial and sexual discrimination, or the command to follow one's leaders at times of war, can support an all-pervading atmosphere of unconscious denial and dominist relationship.

Just as children must engage in some measure of denial to survive, the political denial of a dominist system becomes absolutely necessary for the continuing survival of the system, even if it means massive loss of life for its people. And just as a child's denial only succeeds at dire cost to the child's overall levels of creative energy and intelligence, so systemwide political denial only succeeds through the enormous waste of human and environmental resources and the incessant suppression of free thinking and spontaneous creativity.

The consequences of excessive political denial appear most obviously in modern totalitarian systems. The fascist and communist states of the twentieth century had to commit vast internal resources to their mechanisms of denial: the S.S. and concentration camps, the K.G.B. and gulags, the Red Guard and the Cultural Revolution. The need to keep a populace under constant police scrutiny becomes as energy depleting to a society as a child's continuous suppression of unpleasant events; it eventually wears the system down from within, thus planting the seeds for its own destruction. Totalitarian states ultimately fall apart in strict accordance with the second law of thermodynamics: they become entropic (energy-wasting) rather than regenerative systems. They fail largely because they waste energy enforcing the denial of anything that might threaten the rigidly defined status quo.

Totalitarian states also fall apart because they suppress the continuous flow and exchange of information vital to any regenerative system. This was especially apparent in the breakup of the Soviet Union. After generations of actively suppressing the free creativity of its populace, controlling all information flow within the country, and preventing all exchange of information with those on the outside, the erstwhile superpower collapsed in a condition of sorry and embarrassing ignorance. In the end, the West did not so much win the Cold War as the resource-drained and intellectually stunted Soviet Union lost the will and capacity to remain engaged.

While totalitarian states present stark and obvious examples of the dangers of systemwide political denial, all dominist systems tend toward denial-cloaked self-destruction. America, a nation founded upon the brutal oppression of indigenous cultures and African peoples, has never fully resolved its abusive past and has since added layer upon layer of world-class denial with each passing generation. Though not quite a police state, America has more people incarcerated per capita than any other developed country; has more violence on the streets of its own capital than many battle zones; thrives on fighting prohibitionary wars—against alcohol, drugs, and communists—despite the ever futile and ruinous results; demands capital punishment of its poorer citizens with religious zeal; and, especially, takes great pride in being policeman-to-the-world, eager to jump into armed conflict at any perceived threat to God's own status quo, the American way of life.

This represents a tragic waste of the nation's energy and resources; more frustratingly, one finds it practically impossible to have a productive dialogue about any of this, due to the repressive fog of American denial. As Brian Swimme suggests, modern Americans live at constant risk of the mind going *spronnnng*.

For all the power of its democratic institutions, its free press, and its First Amendment rights to free expression, America has freely evolved into a stultifying stupor. Signs of national ignorance abound: from the decline of an educational system that compares poorly with other industrial nations to the sound-bite mental floss and gloss that passes for an electoral process; from the growing dominance of corporate-controlled media as the primary path to knowledge to the nearly inescapable "consumin' human" force of modern advertising; from the sorry inattention to the basic needs of pregnant women to the brain-maiming violations of poisonous pedagogues. From sea to shining sea, America suffers from the grosser pathologies of a dominist plague, but has become too denial-dumb to fully comprehend the danger or take necessary steps toward genuine change.

Just as dominism feeds into greater dominism, so denial leads to more chronic denial. From the beginnings of the Bush administration—with its Kafkaesque election, its unilateral denouncement of international agreements, its penchant for total secrecy in all its affairs, its determination to pull the country back into the disastrous economic policies of Ronald Reagan, its anti-scientific, oil industry-blessed assaults on the environment—a thick no-think haze seemed to engulf the nation. There was an uncanny absence of real dialogue on these and many other salient issues. It was as if the American people lost all powers of discernment during the election and could muster only a shrugging pass to Bush for whatever he said or did. Yet, bad as it was, with the War on Terrorism it only got worse.

Predictably, post-9/11 America required a gung-ho descent into "my country, whatever" denial. The dominant message of the day—we are good and they are evil and we must violently destroy them at any and all costs—became a countervailing mantra against contrary ideas and discomfiting questions. Americans gave Bush near-unanimous approval for his never-ending, ill-defined war and steadfastly committed to following their leader in his proud avoidance of deep thought and nuanced debate. Bush's America became a standing demonstration of the basic principle that denial perpetuates denial: the more it engaged in the suppression of truth, the more tightly enmeshed in self-imposed delusions it became.

Thus, denial-dumb America withdrew support from international nuclear arms treaties even as Pakistan and India verged on nuclear war; blithely named certain countries as evil untouchables while carrying on business as usual with disreputable others; and announced new policies of unilaterally-decided preemptive strikes (that inevitably kill civilians) to counter the unilaterally-decided, preemptive, civilian-killing strikes of terrorists. The nation trumpeted its proud defense of democracy, freedom, and human rights while enacting draconian new laws and trampling the rights of thousands of innocents and blatantly undermining the freely elected leaders of Venezuela, Palestine, and Iran. The Bush administration rejected all multilateral efforts toward addressing global warming even as its own EPA released urgent calls for immediate action. It continued to shill on behalf of unfettered, unregulated markets, even as a parade of America's finest businesses admitted to sloppy ethics and crooked accounting. And it pressed for full-scale, wholehearted, international participation in its terror war even as it refused to participate in the World Court trials of war criminals or to sign the international treaty barring land mines or to include the United Nations as a vital partner in the war.

In our struggle with denial the lines between the personal and political turn nearly invisible. Childhood denial engenders men and women perfectly suited for the inhumanities of dominist systems. Systemwide political denial allows for legal, institutional, and operational structures that actively suppress every one's energy, creativity, and intelligence. Crippled human beings create crippled systems that cripple human beings. The truth, it's said, will set us free. But how shall we see, hear, or recognize the truth?

Five

The End of Democracy

Throughout our history two strands have coexisted uneasily; a dominant strand of democratic humanism and a lesser but durable strand of intolerant Puritanism. There has been a tendency through the years for reason and moderation to prevail as long as things are going tolerably well or as long as our problems seem clear and finite and manageable. But... when some event or leader of opinion has aroused the people to a state of high emotion, our puritan spirit has tended to break through, leading us to look at the world through the distorting prism of a harsh and angry moralism.

—**Senator J. William Fullbright**[1]

As 9/11/02 approached, America showed little progress from a year of battling terror. Despite the creation of a new federal agency and the reallocation of billions toward homeland security, the country felt no safer. For every potential weakness addressed, a dozen other ways that enterprising villains could inflict terror arose as new threats. Air travel had turned more inconvenient and expensive, but no less vulnerable. Civil liberties had been cast aside like annoying trifles, at grave cost to America's vaunted freedoms but of little consequence to her actual enemies. The great national unity that had blossomed in the immediate aftermath of 9/11 had degenerated into bipartisan bickering, law enforcement turf battles, leadership buck-passing, and the achingly familiar feeling that this supposed new war would only serve to fatten the coffers of the overclass.

America's principal enemy, Osama bin Laden and his al Qaeda terror cells, had come through a year of war remarkably unscathed. Of the more than a thousand individuals arrested and detained worldwide, only a handful had confirmed connections to al Qaeda. Of the several thousand killed in the bombing of Afghanistan, most were Afghani civilians or soldiers belonging to various Afghani factions; few had anything to do with bin Laden, al Qaeda, or the attacks of 9/11.

Yet the elusive bin Laden and company merely led what became an ever-lengthening Bush enemies list. The President made clear from the outset of his terror war that threats to America loomed everywhere and that the war would be omnipresent, all-encompassing, and without foreseeable end. During his 2002 State of the Union Address, he declared that an "axis of evil" was loose in the world and he named Iraq, Iran, and North Korea as centers of state-sponsored evil. He showed no recognition of the progress toward genuine reforms made in Iran and North Korea—after much hard work by previous administrations—nor concerns that his arrogant bluster might agitate sleeping tyrants. He set his sights and his war lust on Iraq especially, pronouncing that "regime change" was an absolute necessity and in everyone's best interest, at whatever the price.

At the same time and with utter disregard for the opinions of others, American policy managed to greatly increase tensions in the Israeli-Palestinian conflict. Though far from successful, peace efforts had been underway in the region and, as will occur in any complex, long-running, emotion-laden conflict, a steady process of negotiation and renegotiation had gradually limned the key points that would have to obtain in any truly viable peace plan. The Saudi government offered a simple proposal that addressed these key points and drew widespread approval. The fact that this initiative had come out of a meeting of Arab states signaled a long overdue engagement of the Arabs in a peaceful resolution of Middle East tensions. It only required America to join the plan and bring its power and influence to a gathering momentum for peace. Instead, Bush chose to ignore the Saudi plan and allowed it, and peace, to wither on the vine.

The President announced that we would see no real movement toward peace until Yasir Arafat, the elected leader of the Palestinians, gave way to new leadership. It was yet another call for regime change, Bush's primary diplomatic tool. (During this same period, the Bush administration also supported an unsuccessful military coup against the democratically elected leader of Venezuela). Simultaneously, he pronounced Israeli Prime Minister Ariel Sharon a "man of peace," though Sharon, like Arafat, had a long history of involvement in acts of terror. Predictably, things got much worse in the region, with a fresh wave of especially horrific suicide bombings by the Palestinians matched by a humiliating Israeli terror-invasion of Palestinian territories.

Inexplicably, the American response to this intensifying crisis was to press the case for an invasion of Iraq. On the first anniversary of 9/11, America was swept up not in grand visions of peace and building a new world (because, 9/11 changed everything). Having spent the year bombing Afghanistan and squirting kerosene on Palestine, the national debate turned to when and how shall we invade Iraq. That we would, in fact, push the world into yet another terror-spreading conflagration seemed inevitable. As Bush mustered America for a reprisal of his father's great adventure, he seemed unperturbed by a dozen niggling details. Among them: that few of America's allies in the previous war were lining up to support this new one; that virtually every reasonable person in the world agreed that an American invasion of Iraq would exacerbate already apocalyptic tensions in the Middle East; and that, while nobody liked Saddam Hussein, most saw better ways to contain and mitigate his particular evil than terror-bombing his people.

In sum, the world had become infinitely less secure after a year of American anti-terror actions. This simple equation eluded America's leaders: the more aggressively they pursued the goal of national security, the more international insecurity they generated. The more forcefully America defended herself, the more dangerous the rest of the world became, and the more America felt justified in expanding its use of aggressive force.

Cowboy Diplomacy

The problem with the Bush administration is that its bully pulpit is all bully and no pulpit.

—**Maureen Dowd**[2]

On September 12, 2002, George W. Bush came before the full U.N. General Assembly to make the case for war. He sought U.N. approval with the greatest reluctance, and only after his advisors—eyes to the polls—warned that the American people would not support a new war against Iraq unless Bush could, as his father did, pull together an international coalition. Yet he presented no compelling evidence that Iraq had working weapons of mass destruction or bore an imminent threat to any of its neighbors. Instead, Bush harangued the gathered diplomats with a long list of U.N. resolutions that Iraq had violated. Ignoring the fact that other countries (including America and Israel) have likewise violated U.N. resolutions, he challenged the U.N. to see Iraq's violations as reason enough to forego any further attempts at diplomacy and to instead unleash the terrors of massive bombing and the violent overthrow of a sovereign (however despicable) state.

What he did not do was ask for the guidance or opinions of other nations or call for a round of renewed diplomatic efforts to peacefully resolve disputed issues. He most certainly did not stand before the world community as a concerned citizen seeking the support of his peers. To the contrary, he strutted his toughness, he accused the U.N. of "lacking spine," he questioned its continued relevance, he issued ultimatums, and he made it clear that if the nations of the world did not unite behind him, then America would go it alone. To all but the most denial-dumb, the speech was anything but a sincere attempt at multilateralism. The American president had served notice: as the one and only world superpower, America would do whatever it wanted.

Immediately after this speech the administration released a 33-page foreign policy tome—the National Security Strategy of the United States[3]—that hammered home all of these key points, for anyone who hadn't been paying attention:

- The world should henceforth think of America as a benevolent hegemon who diligently strives to use its vast wealth and power for the greater good of all.

- All nations should recognize American-style democracy and capitalism as the best ways to run a country and thus the world. Any steps that America takes to spread its forms of government and culture should be understood as for the greater good of all.

- As the world's only superpower, America will justifiably take any steps necessary to assure that no other countries ever approach American military strength, cultural influence, or economic dominance.

- Because of the dangers posed by international terrorism, America will take any actions it deems necessary to eliminate any threats to any American interests (which always coincide with "the greater good of all").

- America will act to preempt "gathering" threats. If another nation engages in behavior that might one day threaten American interests, then America will do whatever it deems necessary to eliminate that possible threat. If another nation, knowingly or not, harbors a group of individuals who might one day threaten American interests, then America will do whatever it deems necessary to eliminate that possible threat.

- While America might seek the approval and assistance of other nations as it wields its hegemonic powers, it does not require such approval or assistance and will act unilaterally when necessary to protect American interests.

• While America welcomes the efforts of multilateral institutions such as the United Nations and the World Court, America will not find binding any international treaties, resolutions, or agreements (including those negotiated by earlier American administrations) that might one day threaten American interests.

• No other nation should aspire to or enact any of the above policies, except in special cases and with American approval.

Most Americans responded to the release of the "Bush Doctrine" with little more than a shrug, if they noticed at all. It merely updated certain principles, including manifest destiny, the Monroe Doctrine, American exceptionalism, and benevolent hegemony, that had been part of the national mindset for generations. Even those who opposed the notion of America as "policeman to the world" did so mostly out of a fear of foreign entanglements. Few Americans, and almost no politicians, questioned the essential thrust of the document: that continuing American dominance, expressed in unilateral action backed by the threat of overwhelming force, represents the best (and only) possible state of affairs for all nations.

Most non-Americans responded to both the rush to war and the release of the Bush Doctrine with varying degrees of frustration, disbelief, rage, fear, and uppity rebellion. Foreign politicians expressed their concerns in the measured halftones of diplomacy and tact while privately shaking their heads at the dangerously self-centered Bush. (When a German Minister of Justice had the temerity to publicly compare Bush's political tactics to those of Hitler, American officials promptly engineered her removal from office, thus proving her point. A similar fate befell a Canadian official who called Bush a moron.) Editorialists and commentators throughout the world joined with the people in the streets to decry American imperialism and to express alarm at the growing international insecurity that it created. An iconic image for foreign pundits and cartoonists became Bush as a yahoo cowboy (emphasis on "boy") with oversized pistols blazing. "Cowboy diplomacy" became the favored term for his under-nuanced approach to global affairs.

Indeed, the Bush Doctrine represented not so much a sweeping new statement for a world shaken by international terrorism as a throwback to America's period of westward expansion. Nineteenth century America felt manifestly destined to move into any land that it found useful, whether for population expansion or resource extraction. The people already living on said lands were considered ignorant savages. Said savages faced the ancient dilemma: they could retreat to new territories, they could surrender to the invaders, or they could fight back. Those who fought back found themselves up against dominant forces and either surrendered, retreated, or resorted to the time-tested tactics of asymmetrical warfare—sneak attacks, suicide missions, and civilian terrorization. Such tactics only solidified their image as savages, adding urgency and force to America's "Indian eradication" programs.

Those savages who tried to appease the invaders made the best deals they could and signed treaties in good faith. They would eventually discover that cowboy diplomats consider treaties and signed agreements as nothing more than short-term dodges on the way to long-term acquisitions. The American government broke most every treaty entered into with native populations during the 19th century. To this day, federal violation of Native American rights occurs with shameful frequency, including a Bureau of Indian Affairs' scandal in 2002 involving billions in "misallocated" funds.

In similar fashion, the cowboy diplomats running the Bush administration feel manifestly destined to take control of any part of the planet that they find useful, whether for corporate expansion or resource extraction (especially oil). Because American businesses require open and secure access to global markets, any interference with American-defined "free trade"—such as local zoning laws, environmental standards, or labor policies—perforce interferes with American interests and may trigger a justifiably aggressive response. Because the American economy requires vast resources from all over the world to keep running, any threat to the cheap and steady supply of those resources (especially oil) likewise threatens American interests and constitutes reasonable grounds for "whatever it takes," including preemptive attack.

The nations of the world have been given fair notice: you're either cowboys or you're Indians, good or evil, with us or against us. Cowboy-think brooks no middle ground, no shades of gray, no relative truths, no multicultural distractions, no negotiations, no compromises, no diplomacy. Real cowboys have no time for diplomacy—they're too busy saving the women and children. Real cowboys have nothing but disdain for the endless debating of the United Nations, all the time wasted listening to inferiors, all the white-color fussing over fine language and namby-pamby resolutions. Real cowboys want to stand before the U.N. assembly and shout: "Speak American!"

Whether we call it the Bush Doctrine or cowboy diplomacy or manifest destiny or American exceptionalism or benevolent hegemony, it all amounts to dominism, pure and simple, and the most all-encompassing dominism the world has ever seen. Dominists have as a sole overriding purpose the expansion of power, by whatever means, at whatever costs. Dominists only engage in diplomacy as a sometimes-effective way to expand power without expending money and soldiers. Dominists dispense with diplomacy if it fails to serve the expansion of their power or if it might expand the power of others.

All of this became abundantly clear in the buildup to the Iraq War. Peace initiatives and diplomatic efforts were dismissed without real consideration. American peace activists were branded as traitors, while foreign calls for peace were simply ignored, even as they approached a near-unanimous crescendo. The cowboy diplomats had their reasons (especially oil), had made up their minds, and all that remained, as Bush's press secretary blithely suggested, was selling the product. Once they got rolling, the engines of war would not be derailed.

What America desperately lacked, in both major political parties and all three branches of government, was even an inkling of how to do things differently. If your only tool is a hammer, the saying goes, then all problems look like nails. Because military force has for so long served as America's primary tool for resolving conflicts, all of the world's problems tend to become militarized. We cannot see, cannot even imagine, any other approach to conflict than a sizing up of each side's capacity for violence. All foreign policy, and a large degree of domestic policy, becomes dictated by the dangerous logic of dominism, which eschews democratic and diplomatic processes. The nation slides (taking most of the world with it) into patterns of increasing militarism, unilateralism, monotheism, sexism, xenophobia, greed, competition, secrecy, and anti-environmentalism.

We the Silenced

Civil disobedience is not our problem. Our problem is civil obedience. Our problem is that numbers of people all over the world have obeyed dictates of the leaders of their government and have gone to war, and millions have been killed because of this obedience. Our problem is that people are obedient all over the world in the face of poverty and starvation and stupidity, and war, and cruelty. Our problem is that people are obedient while the jails are full of petty thieves, and all the while the grand thieves are running and robbing the country. That's our problem.

—**Howard Zinn**[4]

America takes great pride in being the world's oldest democracy, but it's sort of like taking great pride in having the oldest computer.

—Geov Parrish[5]

As the invasion of Iraq grew ever more probable, the economy slumped, markets fell, unemployment rose, and consumer confidence declined. Civil liberties disappeared into the fog of terror war. Responsibility for national energy policies rested in the hands of oil barons, media bias swung sharply and unabashedly to the right, already inadequate environmental regulations caved before the demands of corporate greed, and some 43 million Americans lived without medical insurance. A government already running large deficits eliminated taxes for the wealthiest one percent of its citizens. The President advocated for increasing militarism, unilateral interventions, and preemptive strikes, while people around the world expressed alarm and dismay at America's imperial intransigence, and the US Congress teetered in the most precarious of balances.

With so much at risk and such grave matters to decide, the American people went to the polls in a midterm election. The Republicans picked up two Senate seats and four in the House of Representatives. Though the Democrats won several Governor's races, the Republicans now had control of the presidency, the Senate, the House, the Supreme Court, and, through a rush of appointments to come, the federal judiciary.

The media proclaimed that the American people had spoken *en masse* to give President Bush and the Republicans a resounding mandate. The conventional wisdom held that the Democrats had failed to present a coherent and inspiring vision, and had been especially cowed at the prospect of standing against a popular wartime President. The implications of the outcome loomed large and oppressive: for as long as America remained engaged in the war on terror and the constant work of changing evil regimes, American politics would continue its slide into ever more trenchant dominism.

Yet for all the drama and post-election analysis, the most telling story from the 2002 election concerned not who people voted for, but how many people chose not to vote at all. Some 77 million ballots were cast, which amounted to 39 percent of eligible citizens. Thus, less than 20 percent of the total electorate voted for Republicans, not even remotely a majority of Americans. In the end, 100,000 swing voters in a few key states, less than .05 percent of eligible voters, gave the President his so-called mandate.

This low voter turnout continued a long-term trend toward declining participation in American elections. In sharp variance to the rest of the world's democracies, America has a dismal record of citizen involvement in the electoral process. Not only do fewer people vote in each succeeding American election, the financial realities of the system dictate that most politicians either come from great wealth or must pledge their candidacies to wealthy backers in order to get elected. Democracy (the free and equal right of every person to participate in their system of government) has given way to plutocracy (the rule of society by its wealthiest people), which, following the dangerous logic of dominism, has further contracted into something of an oligarchy (rule of a nation by a powerful few).

Those tracking this gradual degradation of American democracy focus on three key points. First and foremost, the omnipresent influence of money taints, disrupts, and utterly overwhelms every aspect of American politics. Politicians, supposedly servants of the American people, spend more time fundraising than legislating and, given the necessity of keeping major donors satisfied, most legislation amounts to little more than fundraising in disguise. Much like the never-ending war on terror, America has developed a never-ending election cycle with politicians always running for office, so that the fundraising never stops or takes a holiday and the quid pro quo between the elected and their owners never ceases. Candidates spend most of their money on television advertising, which renders meaningful debates of complex issues into 30-second attack ads designed to trigger strong emotional reactions while avoiding rational discourse. Bottom line, the person who spends the most money—not necessarily the best for the job, or the smartest, the fairest, or the most honest—the one who raises the most money usually wins, with occasional exceptions proving the rule. To wit, in the 2002 election Republicans outspent Democrats by nearly $200 million.

A second problem with American democracy stems from its two-party system. The Democratic and Republican parties have dominated American politics for so long that voices from outside the parties have difficulty being heard or exerting influence. Politicians from within either party who wander too far from party doctrine get labeled as mavericks or extremists and remain stuck at the lower rungs of political power. Recurring attempts to launch significant third parties tend toward the perverse effect of draining votes from the major candidate closest to the third-party platform; thus, votes for conservative Ross Perot pushed the election to liberal Bill Clinton in 1992, while supporters of progressive Ralph Nader helped elect fundamentalist George W. Bush in 2000. To make matters worse, both parties have learned that to win elections candidates must "run from the center," which results in bland policy debates that avoid controversial issues and innovative solutions.

Democracy in America especially suffers from in its winner-take-all electoral process. Americans begin with a grossly oversimplified set of choices—Republican/Democrat, Right/Left, Conservative/Liberal—that eliminate outright a diverse host of nonpartisan voices. Then, upon voting, the losing party, and the millions of Americans it represents, loses position and power, even if, as has happened in the past four presidential elections, the winners receive but a razor thin margin of victory. If American political discourse seems increasingly bitter and combative, it certainly does not help that half the voting population (and in 2000, more than half) feels that their votes did not count. By contrast, in the parliamentary systems of most European democracies, the makeup of ruling bodies closely reflect the actual percentages of votes cast; any party or candidate who gets a significant number of votes attains a position and a voice in the resulting coalition government. The leading party of such coalitions must listen to and attempt to accommodate all viewpoints or risk forcing a new election and the possible loss of power. Thus, even if your candidate only received ten percent of the vote, he or she may still have a strong voice in the government, so you know your vote counted. Most European democracies see voter turnouts of more than 85 percent.

Despite the vexing and threatening nature of these problems, and despite many international examples of thriving democracies with high citizen participation, all attempts to significantly address America's electoral issues either bog down in empty debate or result in toothless legislation. The ink had not even dried on the latest attempt at campaign finance reform—the McCain-Feingold bill of 2001—before politicians and political lobbyists had figured out how to circumvent the supposed fixes. Even the glaring and easy-to-understand snafus that plagued ballot casting in the 2000 election have resisted simple solutions.

While we debate about what's wrong with America's electoral system, we ever avoid dealing with the real problem: the dominist-driven mechanics of American government and culture. Over the two centuries since America's birth, and particularly during the last fifty years, the dangerous logic of dominism has twisted the best-laid plans of Jefferson and company into the antidemocratic farce we endure today.

All of the shortcomings in American democracy work to favor dominist elites and the most dominant of the two parties. Most significantly, when 50-60 percent of the people cede their right to vote, the dominists only have to make their case to 20-25 percent of the total electorate. The nonvoters come almost unanimously from the middle and lower tiers of the population. The dominists pick up a good half of their needed votes simply by standing for tax policies and business regulations that favor a continuing transfer of wealth into the hands of the über-rich. For the rest of their votes, they trawl among the underclass and out-groups with single-issue fundamentalist policies for bait: pro-gun, antiabortion, school prayer, anti-immigration, and (you have to admire the chutzpah) antigovernment.

But 20-25 percent will never win elections, or give credible influence to dominist positions, unless a majority of Americans regularly stay away from the polling booths. So dominists have always looked for ways to suppress the vote. The Founders institutionalized such suppression from the very outset by allowing each state to limit the right to vote as it saw fit, an act that left women, people of color, and some underclass white men without the vote. While Americans pride themselves on their democratic traditions, it would take more than 200 years to fully enfranchise the People. Yet even as Americans have gradually expanded suffrage, dominists have worked to reduce turnout of the out-groups on Election Day. From poll taxes, residency requirements, and registration barriers through a thousand and one forms of intimidation to the fraudulent "felon list" that prevented some 80,000 qualified Floridians from voting in 2000, dominists never run short of antidemocratic schemes.

Still, the most powerful of all forces to suppress the vote has come about not by devious design or overclass conspiracy; rather, it simply evolved over the past half-century, the natural result of the Parable of the Tribes applied to elections. Like invading marauders, the Dominist Party (made up in more or less equal parts of Republicans and Democrats) has armed itself with overwhelming wealth, incumbent-protecting legislation, and the inestimable backing of powerful corporations. Those who would stand against the overrunning of American democracy face familiar choices: surrender to or aggressively challenge these antidemocratic forces (both of which ultimately entail adopting dominist ways and means), or run away (by choosing not to vote). That more and more people choose not to vote in each succeeding election makes painfully perfect sense because, with rare exceptions, only dominist positions make it into party platforms and only dominist candidates ever get elected. Americans who find no representation in dominist positions or candidates either waste their time voting for losers or stop voting altogether.

Millions of Americans, predominantly from the underclass and out-groups, choose not to vote because they know that their votes do not count and that voting makes little difference in their lives. Trying to "guilt" such people into voting by appealing to their patriotism and civic duty utterly misses the point: we cannot expect those who have been cast beyond the gilded walls of elite society to show up just on Election Day to affirm the system that's cast them aside. Dismissing these nonvoters as foolishly apathetic likewise misses the point. By in effect voting for "none of the above" they make a far freer and more enlightened choice than most of the 40 percent (and declining) who dutifully voted.

The more that the out-groups give up their votes, the less value that the votes of their social compatriots will have, and thus the greater the validity to everyone's reasons not to vote. Once again we see the workings of viral dominism. Every person who chooses not to vote spreads the pernicious logic of nonvoting to others. No amount of "getting out the vote" will ever overcome the awful truth: the declining participation of Americans in the electoral process manifests as but one more inevitable symptom of the dominist plague that grips the country.

Indeed, with less than 40 percent turnout, how can we even call this a democracy? How different is it, really, from the sham voting of the former Soviet Union? Our so-called democratic system now exists primarily to guarantee an orderly flow of wealth and political power into the hands of fewer and fewer people. Every two years this concentration of sociopolitical power grows more dangerously imbalanced, yet the time between elections gets frittered away on position statements that fit easily in 10-second soundbites.

Representative democracy, with its three branches of government and system of checks and balances, was the Founders' brilliant solution to the dominist tendencies that prevail in other forms of governance and, for that matter, to all of the problems detailed above. The central principle—that all people are created equal and are entitled to an equal voice and vote—remains the single-most effective antidote to political dominism. In any nation or organization that truly follows this principle, power accrues to the voting populace in relatively equal measure. Dominists cannot grow too powerful because when matters get put to a fair vote, small self-serving elites generally get outvoted. In democracies with high voter turnout, populist movements that speak directly to and for the mainstream majority naturally take on greater power.

Of course, Hitler was democratically elected by just such a populist movement and over the years America has endured more than a few charismatic demagogues who seized control of populist positions and votes. However, the danger that a fully enfranchised populace will make free yet foolish choices must not lead to the solution of cynical elites—namely, that we conspire to keep the ignorant riff-raff away from the polls. Rather, the way to stop both populist demagogues and dominist elites from hijacking elections lies in a fully informed and positively engaged electorate. Democracy in America no longer works because its dominism-infected and denial-bound governing and electoral systems produce precisely the opposite—a misinformed and viscerally repelled populace.

Domocracy

My greatest complaint against democratic government as organized in the United States is not the extreme freedom reigning there but the shortage of guarantees against tyranny. —**Alexis de Tocqueville**[6]

As a result of the war, corporations have been enthroned, and an era of corruption in high places will follow. The money power of the coun-

try will endeavor to prolong its reign by working on the prejudices of the people until wealth is aggregated in a few hands and the Republic is destroyed. I feel at this moment more anxiety for the safety of my country than ever before, even in the midst of war.

—Abraham Lincoln[7]

About the only thing more treasonous in modern America than saying "I don't support the war" is saying "I don't support the tax cut." Certainly nothing spells doom for a politician or political party faster than the notion, however well articulated, of increasing taxes on working Americans. Walter Mondale was the last presidential candidate to suggest that raising taxes may be necessary, even healthy, an admission that gave Ronald Reagan a solid mandate for four more years of his fiscal lunacy. Next election, George H. W. Bush made his much-regretted "read my lips, no new taxes" statement, a promise he eventually had to break as President, an act that cost him reelection, a mistake that no politician has made since.

While most everyone will agree that government needs tax revenues to carry on the business of governing, serious disagreements arise regarding exactly what government should spend its money on, how much it should spend, and who should be taxed how much and in what ways. For our purposes, the arguments reduce to whether a system of taxation works progressively or regressively. Progressive taxes take money in greater proportions (as a percentage of income and/or net worth) from the wealthy and spread the money through the nation's economy via government spending on what most people consider essential goods and services. The more you have, the more you give, and the more people that receive the benefits. Regressive taxes take money in greater proportions from the underclass and transfer the money to the overclass via government spending on goods and services essential to dominist elites. The more you have, the more you get, and the fewer that share in the getting.

In a progressive system, such as Canada's and that of most European nations, we see modest gaps in income and net worth between rich and poor along with ample government funding of society's essentials: healthcare, housing, education, childcare, retirement, industrial infrastructure, and the environment. In a regressive system like America's, we see huge gaps between the rich and poor, with lavish spending on the engines of dominism—the military, the Security State, and corporate welfare. Progressive taxation strives to create an all-encompassing social safety net, following the thinking that if everybody has reasonable access to the essentials of life, liberty, and the pursuit of happiness, then society as a whole tends toward peace and prosperity. Regressive taxation expands the wealth and power of the few at the expense of the many; as life inevitably degrades for the underclass, society as a whole tends toward conflict and discord.

For most of the 20th century, America enjoyed the benefits of relatively progressive taxes. The system began to adopt more regressive elements in the 1960s, in small steps at first, quietly taken, before accelerating into a full-scale anti-tax revolution with the coming of "supply-side, trickle-down" Reaganomics in the 1980s. Reagan managed to successfully demonize "big government" as a malevolent force out to steal your hard-earned money for the primary purpose of catering to the frivolous desires of indolent, unworthy others. Tax rates on the wealthy and on corporations plummeted, the federal deficit ballooned, and the gap between the income and net worth of the overclass and underclass steadily increased. Government spending actually expanded under Reagan—big government got bigger—with most of it going into the Cold War military build-up and unprecedented corporate payola. (Remember the Savings and Loans bonanza?) Concurrently, the ranks of the medically uninsured and the homeless grew, while budgets for schools, hospitals, childcare facilities, the nation's infrastructure, the needs of the environment, and the welfare system all declined.

This shift to a patently unfair system that so obviously benefits the über-rich while putting the squeeze on everyone else has never led, as one might have expected in a healthy democracy, to a popular movement to *raise* taxes. To the contrary, with every reduction in progressive taxes, the anti-tax movement has grown stronger, gathering into its ranks the very people who suffer most from the subsequent burdens of regressive taxation. Ironically, as taxes turn more regressive, society gets more mean-spirited, people complain more about the failings of big government, the pitch to cut taxes becomes more persuasive, and the system turns even more regressive. As Lenin predicted, anti-tax politicians have learned to sell their constituents—tax free!—the rope with which they hang themselves.

This clearly amounts to something less than genuine democracy, though neither can we accurately call America an oligarchy. For despite the end product—government by a wealthy self-serving elite—the basic process through which the wealthy gain power in America remains representative democracy. We the People dutifully (if in declining numbers) vote the overclass into power. Though the system has been terribly degraded, Americans still democratically elect their leaders, who still democratically carry on the business of governing. Unlike a typical oligarchy, where the overclass seizes and maintains power through the overt use of vast wealth and control of the military, in America the ruling elite comes to power by winning somewhat open and more or less free elections. And while those living under oligarchic rule typically chafe at the bit and forever threaten palace coups and peasant revolts, even the most downtrodden of Americans will proudly declare their rights and rise to impassioned defense of the land of the free.

Exceptional in all ways, America has come to develop its own unique form of government: domocracy. While the "dem" in "democracy" points to "the people," the "dom" in "domocracy" points to "lord and ruler." In a domocracy, the dangerous logic of dominism gradually perverts the democratic process to produce oligarchic results. It looks for all intents and purposes like democracy in action—politicians campaign, people vote, power switches hands, things get legislated, and the law of the land prevails—but the real action all takes place behind the scenes and under the table where the overclass does its business. The voting public can moderate the inevitable outcome of "rule by a wealthy few," but never really stop it: we may vote some of them out of office, but never out of wealth. In a domocracy, voting ultimately strengthens the positions and adds to the power of dominist elites.

For example, as a number of leading thinkers (including many prominent conservatives) have argued, America's long-running war on drugs has been a monumental failure of social policy. It has overfilled our prisons with young men and women, disproportionably people of color, who go in as nonviolent petty offenders to eventually get released back into society as time-hardened criminals. It has turned the streets of our poorer neighborhoods into squalid and despairing war zones, populated with children who face no better prospects in life than becoming successful pushers. It has made hypocrites of parents, teachers, doctors, law enforcement officials, and politicians, who must carry the standard of "drugs are evil" while shrugging off the greater but legal evils of tobacco, alcohol, and overused prescription drugs. It has delivered obscene profits to the international miscreants who run the drug trade. And, no surprise but so important, it has delivered equally obscene profits to an army of private companies and government agencies—the security-industrial-complex—charged with waging this unwinnable war.

As with the war on taxes, the war on drugs has inflicted such damnable harm on the nation that after so much time and suffering we might expect the voters to rise up and shout, "Enough already, try something different!" But they never do. Even the most reasonable efforts to slow down the drug war, such as the moves to decriminalize medical marijuana or to legalize non-psychoactive industrial hemp, face strong resistance when placed on the ballot. We are as likely to hear a politician pledging to end the war on drugs as to hear one pledging to raise taxes, since either stand spells certain electoral death. So legislators constantly ratchet up the war on drugs, thereby causing the collateral damages listed above, thereby assuring the support of sick and frightened voters for yet more terrible war.

The American public will forever support the war on drugs because voting for war (on whatever) feels safer, stronger, more resolute, and perfectly patriotic. The dangerous logic of dominism has militated a simple public health problem into a moral crisis of epic scope, another battle in the must-win war between good and evil. So people must vote in favor of the drug war, even though, like all wars, it accomplishes little more than the concentration of wealth and power among the overclass.

America's health insurance crisis has followed a similar storyline. Despite the severe social and personal consequences of having nearly 50 million citizens living without insurance, and despite the fact that virtually all modern industrial countries have demonstrated the common sense and effectiveness of government-provided universal healthcare, that most of the people in those countries speak favorably of their healthcare systems, and that most Americans favor a shift to "Canadian-style healthcare," the case for universal healthcare barely makes it into the public discourse, much less into halls of Congress, and never onto party platforms or voter's ballots. Hillary Clinton's much-ballyhooed attempt to reform the healthcare system did not even feint in the direction of universal care and only added to the real problem—the power and profits of big insurance companies. Though polling at the time showed that a bold shift to government-managed healthcare had strong public backing, any such proposals fell on politically deaf ears.

Yet all of the people who make up the U.S. Congress, the federal judiciary, and the executive branch—those who determine the design and implementation of America's healthcare system—enjoy the generous coverage for themselves and their families of government-provided and -managed healthcare. The mind reels, but what seems the worst of contradictions, the most arrant of hypocrisies, makes perfect sense in a domocracy. The dominist principles of excess materialism and self-serving competition have so undermined the democratic process as to render common sense incomprehensible. In this case, the system "works" to keep the decidedly anti-dominist notion of decent healthcare for all citizens off the table and beyond consideration. When the People threaten to vote incorrectly, domocracy assures that they do not vote at all. Again, it manages the look and feel of democracy, but amounts to little more than a puppet's dance, with dominist fingers pulling the strings.

Finally, nothing has a more degrading effect on democracy than war. When the nation's youth go off into harm's way, when the homeland girds for pending invasion, when one's culture, history, religion, identity, industry, and way of life come under attack, when personal and political survival become the countervailing and overarching priorities of the day, the dangerous logic of "with us or against us" spreads through the populace like the most virulent of plagues. Truth, civil rights, and the democratic process always fall among first casualties. During war, people urgently rally behind the toughest-talking leaders and pledge to do whatever it takes to win at all costs. "My country, right or wrong," the nation sings, and no better anthem has ever been crafted for the full-scale industrial mobilizations, draconian civilian sacrifices, rapid deployments, and all-out battles to the death that winning at war requires.

Democracy at such times amounts to little more than farce, theater, and sham—the unanimous vote, the presidential mandate, the absolute proclamation, and the rubber stamp legislation. Genuine debate over the issues becomes impossible as flag-wrapped patriots insist on "war, because you love your country," leaving "anti-war, because you hate your country" to traitorous scum and naïve appeasers. The cloak-and-dagger Security State, with its smug insistence on keeping everything secret, voids the transparency and openness essential to democratic processes. Million-dollar spending programs on needy constituencies that took years to legislate go into the shredder, replaced in a moment and with nary an oversight by billion-dollar weapons systems. Journalism morphs into military propaganda, concern for innocent civilians gives way to an offhanded acceptance of collateral damages, and the bedrock rights of the accused to justifiable arrest, humane treatment, and fair trial all dissolve before the "don't you know there's a war on" demands of martial law.

War grabs democracy by the throat, turns it upside down and inside out, and shakes it till the People become one fear-driven, unthinking horde prepared to inflict mass murder, or at least to cover their eyes and shutter their hearts as compatriots act in their names. Like symptoms of an incipient disease, any lingering impulses among the citizenry for democratic process face stern, even violent, repression. Long-cherished civil rights threaten the Security State's need for absolute national unity, so those who would stand in the way of the nation's path to war—no matter how reasoned or sincere and no matter how much they obviously love their country—get shunned as fools and turncoats, unworthy of consideration and incapable of influence. Conversely, those who fly the flag, wear the colors, sing the anthem loudly, and unthinkingly follow orders take on all the power and glory and absolute righteousness of God's own army.

George W. Bush came into office on a tainted election with modest public approval and little political power. On September 10, 2001 he was nine months into what seemed destined to unfold as a weak and ineffective one-term presidency. A week later his approval ratings reached 90% and he took on the mantle of "most powerful man in the world," despite the fact that he had made no significant decisions and had shown no particularly presidential qualities beyond the capacity to sound tough while reading someone else's well-written speech. He did not engage the American people in spirited debate over life-and-death issues. He did not take to the streets to rouse excited crowds to his brave new agenda. He did not work the legislative process, persuading senators and representatives and hammering out the particulars of his political platform. Indeed, he showed dominist disregard for all things democratic, including congressional powers of advice, consent, and oversight at times of war.

The pampered prince turned suddenly into conquering king because the nation fell suddenly into war. In the immediate aftermath of September 11, as reality dawned on the American people—we've been attacked, thousands of civilians have been wickedly slaughtered, we are at war—the political landscape shifted from a quake of biblical dimensions. All tendencies toward democratic process were overrun by the dangerous logic of militarism. National concerns over the economy and environment and whatever else simply paled in significance, as suddenly all that mattered was national defense and the swift and certain prosecution of the newest war. Mr. Bush, who in the days prior to his inauguration said, "This would be so much easier if America was a dictatorship," had gotten his wish. He had acquired the ultimate in dictatorial powers: he was an American President At War.

History has shown that, in times of war, Americans will stand foursquare—90 percent approval—behind their president as long as they remain convinced that the costs of war answer real and present dangers. The Second World War, for instance, has generally been considered a good war because few doubted the necessity of sacrificing Allied lives to stop the Axis forces. The Vietnam War began as a good enough war, but after too many thousands of American deaths the supposed threat of Communist expansion lost its capacity to inspire the troops or terrify the folks at home. While the American people may have continued reelecting FDR for as long as he and his war went on, when things soured in Vietnam, LBJ became the very opposite of an all-powerful-and-beloved wartime president.

The smart guys at War, Inc. have learned their lessons well from these two seminal American experiences. America now spends more on the engines of war than all of the other nations of the world combined, making America so militarily dominant that the odds of ever coming out of a conflict with major losses approach zero. Even still, America prefers to go to war against toddler countries, such as Grenada and Panama, or when faced with a tougher foe, to fight with low-risk, high-altitude, saturation bombing, as in Iraq, Bosnia, and Afghanistan. America has also learned to seek multinational coalitions before going into battle, thereby spreading costs in casualties and munitions while broadening international agreement. The military's credo is to inflict the greatest amount of damage on an enemy in the shortest possible time, with minimal American casualties or costs. Any deviation from this approach, such as the use of ground troops in unstable civilian environments, as happened in Vietnam and Somalia, runs the risk of turning into a bad war and losing public support. That Bush broke two of these rules for his invasion of Iraq, by failing to form a multilateral coalition and by committing to the occupation of an unfriendly populace, would badly tarnish his war and ultimately doom his presidency.

For as long as the military, with help from a compliant, properly patriotic media, can sustain the image and feel of a good war, then the president's approval ratings stay high, the indivisible and unquestioning force of national unity grows stronger, and democratic processes become increasingly extraneous. The dangerous logic of war guarantees a nation mired in domocracy. For as long Bush's war on terror drones on—peppered with quickie conquests of small evildoing countries—America's most time-honored democratic traditions will only serve to push the nation into more severe domocracy. Politicians who want to stay in power will fully support the President and "run on the war." Those who dare the slightest quibble with the President will sound "weak on security" and go down in defeat at the polls (as happened in 2002 to Max Cleeland, a triple-amputee Vietnam War veteran, and in 2004 to John Kerry, a certified war hero). Faced with the prospect of choosing among marginally different pro-war candidates, more voters will just stay home. Elections will devolve into mud-slinging contests among overclass scions, while the Bill of Rights gets scribbled over with wartime exceptions.

Of the many prescient warnings in George Orwell's *1984*, none cries out with more immediate relevancy than the dangers of permanent war. From the moment that Bush declared war not on a specific country or people but on the idea and tactic of terrorism, he thrust the nation (and the rest of the world) down a neverending road of monumental suffering. War breeds terrorism as surely as any attempt to outgun terrorism plants the seeds for future war, so the war on terrorism can only be a permanent war. We can never win this idiot contest. We will, however, most assuredly lose: our freedoms, our civil rights, her voice, his vote, our precious democracy, everything we proclaimed worth fighting for, we will lose it all.

Part Two

We the Peaceful

I romanticize America. I can't help it. I've always been head over heels in love with Thomas Jefferson and Harriet Tubman and Emily Dickinson and Robert Johnson and roads that go on and on through big, empty spaces, and Walt Whitman's sentences that go on and on, creating their own mental spaces, and the lovely insanity of a bunch of rich, white guys founding a country on the idea that everyone had equal rights, even if they didn't really believe it. In the beginning were the words and the words were so damn good we're stuck forever after trying to make something of them.

— Jeanne d'Orleans[1]

Credo

We believe in the one message
   like a fever chill
   in each mushroom, inside
   the chanterelle, the morel,
   the rose coral and shaggy mane.
We believe the movement of a lake trout
   takes on the sanctity of number
   as the osprey dives. We believe the towhee.
We believe alpine snow water, when it teases the crags
   and outcrops like clear giggling crystal,
   is memorizing sunlight to help oysters grow.
We believe in synchronicity. We believe when a poem is conceived
   the beloved knows. We believe Jupiter touches us with luck
   as we live and live again, and that Jesus knew.
We believe sod holds. We believe there are
   in each of us particles that once
   were stars, that matter is thought,
   and that this belief is the way
   of breathing in.

   – James Bertolino

Six

Thinking Peace

So let us unleash our weapons of mass construction, even as we deploy our gunships and missiles to defend our endeavors. Let us carry the battle into the tent-cities of the Palestinians and the arid crags of Afghanistan, the doctor and the engineer shoulder to shoulder with the U.N. peacekeeper and the U.S. soldier. Let us hurl homes at homelessness, unleash law upon lawlessness, and let justice roll down like a mighty river and wash away the unjust.

—Robert Alberti[2]

One day after strong majorities in the American congress voted for a resolution allowing the president to wage war against Iraq, former president Jimmy Carter won the Nobel Peace Prize. The Nobel Committee cited Carter for the sustaining peace he brokered between Israel and Egypt in 1978; for significant diplomatic efforts in Haiti and North Korea; for his work to bring free and open elections to numerous budding democracies; and for his championing of the cause of human rights around the world. Upon announcing the award in Oslo, Nobel Committee chairman Gunnar Berge stated that the choice of Carter "should be interpreted as a criticism of the line that the current administration has taken." When asked if he thought the timing of his prize might have been politically motivated, Carter suggested that it might indeed act as a "kick in the leg" for Bush and his advisors.

The media gave minor coverage to Carter's achievement. Most reports included a simple history of Carter's life and deeds, stressing the fact that his four-year presidency was considered a failure, followed by an almost embarrassed recitation of his many do-gooder activities since leaving the White House. Rather than dwell overlong on whatever lessons Carter might impart on the actual process of making peace, the media went after the controversial aspects of his selection: that the Nobel Committee had made a "political" choice in Carter and then compounded the dirty politics with Berge's remarks, and that it was unseemly for the ex-president to take swipes at a sitting president faced with war. Pundits strained to make the case that in the current struggle between the forces of war and the forces of peace the doves had taken unfair advantage of the poor hawks. The notion that a group of European peaceniks would resort to underhanded tactics to advance their case and that the self-righteous Carter would acquiesce in such calumny discredited the whole enterprise of making peace. So said the mainstream media.

The entire episode played out as a case of textbook dominism. Not only do the winners in geopolitical struggles take the loot and write the histories, they also set the terms of ensuing policy debates. In a domocracy, voices for nonviolent conflict resolution may find begrudging tolerance during times of relative peace, but once the war drums start beating, everyone must whistle the same martial tunes, including Nobel peace laureates. Contrarians get badly spun in the media, if they show up there at all. Supposed debates in the halls of Congress amount to little more than convoluted digressions on the way to foregone conclusions. Public polling carefully frames debates so that respondents never actually address the complex issues underlying a conflict (95% of Americans agree that Saddam is evil!); pollsters prefer broad sweeping headlines (70% of Americans favor war with Iraq) that neatly elide key data (only 35% favor war without U.N. approval).

The national dialogue, and indeed, the nation's thinking has for so long been subsumed in the all-encompassing and always dangerous logic of dominism that non-dominist thought sounds like so much nonsense, like the babble of children or the imprecise mumbles of drunken derelicts. Talking calmly and respectfully with enemies? Cooperating, compromising, and building consensus? Finding common ground? Making concessions? The dominist mind sneers at such thoughts, then reaches for its gun. While peacemakers encourage adversaries to patiently talk through conflicts, dominists squelch all such dialogue with their taunts and insults and hair-trigger reactions. While peacemaking needs time to allow for a full airing of views and the back-and-forth steps of diplomacy, the dominism virus madly proliferates, overwhelming events, seizing moments, and forcing issues. Dominists thirst after violent confrontation like junkyard dogs straining on the leash, raising such a terrorizing din as to render the best laid plans of peacemakers incomprehensible.

To a dominist people, ideas of violence and aggression just naturally make the most sense; war always comes as a *fait accompli,* an unfortunate but necessary final solution. Peace strikes the dominist mind as unthinkable, unfathomable, and beyond the pale of rational discourse. However diligently peacemakers strive to make the case for nonviolent reconciliation, dominists always have battle-tested counter-arguments: Stress how evil *they* are, how they threaten the women and children, how they would destroy the very fabric of society. Appeal to national pride. Call up historic villains. Dangle the promise of booty. Never allow the weak and simpering agents of appeasement to undermine the nation's will.

The mere suggestion of appeasement can instantly discredit the most conscientious peace proposal. "Thou shalt not appease!" scream the dominists, invoking in a word the horror that was Hitler, the blitzkrieg, the holocaust, the 50 million dead, and laying it all at the feet of Neville Chamberlain. Because appeasement failed so miserably in the 1930s, it will absolutely fail in future circumstances, even those, as in today's Middle East, that bear little resemblance to pre-WWII Europe. Any attempt to address the needs of a belligerent foe, to understand what drives their aggression, or to provide some measure of violence-abating compensation—any attempt think peacefully—gets twisted into the political sins of treason, naiveté, and weakness.

Early in the Iraq War debate congressmen Jim McDermott and David Bonier traveled to Baghdad to meet with Iraqi civilians, to tour the country, to gather information about the effects of U.N. sanctions, and to investigate the issue of Iraqi weapons of mass destruction. Their experiences convinced them that U.S. policies toward Iraq had not only failed to eliminate Saddam Hussein, but had increased his power within Iraq while turning Iraqis and other Arabs against America and the West. McDermott went so far as to say that we should not trust everything we hear from a U.S. administration bent on war. Two well-documented lies—the supposed slaughter of babies in Kuwaiti hospitals and the supposed buildup of Iraqi troops along the Saudi border—fed the dogs of the first Iraq War. Several similar "misstatements," including almost everything the administration said about Iraq's weapons of mass destruction and Hussein's connections with al Qaeda, had been injected into the second war's debate. The two congressmen called for an easing of sanctions coupled with a return to aggressive international weapons inspections; the world should befriend the Iraqi people while simultaneously reducing the threat of their military.

Congressional colleagues either pilloried or ignored McDermott and Bonier, as did the media and, therefore, most Americans. Conventional wisdom held that, much like Carter, the congressmen had overstepped the bounds of good taste and acted just plain unamerican. As with Carter, their thinking on matters of war and peace received only the briefest consideration—appeasers!—while the contentiousness of their means and method became the main event. Their message served mostly to stoke the anger of American dominists, as their actions on behalf of peace got folded into the dance of war.

Meanwhile, in an interesting historic parallel, the gathering conflict between America and a tiny "rogue state" supposedly armed with terrible weapons coincided with the 40th anniversary of the Cuban Missile Crisis. The Bush administration seized the opportunity to strengthen its case for war. Just as

Kennedy had acted unilaterally to remove nuclear missiles from Cuba, they said, so should Bush remove Iraq's weapons of mass destruction. Just as Kennedy had used the full force of the US military to achieve his ends, so should Bush. Just as Kennedy had prevailed through his willingness to do what ever it takes, so would Bush.

Aside from the fact that Russia's placement of nuclear missiles within strategic reach of major American cities bore an infinitely greater danger than the possible arming of an impoverished, militarily diminished, and internationally isolated Iraq, the Cuban Missile Crisis has much more to teach about making peace than waging war. To begin with, it was America's attempted overthrow (oops, regime change) of Cuba at the Bay of Pigs that started the whole mess. Mindful of that earlier fiasco, when Russian plans for Cuba became evident Kennedy refused to act as hawkish as some in his inner circle advised. This caution likely forestalled all-out nuclear war. We now know that, in response to what he perceived as life-threatening American belligerence, a Russian submarine captain had armed his ship's nuclear missiles and was just one final provocation—or tragic misunderstanding—away from firing. At an anniversary conference held in Cuba, American, Russian, and Cuban principals in the missile crisis agreed that we only avoided nuclear conflagration in 1962 through a willingness on all sides to carefully back away from worst-case scenarios. And while American dominists will brag that the Russians blinked first and withdrew the missiles, they ignore the fact that Kennedy negotiated with Khrushchev and ultimately promised to never invade Cuba again.

What really happened in 1962 was that Kennedy did what he had to do to avoid war. By linking the removal of Russian missiles to the cessation of American aggression he created a win-win solution for all three countries. Not a perfect solution, as the decades of continuing tensions between America and all Communist nations would attest. But it allowed for a peaceful resolution of the immediate crisis, and Cuba and America have since lived as hostile neighbors for more than forty years without significant bloodshed. Nonviolent reconciliation does not mean that individuals or countries link arms and skip off to some hippie paradise; it means giving up aggressive force as the principal way to resolve conflicts. It means building connections with others rather than armies against them, and engaging tools of diplomacy rather than weapons of destruction. It means turning one's thoughts to peace and away from war.

The long and arduous road to peace begins with a single thought. Yet only those who make that first thought, and sustain it through troubled times, will ever travel the road or reach the final destination. What Kennedy did in 1962, as did Carter at Camp David, was make the diplomatic quest for nonviolent solutions the primary order of the day. They thought: "We must find a peaceful way through this conflict." Then they persevered through all the naysaying dominists yammering for aggressive force.

The quick and terrorizing road to war builds in the minds of those who can imagine no other way. The cowboy diplomats of the Bush administration, like dominists throughout history, defined "peace" as "all my enemies dead" and dismissed the tools of peacemaking—negotiation, compromise, nation-building, diplomacy, prayer—as weak and ineffective, if they thought of them at all. They reasoned their way through every problem with the dangerous logic of dominism, which forever trumps the hopeful logic of peace. As predicted by the Parable of the Tribes, once a nation succumbs to war-think it undergoes a deformation of essential character: it turns more aggressive, more prone to violence, and less able to approach conflicts in the spirit of cooperation and partnership.

The War on Everything

I do not question that we have a vicious, abhorrent enemy that opposes most of what I cherish — including democracy, pluralism, secularism, the equality of the sexes, beardless men, dancing (all kinds), skimpy clothing and, well, fun. And not for a moment do I question the obligation of the American government to protect the lives of its citizens. What I do question is the pseudo-declaration of pseudo-war. These necessary actions should not be called a "war." There are no endless wars; but there are declarations of the extension of power by a state that believes it cannot be challenged.

—**Susan Sontag**[3]

Our orthodox models in medicine have come to the same fate as the models of the first scientific revolution: they are sadly inappropriate to studies of the living.

—**Larry Dossey, M.D.**[4]

During the fourteenth century bubonic plague struck with devastating results. Called the Black Death, it would wipe out up to half of the population of Europe and much of Asia before it ran its course. Yet, terrible though it was, it left as many survivors as dead. The plague would creep through a town, taking some from this family and others from that, while typically leaving one person behind for every one that died. Among the living were often those who of necessity took care of and thus came in regular contact with the sick—doctors, servants, priests, and nuns, as well as those who would cart the dead off to dispose of and bury. While living in the midst of a horrible pandemic and coming into constant exposure to the infectious bacterium that caused the Black Death, some individuals not only stayed free of the disease, they lived on in relative health.

Since the fourteenth century, we have learned a lot about bubonic plague. We fully understand the bug that causes it: what it looks like, how it lives, how it travels, how it affects the human body, and how to kill it, which we have proven successful at doing. Yet we know little about those who survived the Black Death and how and why they lived on. Indeed, we have barely even considered them. While we have conscientiously studied the half of Europe that died we have blithely ignored the half that survived.

Doctors now say, "The survivors just had greater resistance; they had natural immunity." But what does that mean? Was it God's will? Were they born with it? Were they just lucky? Or could it have been something in their diet, or their manner of thinking, or the way they processed their emotions, or how they prayed, or perhaps some combination of any or all of these factors? More importantly, as we come to better understand the survivor's experience, can we successfully transfer it to others?

In fundamental ways, Western medical science over the past few hundred years has avoided addressing these questions. We have enthusiastically dissected the dead while showing little interest in the living. We have stayed away from questions of individual immunity and natural healing while focusing our intellectual energies and research on defeating specific disease symptoms, battle by battle, with an increasingly complex array of medical weaponry. Rather than a peaceful investigation into the nature of wellness—How do some people manage to stay healthy without resorting to doctors or medicines?—we have chosen to wage war on the real and imagined agents of disease.

Born out of dominist culture, this wage-war approach to medicine reaches its zenith in modern America with the War on Cancer. Since Richard Nixon declared the war in 1971, American medicine has fought an all-out crusade against a single disease, spending some $100 billion on research and more than a trillion on treatment. Yet, 1.2 million Americans receive new cancer diagnoses each year and 1500 die from cancer every day. A huge anticancer apparatus has been funded and erected—universities and teaching hospitals, research centers, biomedical laboratories and startup companies, much of the pharmaceutical industry, several major charities—all geared to the continuing search for a cancer cure, year after year, one breakthrough treatment after another, even as new cancer rates remain steady. After more than thirty years on this expensive quest, we still have little understanding of why cancer arises in one person but not another, or of why some people die from it while others live on. We have, however, waged one hell of a war.[5]

Waging war requires weapons, the more lethal the better, and all weapons inflict collateral damages as a matter of course. The two primary weapons in the War on Cancer, radiation and chemotherapy, attack cancer cells with military zeal, but produce terrible side effects and unintended consequences, sometimes worse than cancer itself. Both radiation and chemotherapy have especially toxic effects on the human immune system; such "remedies" undermine the very capacities for self-healing that patients most need. While the latest advances in cancer treatment strive for "magic bullets" that target only cancer cells, mostly sparing healthy tissue, even the best of these treatments fail to alter the systemic conditions that trigger cancerous growths in the first place.

Waging war also requires a one-minded obedience to the commanding ideology. Paradigm-challenging theories get brushed aside and dissenting opinions face active suppression. Throughout the War on Cancer, medical authorities have abused the powers of state and federal law enforcement to squelch innumerable alternative therapies. Serious doctors and medical researchers, often supported by a host of grateful patients, have been dismissed as quacks, jailed as charlatans, and driven out of the country as dangerous felons. Though cancer-war authorities early on saw the wisdom of reducing tobacco use—its single most life-saving "battle" to date—it was decades slower in accepting that diet might play a role in the genesis of the disease. To this day, the medical establishment seems reluctant to acknowledge or investigate the likely link between cancer and the rise of the petrochemical and nuclear industries in America. And even when, as we have seen since the mid-90s, the cancer warriors begrudgingly admit the effectiveness of some low-cost alternative therapies—especially diet and stress-reduction—it does nothing to stem the flow of dollars into the search for, production, and use of more exotic weapons.

Above all, waging war demands the silencing of peaceful voices and a rigid avoidance of viable peace plans. In the War on Cancer this has meant paying no heed to the countless well-documented cases of people who have recovered from cancer through alternative means. One would think that a single such story, let alone thousands, would propel researchers into fervent study. One could imagine cancer detectives excitedly seeking out a few hundred of these "once cancerous, now healthy" people to test their blood and examine their immune systems and to earnestly dissect their histories of recovery. One might even dream of a worldwide database filled with documented stories of cancer recoveries, and at every new cancer diagnosis the patient could be told, "Here's several people just like you, who suffered just as you do now, and they fully healed, and here's how they did it." But no, cancer warriors simply ignore these living bodies of potent evidence, while steadfastly denying the possibility of any better way than continuing down their battle-worn path. The mere suggestion of a peaceful solution can cause violent paroxysms for those committed to war.

As he retired from office, President Dwight D. Eisenhower imparted a scary warning about the "military-industrial complex": an insidious merging of America's security apparatus with private and corporate profiteers that gobbles up vast national resources while spewing waste and destruction in its wake. The War on Cancer marked the rise of a similar danger—the medical-industrial complex—that likewise grabs a huge chunk of the public treasury while providing a too-often-unhealthy medical product. These mammoth conglomerates share a number of traits: they redirect huge portions of public tax dollars into the private pockets of the corporate overclass; as major sponsors of politicians, they achieve oligarchic influence over key social issues; through the sheer size of their businesses and bureaucracies and the millions of jobs they represent, they become too important to question, too big to fail, too byzantine to investigate, and too entrenched to change; they attack mere symptoms of problems, while exacerbating root causes; and through their dominist determination to solve all problems by waging war they inflict inevitable terrors, great and small, on an already war-torn world.

As another example, one year after the war-obsessed Nixon began the War on Cancer, he formally declared a War on Drugs (which had been festering undeclared since early in the 20th century). There followed a rapid rise of the drug-war-industrial-complex—a constellation of new law enforcement agencies, programs, and directives, hundreds of new prisons, increasing sales (legal and illegal) of firearms, and a rush of technological innovations for the benefit of a burgeoning Security State. Like all other wars, the drug war has squandered public resources, perverted the political process, proven impervious to the most finely reasoned counter-arguments and suggestions for reform, and left a collateral trail of broken bodies, burned out neighborhoods, and impoverished families. Like all other warriors, anti-drug warriors intimidate proponents of peaceful solutions to substance abuse and deny all evidence of those who have resolved such abuse in nonviolent, non-punitive ways.

Now the wage-war mentality has turned its steely attention to the problem of international terrorism. Though slow coming into form, the security-industrial-complex promises to become the mother of all wage-war conglomerates, as it subsumes the US military, all local, state, and federal law enforcement, the judiciary, the Customs Service, the Coast Guard, several intelligence agencies, and the Immigration and Naturalization Service, and with the blessings of both political parties places it all under the auspices of a single bureaucracy, the Department of Homeland Security. Economic forecasts portend huge state and federal deficits for years to come as the usual wartime transfer of public monies into private pockets unfolds. Collateral damages litter the landscape, with civil liberties shoved through the shredder, secret prisons filling with uncharged and unrepresented suspects, government surveillance schemes working overtime, international relations with enemies and allies dangerously strained, and non-war domestic programs facing deep cuts in essential funding. At the helm of this battleship of state, we have a gang of cynical dominists who understand too well that as long as they can keep the war-think going, it will secure them wealth and political power. They constantly warn of a war with no end and issue regular security alerts to hold the whole nation in a fear-stoked state of my-country-whatever patriotism. In the end, all of their warring on terrorists and terror bombing of third-world nations will only increase recruitment for the cause of anti-American terrorism.

Nowhere in the gargantuan security-industrial-complex will we find a Peace Department, nor any think-tank scholars working out the details of nonviolent conflict resolution, nor position papers on achieving peace without excessive force, nor speeches stressing the need for unhurried negotiations, for making tough compromises, for talking sensitive issues through to consensus. The wage-war logic of dominism acts to eradicate make-peace thinking before it reaches the hearts and minds of too many people. Before it weakens our resolve, before it captivates our young, before it flaunts our freedoms, before it divides our numbers, before it compromises our plans, before it undermines our leaders, before it gives succor to our enemies, before it appeases evil—before peace-think can gain the slightest traction in ever-conflicted human affairs, we must nip it in the bud, stamp it out, discredit it, burn it, drown it, kill it.

For the war-minded and warmongering, conflicts invariably lead to escalating aggression and the eventual domination of one side by the other. Peace runs absolutely counter to such thinking and threatens the war. Whatever the presumed purpose of a particular war, it always begins as a war on the mere thought of peace and ultimately becomes a war on everything.

Waking Up

We have an opportunity, now laid so grievously before us, to start and win a war with our most powerful and uniquely American weapons: love, opportunity, education and hope.

—**Robert Alberti**[6]

Affairs are now soul size.

The enterprise is exploration into God.

Where are you making for?

It takes so many thousand years to wake,

but will you wake for pity's sake?

—**Christopher Fry**[7]

In 1985, after suffering for more than a year with a set of increasingly debilitating physical symptoms, Niro Markoff Asistent tested positive for HIV and was diagnosed with what was then called AIDS-related complex (ARC). Three months later, the results of a second blood test brought dire confirmation: she should expect to die of AIDS within the next eighteen months.

Asistent not only survived for many years beyond her prognosis, she thrived in good health. She movingly recounted her experience in the book *Why I Survive AIDS* and lectured widely. Yet, even more significant than her continuing survival, Asistent tested HIV negative. This was not supposed to happen, even for patients following the most sophisticated drug regimens. While the global War on Aids has managed containment, turning AIDS into a chronic but survivable disease (for those who can afford the medicines), it has yet to find an actual cure. Yet Asistent lived on to tell the tale, with medical records to chart her journey into AIDS and out again. The medical-industrial-complex, predictably, ignored her experience: "I cooperated fully with my doctors, who drew quite a few pints of blood from me, but unfortunately I never heard from them again to know what they did with it. I guess I was naive to have believed that the medical establishment would be open to and willing to explore alternative possibilities."[8] For those who will listen, however, she presents a living, breathing testament on dealing with the most dominating of viruses.

Asistent does not give a simple, how-to prescription for all those living with AIDS. Her healing grew out of her unique history and life circumstances. Still, one clear message leaps from every page of her extraordinary book: "This condition was my 'wake-up call.' I could have chosen either to respond to the message or to roll over and go back to sleep....Every crisis, whether it be illness, the consequences of addiction, or the loss of a loved one, offers us an opportunity to wake up."[9] Though she accepts the biochemical dimensions of viral disease, she views them as secondary to the psychoemotional reality of the infected person. She makes the bold promise that becoming consciously aware of one's psychoemotional reality—waking up—turns the key to ecstatic living and "healing into death."

During her healing process, Asistent developed what she called her Daily Awareness Routine. A combination of meditation, diet, exercise, and long walks along the ocean shoreline, the routine became her moment-by-moment commitment to an unflinching awareness of all aspects of her life. She opened to the suppressed energies and conditioning of her childhood, to the dominant/submissive patterns in her current relationships, and to her deepest fears and furious rage at facing death from AIDS. "I had begun to lift the veil of denial, open my eyes, and honestly view my life. I had taken my first step on my path of healing."[10] Ultimately, she did not wage war on the virus in her body; instead, she used the illness as a call to radical wakefulness and for the embodiment of living peace.

Before we shrug Asistent's story off as but a meaningless anecdote or misdiagnosis, or an odd freak of nature, or as proof that miracles do happen, we might spend some time listening to the testimonies of other long-term AIDS survivors. Thousands of such people exist, on record, and a number of studies have tracked their experiences and compiled data. In America, survivors show up in all major at-risk groups: gay men, intravenous drug abusers, the sexually promiscuous, those who received tainted blood transfusions, and the children of HIV-infected mothers. According to the research, as many as ten percent of those infected with HIV do not, and perhaps never will, progress into full-blown AIDS. The medical-industrial-complex calls these people "slow progressors," insinuating that they do indeed have an incurable disease that will catch up to them someday. (Who doesn't?)

Mainstream AIDS researchers explain that all HIV cases sort into a classic bell curve—the slow progressors merely balance out those who progress rapidly and die within months of their diagnosis, while the majority fall in the middle, gradually progressing, declining, and, short of a medical breakthrough, dying sooner or later from their incurable condition. Like the half of Europe that died from the plague, most of those with HIV fall victim to some combination of bad genes, bad luck, bad habits, and bad medicine. Inexplicably, just as medical researchers have showed little interest in the half of Europe that lived on, they have for the most part ignored the experience of AIDS survivors, while continuing to trumpet the incurability of AIDS.

From a collection of studies[11], three key points emerge. First, long-term survivors of AIDS forcefully reject the very notion of "incurable disease;" in immediate response to being diagnosed with HIV, they *think differently* than typical AIDS patients and boldly affirm their determination to achieve full health. Second, they all speak of total lifestyle changes, involving diet, daily habits, occupations, avocations, relationships, and spiritual outlooks and practices; just as Asistent developed her Daily Awareness Routine, survivors invariably "wake up" to profound changes of mind, heart, body, and life. Third, most never used AZT or any of the other anti-viral drugs prescribed by the medical-industrial-complex; by avoiding the collateral damages of such harsh weapons, survivors spared their bodies the ruinous dangers of iatrogenic (treatment-induced) disease.

These long-term survivors of the modern world's most horrific plague have much to teach us about transcending viral dominism and moving our societies from war to peace. Most significantly, they underscore the importance of rousing to a clear, focused, and unswerving commitment to the idea of personal and political peace. As Gandhi put it, "We must become the change we want to see in the world." The practices and processes through which individuals, groups, and whole nations go about creating peaceful relations can only emerge from minds that experience peace as a tangible, manifest reality—from minds that find war utterly unthinkable. Until we supplant the dangerous logic of dominism within ourselves we shall see nothing but the results of that logic in people, circumstances, and events. Only when we make the life-affirming logic of peace our daily, routine awareness, will we naturally act in ways that generate the effects of a more peaceful world.

This does not mean that we must wait until all parties in a conflict have reached a state of personal peace (a fairly hopeless proposition). For the process of peace to move forward, it is enough that at least one party firmly commit to the ideas and practices of nonviolent conflict resolution. Of course, the more the merrier and, as we shall see, the more intrinsically powerful the individual, group, or nation that thinks, speaks, and acts for peace, the better the chance that conflicts will resolve in peaceful ways.

Conversely, when dominist-driven and denial-bound people work for peace, despite their best intentions they tend to generate the very conflict, hostility, denial, and dominism that they so much want to end. When we try to make peace before we actually think, feel, and believe peace, we mostly make things worse. This explains the mixed legacy of the antiwar movement of the 1960s. Contrary to the slogan "Make love, not war," most of the era's protestors knew little about the process of creating more loving lives, or a more loving world. The so-called peace movement was driven by a handful of power-tripping militants and afflicted with racism, sexism, and a petulant, privileged dominism given to bouts of unfocused rage. Like the other important movements of the time—civil rights, women's and gay liberation, environmentalism, holistic healing—the '60s anti-war movement planted seeds, marked a beginning, and pointed the way for years of hard work to come. People simply were not ready for peace yet, had not done their personal work, were trapped in waging a war against war, were not thinking, talking, and making peace.

In the Bush administration, we strained to find a single prominent member who showed even a trace of peace-think. We saw instead the very opposite—fire and brimstone mixed with piss and vinegar to spit in the eye of all our enemies (and most of our friends). Instead of calm and carefully nuanced peace-talk, we heard absolute adherence to war-talk: tough, nasty, threatening, unforgiving, unyielding, and uncompromisingly militaristic. They laid out an agenda that called for a continuous worldwide war on terror punctuated with a series of preventative terror bombings of designated evildoers. From the outset they displayed nothing but disdain for peacemaking activities—they tore up treaties, walked away from agreements, spurned the International Court, dismissed the UN as irrelevant, and avoided involvement in the Israeli-Palestinian conflict. It was hard to imagine any of these men and women ever pondering an international crisis, thinking, "How do we do this in the most peaceful way?" To the contrary, the evidence strongly suggested that they think of peace as that quiet feeling of security when all one's enemies have been silenced or killed.

But genuine peace-think entails so much more than just an absence of enemies or a cessation of war. Peace must become an active presence—an all-encompassing state of mind and all-enlivening pulse of feeling, a constant mantra and ongoing prayer, one's first thought in the morning and last thought at night. We must make peace our top priority and bottom line, our non-negotiable demand, overarching principle, core value, prime directive, marching order, raison d'etre and d'etat. We must have an absolute and unimpeachable commitment to the creative logic of peace, a commitment that can sustain peace-think through the hard twists and turns of violent conflicts, through the inevitable setbacks of complex negotiations, through the dark and tortured realpolitik of dominist war-think run amok.

Making peace begins with waking up—to a new day, a new world, and a whole new way of thinking. It means shaking off the shrouds of denial that keep us trapped in nightmare realities, that cause us to expect nothing but the worst from others, that prevent us from opening and trusting, that make us see war as inevitable, justifiable, and righteous. As individuals, waking up requires a great leap of the imagination, a sober commitment to wild dreaming, and an unswerving belief in progressive human values. For societies, waking up means bringing America's fundamental promises—democracy, freedom, equality, and the right to peacefully pursue happiness—to all of the people, in all countries, all of the time.

"Affairs are now soul size," indeed. We face the challenge of ending the age-old prisoner's sleep, of coming into radical wakefulness, of spreading hope and light and songs of peace to and through all our relations. In the end, we face nothing more than a change of mind, a simple choice. But will we wake?

The Light of Awareness

The breezes at dawn have secrets to tell you.

Don't go back to sleep!

You must ask for what you really want.

Don't go back to sleep!

People are going back and forth across the doorsill

where the two worlds touch;

The door is round and open.

Don't go back to sleep!

—**Rumi**

The experiences of Niro Asistent and other long-term AIDS survivors suggest that waking up to a new way of thinking marks an essential beginning, but just that. Like achieving radiant health, manifesting peaceful relations requires that we stay awake—that we sustain our commitment to radical wakefulness and perseverant peace-think through bad news, hard times, and chronic backsliding into dominist denial. A single epiphany, breakthrough, or paradigm shift will not produce a lasting transformation of individual lives, much less entire cultures. While awakening to peace-think can occur in a single moment, the work of making peace viable in personal and international relations can take years, if not lifetimes.

For the individual, becoming more peaceful requires steadfast dedication to the mostly inner work of personal growth and transformation. Whether through some form of therapy, the process of intimate relationship, regular meetings with a twelve-step group, a religious or spiritual practice, or some combination of any of these approaches and too many others to list, would-be peacemakers must undergo a journey of self-realization. A myriad of methods, systems, programs, and teachings can help the conscientious seeker along his or her way. The best approaches bring unflinching awareness to the varied aspects of one's life, illuminating inward processes of thought, feeling, desire, and believing, of past events, and of dreams for the future. "An unexamined life is not worth living," warned Plato, to which we can add that without sustained self-examination we will never live free of viral dominism. Only the unvarnished truth will set us free. Getting to the nitty-gritty, deep-down truths of one's life requires a regular, long-term discipline—a daily awareness routine—of shining a bright light inside and seeing where we've been, what we've done, and who we have become.

Whatever approach one takes, this inward exploration of self involves confronting, wrestling with, and undoing the beliefs, perceptions, and behaviors of dominist relationship, and long before the truth ever sets you free it can make you pretty miserable. Bringing one's life into the light of awareness means learning a whole new way of thinking. It entails honestly evaluating the power dynamics of all one's relations and facing up to and then ending addictive behaviors, bad habits, and unconscious obsessions. It demands that we become more vulnerable to others, while opening to their vulnerabilities, that we learn to forgive those who have trespassed, to trust those who have betrayed, to believe in those who have failed, and to love those who have hated. It means, ultimately, making peace with all that has gone before and claiming peace for all still to come. In the end, it means stepping free of deeply-ingrained patterns of viral dominism—like waking from night terrors, like shaking off the hated monkey forever—and becoming, embodying, the peace we long to see in the world.

Along the road to self-realization we see others in the breakdown lane, some just resting, many more giving up and sinking back into the prisoner's sleep. The temptation to quit growing never really goes away. Viral dominism has insinuated so deeply into the fiber of our beings, has woven so tightly into the tapestries of our lives, that half measures and faint-hearted efforts just will not do. We must commit to utterly purging ourselves of all dominism, since any dominist tendencies left in place can serve as seeds of future reinfection.

To make matters more difficult, undoing our personal patterns of dominism seriously undermines our ability to succeed in dominist realities. As we purge ourselves of dominism within, we become, in the short-term, less effective at dealing with the dominism around us. We give up the very psycho-emotional strategies and protections—militarism, hostility, aggression, distrust, greed, competition, secrecy, authoritarianism, absolutism—that make one more effective in a dominist world. This unilateral disarmament of ourselves makes the dominists around us that much stronger, that much more threatening, and that much more virally infectious.

Moreover, the dominist world treats the whole notion of inward-looking self-examination with utter contempt. The typical rough-and-tumble dominist could barely get through the past few paragraphs without erupting into insulting tirades and pitying sneers. Dominists pride themselves on not self-reflecting, on never feeling vulnerable, on having no need for changes of heart, mind, or direction in life, on never looking back or asking why or worrying over the feelings and motives of others. All this therapeutic process and endlessly talking things through and opening to emotions and navel-gazing amounts to so much sissy nonsense—irrelevant play for silly narcissists who have convinced themselves that it actually matters how they think and feel. Dominists have too many important things to do to waste time trifling with hippie parlor games, especially since all this so-called self-realization just makes one weaker and less capable in a dominist world.

The anti-introspection of individuals, expanded to the masses, creates a populace ignorant of history, afraid of multicultural influences, and unwilling to even consider the psycho-political realities of other peoples. Such a nation can engage in cataclysmic war against a handful of guilty tyrants, while dismissing as unpatriotic any thought for the entirely innocent women, children, and men—the obscenely-labeled "collateral damages"—who suffer most terribly in high-tech wars. Only the weak and self-divided worry over such matters. The tough-minded and hard-hearted have no concern for historic grievances, root causes, questionable motives, hidden agendas, civilian casualties, or environmental fall-out. Those who really love their country just button up their brains, lockstep into line and follow orders, no thinking required. Self-examination—of the individual, of the nation—can only lead to nagging doubts, to probing questions, to faltering denial, to unauthorized thinking, and even to transformational insights, to alternative visions, to the crowning possibility of a post-dominist world.

Just as individual recovery from viral dominism demands a continuing practice of expanding personal awareness, so the progressive transformation of America means finding ways to bring the disinfecting light of truth to all of the nation's business and affairs. This starts in the business of government itself and, to America's credit, many key policies and procedures have already been worked out and put into use. Of primary importance, all governments (and most organizations) need tough and easily accessed and implemented freedom of information policies that make the revelation of their inner workings to the people they represent simple second nature. The cult of secrecy must give way to conscientious practices of honest governance, reinforced with high-powered investigative committees when necessary. Clearly designed and rigorously enforced sunshine laws can keep truly sensitive information secret for a reasonable time while assuring that all information—the whole truth and nothing but—becomes public knowledge in due course. Whistleblower laws can encourage and protect those on the inside of power structures who bring knowledge of malfeasance to light. And the legal system must mete out harsh punishments to those who attempt to circumvent these laws, making the nation's commitment to free-flowing information and the end of secret governance painfully clear.

Of course, all such laws require first and foremost a genuinely democratic system in which to take root and flourish. To the extent that America has turned into a domocracy it has simultaneously turned away from its commitment to open governance. In order for the people to engage democratically, they need to know who got elected and what got decided and why it all matters. Yet only a people who experience true democracy will ever understand the importance of free-flowing information, much less have the capacity to make it so.

With fits and starts and inevitable regressions, America has steadily been bringing its inner workings out of the shadows, especially since the days of Nixon and Watergate. We have seen a constant progression of special prosecutors, congressional committees, and blue-ribbon panels that have yanked the nation from one scandalous "gate" to the next, revealing all manner of overclass shenanigans, hijinks, and illegalities, culminating in the 8-year show-and-tell that was the Clinton presidency. Though there have surely been excesses and abuses of this process of shifting to wide-open governance, the absolute necessity of continuing the process has never been clearer. America cannot hope to overcome the insidious demands of viral dominism, much less provide a much-needed model for other nations, unless it once and forever ends all manner of secret governance.

We should never expect dominists to initiate or sustain practices that will undermine their dominist powers. America's honest-and-open government policies of the 20th century all came about as long-overdue reforms triggered by gross abuses of political power. Such abuses rarely come to light through the voluntary self-examination and revelations of the political overclass or its bureaucratic underlings. Rather, it requires a committed, tenacious, and independent media to alert and educate—to wake up—the people to the most serious problems of the day. Without such media, the inmates will never glimpse their imprisonment, nor rouse to change, nor truly understand.

The Best Disinfectant

The major media are much less major than they used to be, but the coverage of dissent within their circles hasn't changed much since the 1960s. When elites coalesce, the media readily follow suit. Then it takes a strong surge of public opinion to shift the sense of what is speakable.

*—***Todd Gitlin**[12]

And say, finally, whether peace is best preserved by giving energy to the government, or information to the people. This last is the most certain, and the most legitimate engine of government. Educate and inform the whole mass of the people. Enable them to see that it is their interest to preserve peace and order, and they will preserve them.... They are the only sure reliance for the preservation of our liberty.

—Thomas Jefferson[13]

In 1937 Adolf Hitler came to the aid of fellow fascist Francisco Franco in the generalissimo's efforts to end the Spanish Civil War. The Nazis introduced the terror tactic of massive aerial bombing to the modern age by decimating the tiny Basque village of Guernica. After three hours of nonstop bombing, the village lay in ruins and 1500 innocent civilians had been slaughtered. Pablo Picasso responded to the then unprecedented horror by painting *Guernica*, a masterful cubist mural, rendered in seething shades of gray and black, that depicts the visceral realities of war—the decapitated soldier, the terror-stricken eyes of a lanced and bloodied horse, the torn and dismembered bodies, the wailing mother holding her dead baby.

Since its painting, *Guernica* has stood as one of the world's more potent antiwar statements. In 1987 the United Nations hung a tapestry reproduction of Picasso's work outside the doors of the Security Council meeting room. Whenever diplomats gather to seek resolution of difficult international conflicts, they must pass by this grim reminder of the true nature of war. On the day that Secretary of State Colin Powell stood before reporters in that hallway to press America's case for a massive terror bombing of Iraq, US officials insisted on draping the painting, so no one would dare to match Powell's words to Picasso's imagery. Never has the term "political cover-up" been more poignantly on the mark. Sadly, most American media compounded the cover-up by failing to adequately report what had happened. What could have been a rich and insightful media event, as artistically powerful in present terms as Picasso's original effort, was allowed to pass with hardly a mention.

Unfortunately, as we've already seen, the steady consolidation of mainstream media into the control of but a few dominist corporations, coupled with the personal wealth (or desire to attain wealth) of so many prominent journalists, has stifled free and independent public voices while stemming the system-wide open and honest flow of information necessary for a healthy democracy. To the extent that the media has abdicated its responsibilities of breaking through cultural and political denial, of waking and informing the people, and of telling, even yelling, truth to those in power, the world has lost a vital cog in the machinery of positive social change. We need autonomous journalists with the courage to track down malevolent dominism wherever it hides, to rake through the muck, and to shine the bright and disinfecting light of truth until people arise and undertake progressive reforms. Just as Niro Asistent practiced self-awareness as an essential step toward transcending HIV, people everywhere must engage in a media-mediated program of expanding social awareness if we ever hope to transcend political dominism.

And hope we may, with some good reason, precisely because of the potential powers of modern media. Until midway through the 20th century there was not really much to do about the spread of viral dominism. Individuals had little capacity to grasp the cultural gestalts of their own situations, much less to see deeply into dominist tides of international relations. The human species suffered from a chronic disease of no name, with symptoms that had long been accepted as absolute human nature. Those who managed to sense the raw outlines of the problem were sorely challenged just to heal themselves; reaching the infected and contagious masses was utterly impossible. Until, that is, the advent of mass, electronic media.

Just as media can unconsciously spread viral dominism far and wide with broadcasts of emotion-laden events of violence, war, and terrorism, so, with conscious and responsible direction, media can spread the transformational forces of awareness, truth, love, compassion, trust, tolerance, empathy, and hope. The same principles apply: the media act as vectors for carrying emotionally-charged beliefs and ideas from a specific human drama to readers, listeners, and viewers everywhere. The more emotional force that communicates from the original source, the more that channels through media outlets, and the deeper the impact on the consuming public; and, the people behind the keyboards, cameras, and editorial desks of media productions act as first recipients of the emotion-laden content and thus typically bias their broadcasts.

Mass media spread infectious beliefs and ideas to the masses. The full import of what is spread—viral dominism or transformational awareness, denial-cloaked lies or liberating truths—depends on the intentions and choices of the producers, managers, and owners of media content, in conjunction with the existing perceptions and biases of the reading, listening, viewing public. For those who have begun to rouse from personal denial to radical wakefulness, modern media can serve as vital tools for dealing with socio-political dimensions of dominist reality.

The ever-expanding electro-informational web of computers, telephony, and television and radio waves now encompassing our world has made a global spread of transformational awareness and liberating truth both possible and probable for the first time in history. As human-to-human electronic connections become more ubiquitous, more everyday, yet ever more meaningful and potentially intimate, critical information can pass instantaneously between individuals and from one group to another, breaking former barriers of time and space, as well as ancient rules of human relationship. Information speeding through modern communication systems gives fresh meaning to the term "current events"—emotionally-charged content that spreads along the vibratory currents of telephones, radios, televisions, and Internet connections can affect people more deeply and seem ever more here and now than ordinary unwired reality.

On the day that American revolutionaries signed the Declaration of Independence, King George of England wrote in his diary, "Nothing of importance happened today." It would be weeks before he learned of that earth-shattering event, before viral democracy reached the people of Europe, before America's upstart shot was heard round the world. Even as the news spread, it came in whispered gossip, rumors, and innuendo, in tales many times removed from the original event, and in official documents replete with bias. Were the same event to happen today, people everywhere would follow it as it happened—transfixed by their TVs and gathered around radios and surfing the web and talking on phones—taking in layers of truth and half-truth, ingesting it all, their emotions aroused, the underclass inspired, and who can say how far the revolution would have spread, how irresistibly contagious democracy might have been, how overwhelming we the people could have become.

These days, a few well-written paragraphs, posted to a hundred friends, can by tomorrow touch millions of readers around the globe. Footage from a home video camera, picked up by a local cable station, will soon show up in network news reports, then proliferate wildly, airing repeatedly, its images sinking deeply into the public psyche. A single photograph, rendered well and widely broadcast, can spread to the hearts and minds of people everywhere, can affect a billion souls, set loose waves of viral emotion, and change the course of history. Universal access to electronic media means that uncensored truth has a much greater ability to penetrate mainstream thinking. As enough people really wise up, the dangerous logic of dominism gives way to the creative logic of peace.

Ever since America dropped its atom bombs on Japan we have been inching our way toward this "global spread of transformational awareness and liberating truth." The mushroom-cloud photograph of massive Japanese death has been reproduced and spread throughout the world to each new generation of growing children (as have been the equally horrific photographs of the Nazi holocaust). For the first time in human history, everybody saw—felt—the savage and indecent act. Everybody bore witness to the dominist's mentality and behavior, and everybody bore witness to the horrible aftermath. This explains why Hiroshima marked the end of the last good war: the whole world bore stark witness to the ugly truth of war and—a source of hope—we have had growing difficulty with warring ever since. The media-spread visions of absolute war-think carried vital seeds of eventual peace-think. The thoughts "never forget" and "never again" have taken root in millions of minds. A sleeping giant of human potential has been shocked awake and scalded with truth.

The modern peace movement was born in the ashes of World War II, evidenced in part by the formation of the United Nations. The movement tenuously struggled through a long infancy and then burst into inarticulate, narcissistic, raging adolescence with the antiwar protests of the 1960s and early '70s. It was a movement beset with difficulties and contradictions, yet through its excesses and failures it nonetheless managed to carry on, in nascent form, but gradually developing over the next four decades. Throughout this development, the peace movement has risen and fallen on its fluctuating ability to effectively use the media. The photo of a naked Vietnamese girl screaming from napalm burns, the scenes of self-immolating Buddhist monks, the daily footage of body bags and coffins arriving at American airports, the media representations of a weary, crestfallen LBJ and a mean, vindictive Richard Nixon, the Kent State student crying over the body of a slain protestor, the burning draft cards, the peace signs and posters, the unprecedented marches on Washington, the costumes, the street theater, the revolutionary music: as never before, we saw that the media, unrestricted and decidedly anti-establishment, had the power to ignite public opinion, change government policies, and inspire a wide range of activities than ran wildly counter to dominist culture.

Yet, like a fireworks extravaganza, the movement would peak, furiously climax, and then gradually fade into less revolutionary times. The movement issues of world peace, social justice, women's liberation, civil rights, and the environment all carried forward, but in the hands of former radicals who traded in the their tie-dye for suit and tie, pledging to work within the system, running for public office, starting businesses, becoming community stalwarts. Others totally dropped out of the revolution, shifting from the work of transforming politics to the more manageable work of transforming themselves, while proclaiming that a "new age" had arrived. Many found that just dealing with the demands of everyday life—making money, building a home, raising kids, staying healthy—left little time or energy for even the most worthy of causes, much less the total transformation of Western civilization.

Soon after the conclusions of the Vietnam War and the Nixon presidency, the media likewise began a gradual change. The conglomerating of radio and television stations, newspapers, and magazines into ever fewer mammoth corporations left most of the fire and muckraking fury of the 1960s countercultural media without sponsors or outlets. Mainstream journalists tiptoed through the Reagan years, unwilling to cause disturbances in the halls of power despite a series of high-level scandals that would have made Nixon proud, culminating in nothing less than the Iran-Contra disgrace—the secret selling of arms to the enemy—an affair so poorly covered by the media that multiple felons and bird-flipping scalawags like Oliver North and Eliot Abrams ended up as heroes of the tale. For Bill Clinton's presidency, not only did this failure to meaningfully cover the machinations of dominist power-mongering continue, but a handful of wealthy right-wing patrons funded a perpetual scandal chase that undermined every effort of progressive government while sinking American media even deeper into tabloid journalism and faux news. Significantly, the American underclass spoke truth to power by giving Bill Clinton his highest approval numbers *af-*

ter his impeachment (though the dominist media got even by skewering his would-be successor Al Gore in an election that historians will look back on as a singular, shameful failure of American journalism).

Gore was pulled down in large part by the constant repetition in the media of a series of canards, most notably his supposed claim to have invented the Internet. Ironically, Al's Internet now gives us our best, perhaps only, chance of reviving the revolutionary powers of a free and independent media, of restoring democracy to the America people, and of effectively waging peace throughout the world. People now have the ability to link with like-minded others, everywhere and simultaneously, and to share all manner of communications—words, pictures, sounds, and video. Really potent peace-think gets repeatedly mass-forwarded, spreading further and faster than the most virulent of bugs, causing powerful changes in people's thinking, as well as organizing their behavior. All of this happens beyond the control of government, the direction of bosses, the rule of money, the perquisites of fame, and, most importantly, the twisted logic of dominist violence. For now at least, the Internet thrives as a fairly democratic town square, university, research lab, salon, and marketplace, in which most all people have more or less equal access—as passive observers and active participants—to the ebb and flow of "current events."

The Internet has enabled unprecedented, almost humanity-wide conversations. As America pressed its case for the invasion of Iraq (and, to a lesser degree, before the invasion of Afghanistan) an incalculable number of meaningful communications occurred, with people everywhere engaging in a common "omnilogue," exploring the issues, debating points and counterpoints, devising strategies, forming alliances. Hundreds of thousands of new websites and web logs (blogs) appeared, creating smaller, more intimate conversations within the greater omnilogue, generating fresh new insights, birthing new movements, and making new friendships. There has never been anything remotely like this, as if a billion people gathered around a common fire to pass the pipe and take turns talking, until everybody's voice could be heard and the outlines of a genuine consensus could emerge.

In the run-up to the Iraq War, Internet-issued calls to protest brought millions of people to the streets of cities worldwide, led to a "virtual march" of faxes and telephones calls that shut down the White House switchboards for a day, and, on the eve of war, created a night of candlelight vigils that circled the globe. One poet's frustration with the Bush administration's intransigence resulted in a flood of original poems posted to a new website, as poets around the world spoke in one voice. Another artist shared on the Internet her notion to stage a reading of the antiwar play *Lysistrata*; ten days before the onset of war, versions of the play were performed in some 900 different locations worldwide. Though in the end nothing could stop America from having its war, the peace movement had blossomed and matured, had gathered momentum, and had just begun to understand the creative potential—the powers-with—of an Internet-connected and -enabled people.

Assuming that we can keep the Internet relatively free of government and corporate controls (no easy task), and assuming that we continue to expand broadband access, the Internet will become the media of the 21st century. Not only will most print, radio, and television news content get posted on the Web, thus allowing for timely worldwide distribution, but mainstream journalists will increasingly use the Web for much of their research. As democratic access to information becomes a basic civil right, journalism will build on the support of a highly informed, proactive public. Reams of government and corporate secrets will appear online, through the efforts of insider document-posting and outsider hacking. The darkest reaches of human thought and behavior will open before a billion Internet surfers, so the disinfecting power of human awareness can work its healing transformations. Dominism has always been a creature of the dark; the 21st century media have just begun to drag it into the light.

The spread of open software and open data streams has birthed an age of open governance, at all levels, from the family to the mega-corporation to multinational relationships. The dangerous logic of dominism, in all its arguments, will not stand up under the common and collective scrutiny of a truth-connected people; only the closed-off, separate, and denial-dumb can sustain the foolishness of "might makes right," of "with us or against us," of "only one God," of "different and unequal," of the subordination of women, of greed, competition, secrecy, and anti-environmentalism. If the Internet can stay free enough to fulfill its promise, then we will find ourselves positively charged for the common tasks of living cooperatively and making peace.

Seven

Living Peace

When George W. Bush spoke on national television to announce the start of "war" against Iraq, he looked into the camera and asked to speak directly to the Iraqi people. He could have appealed to their nationalism, and asked them to join our soldiers (or at least not shoot at them) in toppling Saddam. He could have appealed to their knowledge of the peaceful side of Islam and asked them to go to their mosques, which we would protect from bombing, and pray for a quick resolution of the conflict. He could have apologized in advance for the death and destruction he was about to unleash on their land, that would kill many times more innocent civilians than died in the World Trade Center, and promise that the US would do our best to make it good after the war.

But these were not the things on Bush's mind. Instead, he said, "And all Iraqi military and civilian personnel should listen carefully to this warning. In any conflict, your fate will depend on your action. Do not destroy oil wells..."

—Thom Hartmann[1]

The major news in early November 1989 concerned the rising tensions in East Berlin and throughout Eastern Europe. Since that May, when Mikhail Gorbachev declared that the Soviet Union would no longer use force to stifle dissent, over 200,000 East Germans had passed over to the West. More than a million had gathered for a November 4th protest in East Berlin, which forced the resignation of most East German leaders. In retrospect, it seems obvious that the fall of the Wall was imminent and inevitable.

Still, the conventional wisdom of the day was anything but optimistic. Only six months earlier, a similar democracy movement had been brutally suppressed by the Chinese in Tiananmen Square. Though Gorbachev had forsworn the use of Soviet troops, the East Germans had a more than ample military and security apparatus of their own. Visions of the iron fist of totalitarian suppression—tanks rolling on the protesting crowds, preemptive arrests of leading dissidents, the rigid enforcement of the Wall and other borders—filled the airwaves and newspaper columns. Though Ronald Reagan had given voice to the possibility, urging, "Mr. Gorbachev, tear down this wall," and Gorbachev himself had announced at the East German Palace of the Republic, "whoever comes too late is punished by life," it remained hard to imagine that the Berlin Wall could actually fall, along with a forty year-old Communist dictatorship.

Yet in the end it came down with hardly a struggle, with no shots fired, and no more deaths. That first day, November 9th, families throughout East and West Berlin who had been physically and ideologically separated for decades were tearfully reunited. Within weeks, they finished the heady process of dismantling the Wall, smashing concrete with the raw, determined joy of freedom. Over the next several months, a new parliament was formed, new proclamations issued, new alliances forged. October 1990 brought the final reunification of Germany; the implosion and breakup of the Soviet Union was well underway.

The fall of the Berlin Wall and the ensuing collapse of the Soviet empire stand as a lesson-rich study in our current struggle against the forces of viral dominism. The Soviet system inflicted the worst of dominist coercion on all of the people who came under its totalitarian influence. Communist ideology showed utter disdain for any semblance of basic civil rights, of democratic processes, or of the sovereignty of other nations. The State slaughtered millions of people, and consigned millions more to the machinations of its secret police, its Kafkaesque courts, and its hellish gulags. The free and vital flow of information, within the media and the educational system, was replaced by a stupefying State propaganda apparatus. The people's impulse to worship and spiritual practice was banned, ridiculed, and forcefully suppressed. National resources were squandered on the military and domestic police. For forty years, the Soviet State and its people lived with war-think and terror as unchanging facts of life, made bearable only by a dark and smothering fog of personal and political denial.

From its inception, Soviet communism spread like the most infectious of plagues. Wherever dominist imbalances left a nation torn and vulnerable, communist ideology and practices threatened to take root, fester within the body politic, and eventually erupt into revolution and government collapse. Even in the developed nations of the democratic West, the Communist Party wormed its way into every political system, in some places as merely a chronic bother, but in others threatening to gain ruling powers. With its global network of undercover agents and its penchant for the darker arts of espionage, propaganda, and disinformation, the Soviets projected a viral wave of malevolent influence—misleading, undermining, corrupting, and destroying—that could capture the best minds of a generation and turn well-meaning idealists into spies.

America deserves eternal credit for recognizing the dangers of 20th century communism, for mobilizing to meet the viral wave of dominist expansion head-on, and for persevering through a forty-year struggle to ultimate victory. We shudder to think of what the world might have become had the aptly named "domino theory" played out without meeting any resistance from anti-communist forces. With its strategy of infiltrating other countries, fostering revolution, and then taking over from within, Soviet communism brought the Parable of the Tribes to a perilous edge since fighting back invited all the horrors of civil war for the invaded population, at little cost to the invaders. Without some countervailing force to stem the growth of global communism—without the bulwark of American power—we could be living in a very different world today.

In its cold war victory over the Soviets, America demonstrated many of the practices of active pacifism. At the conclusion of WWII, America assured a "good peace" with the Marshall Plan rebuilding of Germany and Japan, followed by years of generous aid to developing countries. America was instrumental in the formation of the United Nations, of NATO, and of other international alliances, laws, and treaties. It charged all nations with the essential tasks of nonviolent diplomacy and multilateral cooperation, and helped spread the positive contagions of democracy, freedom, and concern for human rights. America met the specific Soviet threat through a combination of containment and deterrence, answering power with power, while gradually working toward mutual disarmament. Whenever possible, America encouraged economic, scientific, and cultural exchange and engagement with its adversaries, understanding that even just a taste of a better life can work miracles for an oppressed people.

Though most will stress the militarism of the time—the buildup of nuclear arsenals, the espionage, and the many places around the world where the cold war flared into hot and horrible conflicts—the active pacifist tells of two superpowers, armed for Armageddon and stoked with seething hatred for one another, who faced off across a narrow void for forty years while generals on both sides clamored for all-out war, and yet *did not fight*, never unleashed a single missile, and ultimately came to a place of peace and partnership. In the end, the people's desire for peace, coupled with the practices of active pacifism, proved stronger than the dangerous logic of dominism. We avoided the horrors of an all-destroying World War III because the fundamental human preferences for love, tolerance, and cooperation prevailed over chronic habits of fear, hate, and violent struggle.

Yet, while America's initial thoughts may have been toward the principles of active pacifism, its long, to-the-death, with-us-or-against-us struggle with Soviet dominism ultimately added to the nation's viral load of dominist tendencies. In ridding the world of a tyrannical superpower, America greatly expanded its own powers and, as the Parable predicts, increased its own propensity for tyrannical actions. In the wake of its battle against the dark forces of communism lay a bleak and forbidden history of American transgressions and misdeeds, at home and abroad. Anticommunism served for decades as the overarching principle in American politics and public life, spawning the excesses of grade school atomic war drills and backyard bomb shelters, of Joseph McCarthy and J. Edgar Hoover, of Red scares, professional blacklists, bloated defense budgets, and unwarranted domestic surveillance. Moreover, America's visceral fear of anything even remotely communist would over time cause it to undermine the labor movement, to seriously underfund all social welfare programs, and to flatly reject many reasonable policies of European democratic socialism, such as universal health and childcare.

Internationally, the noble impulses of America's war on communism gave way to the dangerous logic of militarism, unilateralism, monotheism, and xenophobia. What began as a great notion—to stand up to the communist threat on behalf of people everywhere—became a narrowly self-serving, endless war against any who dared to stray from the American script. America meddled in the affairs of sovereign nations with the same techniques and same sorry ignorance of unintended consequences as the evil Soviets. The wise and benevolent America of the early cold war turned foolish and ugly as it sanctioned the assassination of foreign rulers (Patrice Lumumba, Salvador Allende, Ngo Dinh Diem, Fidel Castro). It undermined democratically elected governments in Guatemala, Guyana, the Dominican Republic, Brazil, Chile, Uruguay, Syria, Greece, Argentina, Bolivia, and Haiti. The U.S. poured arms into explosive conflicts everywhere, and propped up vicious, antidemocratic regimes in Turkey, Zaire, Chad, Pakistan, Morocco, Indonesia, Honduras, Peru, Colombia, El Salvador, Haiti, Cuba (under Batista), Nicaragua (under Somoza), Iran (under the Shah), the Philippines (under Marcos), and Portugal. We supported terrorists in Nicaragua and Afghanistan, abandoned once-important clients (Iran, Iraq, the Kurds), and invaded minor countries that posed no clear and present danger (Laos, Cambodia, Grenada, Panama, Iraq). While managing to avoid the global conflagrations of a nuclear holocaust or another world war, America succumbed to an all-encompassing war-think, with dire costs in national resources and international relations.

Along the way to becoming history's most dominant nation, America would abandon the very principles and practices that powered its ascent. Gone, the noble generosity of the Marshall Plan and non-military foreign aid. In 2002, America ranked 21st among nations in such aid. Gone, the Wilsonian idealism that built the United Nations and formed enduring alliances and took the initiative in writing key treaties. Gone, any commitment to international affairs as cooperative, win-win engagements. Never has the contagiousness of dominism been so dramatically demonstrated, as America's cold war struggle for the cause of freedom morphed into a military machine bent on pox Americana. War-think took over the national psyche till all that mattered was having the biggest bomb, the largest army, and the deadliest arsenal.

In forty years America shifted from the global beneficence and multilateral engagement of Franklin Roosevelt to the narrow parochialism and unilateral bullying of George W. Bush. Witness the Iraq War: though containment and deterrence—relatively nonviolent tools—had proven effective for dealing with the monstrously armed and globally festering malevolence of the Soviet Union, the same approaches were pronounced as inadequate to deal with the poor, puny, isolated tyranny of Iraq. Although the full international community, including most Arabs and Muslims, stood behind a United Nations-led process for dealing with Saddam Hussein's excesses, Bush chose a preemptive, with-us-or-against-us terror bombing and invasion of a sovereign nation, with death and humiliation for the Iraqi people. Even though the Marshall Plan powerfully demonstrated that the real work of winning a war comes after the shooting stops, America failed to follow through with the necessary rebuilding of Iraq, just as it failed to honor its post-war commitments in Afghanistan.

Today's America bears little resemblance to the country that saved the world from fascism, turned the vanquished, criminal nations of Germany and Japan into proud and prosperous friends, and, without missing a beat, took on the serious threat of global communism. Too many years of violence and cutthroat competition and waging war on everything left America infected to the core with viral dominism. Though it stands as the most dominant nation in history, America suffers from all the symptoms of systemic chronic infection, given to periodic bouts of acute crisis. The rapid collapse of the Soviet empire (and those of the English, the French, the Prussians, the Ottomans, and the Romans) surely warns that all of the planes and tanks and missile silos, the ribbon-breasted generals and clever spies, the patriotic songs and marching bands, that all of it runs only to grief and destruction and thus ever grinds the nation on toward its own vainglorious death.

If it follows unabated on this course of chronic dominism, then America can look forward to its own Soviet-like implosion, as it rots from within and eventually loses the ability to keep its own people under control, much less those of other nations. Conversely, if America rises to the challenges of active pacifism, it can retain all of its power and prominence while leading the world in resolving the ancient cycle of violence and establishing at last a global continuum of peace. In giving up the self-destructive powers-over of dominism, America could come into the life-creating powers-with of partnership, cooperation, and the free pursuit of happiness for people everywhere.

Rational Defense

Our paradigm now seems to be: something terrible happened to us on September 11, and that gives us the right to interpret all future events in a way that everyone else in the world must agree with us. And if they don't, they can go straight to hell.

—**Bill Clinton**[2]

If punishment were what I felt was most important, perhaps I could share in the grim patriotic fervor of this moment. But I care about keeping people safe, about making the world a better place to live, about protecting the values America claims to cherish. I feel a sorrowful certainty that this war will do the opposite—will decrease life, decrease liberty, decrease the perennially endangered and quixotic quantity we call happiness.

—**Marion Winik**[4]

Within days of the overthrow of Saddam Hussein—ostensibly to prevent the use and spread of weapons of mass destruction—the Bush administration signaled its intentions to develop, test, and build a new class of battlefield-ready nuclear weapons. These "bunker-buster" bombs would target the caves and underground installations where America's enemies might hide to frustrate more conventional weapons. Super-smart and ultra-lethal, one computer-guided, nuclear bunker-buster could atomize the entire command structure of a designated enemy, effectively preempting the trouble and expense of all-out war, at the cost of a couple of radioactive mega-pits on foreign soil. Or so went the theory.

In reality, guaranteeing the location of a stealthy enemy will always prove difficult. Even the smartest bombs sometimes go awry, whether due to mechanical failure, operator error, or bad intelligence on the ground. Some degree of radioactive waste would linger for years, poisoning the environment, and driving civilian populations to new levels of America-hate (we should not expect all nuked cultures to be as gracious as the

Japanese). America's decision to abrogate critical arms control treaties would trigger the global proliferation of weapons of mass destruction. Given that, in the half century since America dropped two nuclear bombs on Japan, there has been an international consensus, backed by every American administration, never again to use such horrible weapons, we're left to some scary conclusions: the people who dream of using such weapons follow a biblical-apocalyptic script that demands a world-ending conflagration, they stand to make great fortunes as arms dealers, and/or they've become such unhappy, hate-wracked souls that they can neither imagine living in peace and cooperation nor grasp the utter insanity of their war-warped worldview. Just as Reagan's obsessive pursuit of a space-based missile defense (which George W. Bush revived) was rendered irrelevant by the fall of the Soviets, the development, testing and threatened use of a whole new class of nuclear weapons would provide little defense against the actual dangers of the 21st century, while further inflaming and (in the minds of the threatened) justifying continuing waves of suicide bombers and anti-American zealots.

Despite such compelling reasons to stay the course on arms control and to continue working toward a nuclear-free world, Bush and his advisors proceeded hell-bent on their bomb-mongering ways, with nary an objection from the US media or either political party. The notion that the American military, fortified with the most lethal weapons and sanctioned for preemptive strikes, would wage an unending, shock-and-awe, radioactive war against tiny bands of terrorists hiding among civilian populations all over the world—that *that* would make America safer—was presented with the self-righteous assurance of those too denial-dumb to comprehend the sheer lunacy of their thinking. American foreign policy had transmogrified into an Orwell in Wonderland scenario of bluster and blunder, of arrant hypocrisy, convoluted contrariness, and outright, smug, and unashamed dishonesty. To foes and friends alike, America acted as the ultimate aggressor, offensive in every way, a testosterone-crazed bull in the china shop of international affairs. Obvious to all, the more zealously Bush prosecuted his endless war, the more dangerous the whole world became.

Which brings us to the first tenet of active pacifism: no offense. In elementary physics, every action causes an equal and opposite reaction; in the realm of interpersonal and international affairs, the offensive behavior of one invariably causes offensive behavior in others. The party who acts offensively—through verbal assaults, aggressive demands, coercive expressions of anger, physical attacks upon body and property, or invasions of territory—projects a viral wave of threatening force to which the offended party must react, with as equal an answering force as possible. The Parable of the Tribes ever begins when one group (or individual) decides to resolve conflicts by going on the offensive, acting aggressively, moving violently upon another. A single offensive action can spur a cycle of violence that will last for generations or seed a dominist contagion that infects millions.

George W. Bush wrote the book on the pitfalls of offensive behavior. With his penchant for branding his enemies as evil and verbally slurring their leaders in public statements, and all his cowboy rhetoric of "with us or against us" and "trackin' 'em down and smokin' 'em out," and his undisguised, sneering contempt for opposing viewpoints, and his flippant disregard of the practices of diplomacy, and his infamously fumbling attempts at sincere expressions of compassion, Bush's first instinct in every conflict was to go on the offensive. Domestically and internationally, Bush picked fights with reckless abandon, like a schoolyard bully who woke up each morning wondering who he would intimidate next. Though he came into office on a tainted election, without a clear mandate, and with promises to be a "healer, not a divider," he soon discovered that the American people prefer the in-charge, do-it-now, swagger of offensive actions (however lame-brained or dishonest) over the slow, tempered uncertainties of defensive response.

So it was that thirty months into Bush's crusade against evil, the world had become vastly more dangerous. The al Qaeda terrorists, mindful that America had its omnipotent guard up, went after a series of softer targets, beginning with the tranquil island of Bali. Afghanistan and Iraq, their civilian infrastructures badly damaged, each teetered on the edge of total anarchy. The Israeli-Palestinian conflict steadily degenerated, showing no signs for hope but every reason to fear the worst. The North Koreans, rightly imagining that Bush would like to do unto them as he did in Iraq, reacted with increasing belligerence and the expansion of its development of nuclear weapons. America was barely on speaking terms with such longtime friends and allies as Canada, Mexico, France, Germany, Turkey, and Saudi Arabia, had strained its critical new alliance with Russia, had undercut and undermined the United Nations, and had rendered irrelevant the very concepts of international diplomacy and multilateral agreements. At home, the economy remained mired in a long recession, with 2 million jobs lost, nearly 50 million Americans without health insurance, spiraling deficits, and a bitterly divided Congress that spent all its time bickering over the annoying tax burdens of the über-rich. The crashing economy, combined with the massive military commitments of Bush's War on Everything, meant that there was little money left to fund a comprehensive and balanced defense of America against the sort of low-tech attacks that terrorists favored. Civil liberties declined, the environment degraded, the social safety net disappeared, and political discourse, from the loud-mouth insulters of squawk radio to the screaming heads of pundit TV, became ever more vituperative, mean-spirited, and intentionally provoking.

While offensive, aggressive, dominating action may sometimes solve short-term dangers, it only does so at the detriment to long-term safety. Offensive behavior always gives offense—it creates and spreads offensive behavior—and a world filled with offensive people remains forever doomed to violent conflict. Contrary to Bush-think, we cannot not solve this conundrum by becoming yet more offensive, by developing even bigger bombs, or by destroying other nations more efficiently. Rather, we make the world less dangerous by behaving less offensively, while developing a more than adequate defense.

Behaving less offensively means honoring the practices and measured language of diplomacy and believing—then proving—that nonviolent communication offers the preferred solution to all problems. It means working diligently to build respected multilateral institutions and having the patience to pursue consensus in the resolution of conflicts. It means establishing widely accepted codes of conduct—laws, treaties, and agreements—that further and uphold the principles of democracy and that distribute power equally among parties. It especially requires the discontinuance of offensive ways and means; one must stop developing and start dismantling offensive weapons, tactics, strategies, and plans. By disarming ourselves, we become an active force for disarmament among others.

Obviously, total unilateral disarmament in the face of offensive others may only feed their aggression and open the way for increasing violence. The practice of active pacifism recognizes that the causes of aggression, violence, and war persist in the world and that every nation (or individual) has the right and the responsibility to defend itself against clear and present dangers. Such legitimate self-defense requires: first, a sober assessment of potential threats; second, the development of weapons and tactics that will best utilize one's unique position in history and geography; and third, a commitment to remaining purely defensive in relation to others, especially when working through difficult conflicts. When every nation focuses entirely on defense, while disavowing offensive aggression, the world will have greatly diminished the prospect of major wars and made it far more difficult for non-state terrorism to flourish.

The Swiss, for example, combined a mountainous terrain and well-armed populace with their essential role in world finance to establish a strong enough defense to keep them unscathed in the middle of two world wars. They resolved the Parable of the Tribes neither by fighting back nor surrendering, but by making themselves too difficult to invade. We make the world less violent neither by returning violence nor fearfully fleeing the violence of others, but by becoming strong, capable, and well defended. We end war neither by waging more furious war nor by weakly appeasing evil, but by steadfastly developing the requisite powers of containment and deterrence to meet present and future threats.

With the peaceful nations of Canada and Mexico on its borders, and a pair of oceans insulating it from ancient and persisting war zones in Europe, Asia, and the Middle East, America has from its beginnings been naturally suited for non-aggressive, effective, rational defense. Though America should always stand as a valued partner in the multilateral coalitions that arise to meet global threats (a point we will return to), it can no longer act as sole superpower and policeman to the world, unilaterally preempting whomever it deems evil, without generating offensive cycles of aggression, violence, and war. America would make the world much safer if it used its considerable powers to wind down and defuse the nuclear arms race, retaining just enough missiles in place to deter the development and use of weapons of mass destruction by other nations. It could transform a large portion of its war corps into a revived and deep-pocketed peace corps that would set about addressing planetary conditions that lead to violence. With all the resources it would save from ceasing its imperial overreach, America could then wisely focus on its own domestic concerns.

Above all, the development of and commitment to rational defense means an end to unilateral invasions of sovereign nations. In a world that has moved beyond war, nations (and individuals) resolve problems through some combination of economic redress, diplomatic arbitration, and nonviolent communication. At those times when war looms as the only solution, as when one dominist-driven nation invades its neighbours, or when a country disintegrates into fratricidal civil war, then internationally sanctioned and supported defense forces—armed and maintained at levels superior to that of any individual nation—can mobilize to stop the bloodshed and to occupy territory for as long as necessary to keep the peace.

In the martial arts traditions of tai chi and akido, the highest masters are those who develop their awesome abilities through a lifetime of discipline yet never actually fight. They understand that once a violent battle begins, everyone loses, whatever the outcome, and that the real art of war—the best use of power—lies in defusing rather than feeding conflict. Only the strongest have the power to stop the cycle of violence and become an active force for peace. America has that power now; pray that it does not squander its fleeting greatness on the continuing follies of offensive action.

E Pluribus Unum

The cause of America is in a great measure the cause of all mankind.

—Tom Paine[4]

The question behind peacemaking is: How be consistently peaceable within oneself and with others? As a nation, we have a mistaken idea that peace can be achieved through the diplomatic efforts of intrinsically argumentative, belligerent people. We strategize peace without living it.

—Deena Metzger[5]

During the build-up to the invasion of Iraq, George W. Bush made several hectoring references to the irrelevancy of the United Nations. He warned that if the U.N. did not accede to

American views and methods, then America would go it alone, and the U.N. would forfeit its whole reason for existing. According to Bush-think, the U.N.'s real purpose, after all the community powwows and diplomatic chit chat, was to get the rest of the world to fall in line behind America. That other nations might disagree with Bush's plans was simply inconceivable; that this collection of has-beens and weak sisters might actually use U.N. procedures to block American action proved that the very notion of multilateralism had reached the end of its utility and was no longer relevant since America would have its invasion anyway, no thanks to y'all.

What the whole episode really proved was that the offensive, self-centered dominism of a single party can undermine, if not destroy, the delicate balance and careful workings of a loosely aligned and defined group. It only takes one stubborn unilateralist to upset the game for everyone else. This especially applies when the unilateralist happens to hold the most power, and even more so when its power dwarfs that of all of the other parties combined, as in the present case of America in relation to the rest of the world. For as long as the international community lacks an effective check on America's offensive powers and ever-expanding (however benevolent) hegemony, then world affairs can only continue down the dangerous road of viral aggression and endless war.

If America really cared about the relevancy and effectiveness of the United Nations it would bring its awesome power to the international table, not as a clumsy bludgeon for forcing its will, but as a calculated offering that would strengthen its own position, while simultaneously strengthening others. This was so apparent in the immediate aftermath of September 11th. The whole world stood ready to join Team America in its worthy battle against the common scourge of terrorism. We can only wonder what a more internationally-minded President might have done with that moment and how a fully sanctioned and empowered United Nations might have addressed the terrorist threat. As it was, Bush abruptly alienated would-be allies with his militant unilateralism; the resulting Divided Nations have spent more time struggling with global Americanism than global terrorism.

The second tenet of active pacifism—multilateralism—asserts that, when dealing with serious conflicts, anything less than a consensual resolution that addresses all parties and viewpoints merely defers the conflict to another time. This pertains to the tyranny of dictatorship, where the oppressed never fully accept their forced conditions; to the commands of unilateralism, however benevolent or well-intended; and even to the bilateral processes of majority-rule democracy, in which every decision has a losing side and difficult problems fester unresolved for generations. Domination never solves anything. While having the most power in a relationship *could* give one the greatest facility and range of options for working with others, using that power to unilaterally force one's way merely sows the conditions of future conflict.

The world has long recognized the need for multilateral institutions and made its first serious attempt at such with the League of Nations at the end of World War I. Out of that failed effort grew the conditions for yet another, even more catastrophic global war, and then another, even more hopeful global creation, the United Nations. Though neoconservative Americans have been railing for years about the failings of the U.N., refusing to fully fund U.N. activities, and even raising fears about the U.N.'s supposed plans to wage war on America from an armada of black helicopters, the achievements of this institution in its first fifty years could fill several books. The U.N.'s work toward furthering human rights, protecting the environment, preventing disease, improving conditions for women, spreading democracy, fostering sustainable development, alleviating hunger, reducing child mortality, aiding victims of natural disasters, and physically keeping the peace in dozens of global hotspots has made the world a vastly better place. It not only achieved these accomplishments while standing in the middle, for most of its history, of two bitterly divided and armed-to-the-teeth cold war superpowers, it had to contend throughout the period with its own cold war contradictions and divisions. That it has managed to do so much good despite such obstacles bears solid testimony to the creative power of nations working together.

Of course, the U.N. has also experienced more than a few failures. We should expect as much as such a brave new enterprise evolves, remembering that the world has lived through so many generations of chronic dominism that it has come to think of violence and war as normal and natural and of peace and cooperation as subversive foolishness. So we may forgive ourselves if we sometimes stumble during early efforts at multilateral peacemaking.

We must especially press on with the U.N.'s most important task at the beginning of the new millennium: the co-creation of a multilaterally armed, internationally sanctioned, and militarily superior peacekeeping force. Rogue nations bent on illegal weapons development, severe transgressions of human rights, and/or the invasion of other nations must know that they face the unified wrath, combined might, and unyielding defense of the world community. Likewise, international terrorist cells must know that every police force on the planet, empowered with the most advanced investigative and forensic tools, will work together to bring swift and certain justice to all perpetrators of terrorizing violence. People everywhere must come to understand that aggressive dominism will always invoke an answering force of multilateral, cooperative, active pacifism.

Early U.N. efforts at international peacekeeping forces have brought a mixed bag of successes and failures. America's resistance to these efforts, and at times blatant subversion of them, has contributed largely to the failures, just as America's decision to bring its powers and to cooperate with new efforts will turn the key to future successes. America has to get over its juvenile and parochial loathing of consensus process, its insistence on always being right, first, best, and strongest, and its fear of losing its sovereign freedoms in the cooperative play of multilateralism, to at last sit down at the gathering of all nations as one peer among equals. That act, bolstered with the commitment to follow the will of global humanity, will transform the U.N. overnight into a super-relevant institution, the ultimate benevolent hegemon.

Practically speaking, this means turning most of America's awesome weapons and a portion of its military over to the shared controls of an international force. Neoconservative and benevolent hegemonic theorists have long been correct in arguing that only a super powerful force such as America's in World War II can put a stop to rampant evil in the world. They've been mistaken, however, in thinking that one nation acting unilaterally could play that role without falling into the traps of imperial overreach and viral dominism. No single nation can, not America, nor any other in history. As the Parable predicts, the most well-intended efforts go awry, because the domination of one sovereign power over many others can only engender future conflict, future dominations, and future cycles of aggression and violence.

Only a multilateral, U.N. peacekeeping force, strong enough to defeat any single aggressor, can bring a full and final resolution to the Parable: by spreading the answering aggression among many parties acting as one, we insure that nobody has to flee, nor surrender, and that in fighting back the cause is just and the methods appropriate. It falls to America to take the big steps, to grow beyond its myopic nationalism, to desire meaningful connection with the rest of the world's people, to channel all of its super powers into the creation of more equitable and just societies, and to take pride in serving as one among peers in international, multilateral institutions. America faces a monumental choice: we can stand with other nations to resolve conflict in non-dominist ways, or we can follow our separate, unilateral path to its ignoble end.

One People, Many Gods

The problem is fundamentalism. Not Islam, not Christianity. Once you say that only your version of the truth is acceptable, it is a short hop to crashing airplanes into buildings, or burning witches at the stake.

—**Sean Driscoll**[6]

Though early America was comprised for the most part of god-fearing, Bible-toting Christians, a strong current of Deism flowed among the Founders, most notably Thomas Jefferson, Tom Paine, George Washington, Benjamin Franklin, and Ethan Allen. While Deists (then, as now) believe in God, they deny the validity of "revealed" religions that derive purely from the divine revelation of individuals or sacred writings. To the Deist, a belief in God comes as a supreme act of reason based on simple observation of manifest creation. One must learn, as Jefferson advised in a letter to his nephew, to "question with boldness even the existence of a god; because, if there be one, he must more approve of the homage of reason, than that of blindfolded fear." One must forswear all prophets, sects, and holy books, as Paine wrote in *The Age of Reason*, because "the Word of God is the creation we behold and it is in this word, which no human invention can counterfeit or alter, that God speaketh universally to man." The great failing of revealed religion was that, as Allen wrote in *Reason*, "such people as can be prevailed upon to believe that their reason is depraved, may easily be led by the nose, and duped into superstition at the pleasure of those in whom they confide, and there remain from generation to generation."

Deism stresses that all men and women have the essential right and responsibility to reason for themselves, to comprehend the mysteries of creation, to establish their ideal forms of government, to pursue their unique notions of happiness, and to negotiate their own understandings of and relationships to the Creator. The People have the power within, and therefore must have the freedom among others, to individually develop and collectively progress without the excessive domination of sociopolitical rulers, nor the religious command of pastors, parsons, priests, and popes. This was perhaps the most revolutionary thought of the whole Revolution: a genuinely free people have no need for dominist intercessors of any sort. "The government which governs best, governs least," said Jefferson, an insight that applies to all forms of institutional authority. The best religions, then, have the least dogma, the fewest commandments, and the greatest respect for the individual's capacity for self-guidance and meaningful practice.

The influence of the early Deists, combined with the fact that so many of the colonists had fled the constant religious warring and persecution of Europe, led the Founders to strive for a constitutional separation of church and state. Even the most emphatically Christian must have understood the danger when any specific religious revelation or practice assumes the power and authority of the government. Just as America would no longer honor the divine rights of royalty, so the State would not give sanction to one religion above all others. The People should have the same unimpeachable freedom to practice the religion of their choice, or no religion at all, as they do to elect their governing representatives, to speak their minds, to congregate in protest, and to bear arms for the purpose of rational defense.

America has certainly gone a long way toward separating church and state and thereby establishing real freedom of religion. No country in history has evinced such a wide diversity of religious faiths and practices, from the Amish to the Zoroastrians, with Jews, Muslims, Buddhists, Hindus, Sikhs, Jains, Taoists, Deists, and pagans scattered about, along with a thousand different flavors of practicing Christians. America was built on the constant immigration of people from all over the world, who carried their religions with them to add to the nation's ever growing spiritual melting pot. At the same time, in keeping with its penchant for entrepreneurial invention, America has given rise to numerous new prophets, sects, denominations, and sacred texts.

Still, America began as a primarily Christian nation and, according to a 2002 Gallup poll, 72% of Americans still declare themselves as Christians, with 2.3% claiming to be Jewish, 10% "of all other religions," and 15% agnostic, atheist, or no religion/no answer. While the Christian majority has proven tolerant of minority faiths, it has for the most part been the grudging forbearance of superiors to their underlings. Christian America has allowed other religions to take root and even flourish, but only on the outskirts of the realm, like tiny gardens on the far borders of a sprawling farm. It has always been clearly understood and expressed through a myriad of customs, laws, and social mores that Christianity comes first and foremost in all matters of import. With few exceptions (most them Jewish), Christians still run the government, judiciary, military, law enforcement, the media, and the major corporations. Moreover, Christian ideology dominates the political sphere to an extent that recalls the worst fears and dire warnings of Jefferson and Paine.

In recent years, America's commitment to freedom of religion has come into increasing conflict with its equally strong commitment to the monotheism of Christianity, with pitched cultural battles on many fronts. Should we force non-Christian children to participate in Christmas celebrations or should we deprive the Christian children—most of the school—of such vital traditions? Can we find some way to bring prayer into the schools that does not, by its very form and substance, offend somebody, or do we deny the many to protect a few? Can a judge who displays the Ten Commandments in his courtroom show fairness and impartiality to those who deny the Bible's validity as God's word? How can non-Christians possibly feel included in critical legal, political, and civic affairs that begin with "swearing on the Holy Book?" What of homosexuals, many who consider themselves good Christians, but who run afoul of narrowly interpreted revelations of scripture? How do we fairly resolve the abortion debate, ultimately a conflict between what the early Deists would have seen as bodies of revealed truths concerning life, death, birth, motherhood, and individual sovereignty?

As long as we remain stuck in a dominist system, our most sincere attempts at resolving these issues only take us deeper into conflict, for no amount of effort can overcome the fundamental prerogatives of monotheism. "My way or the hell way" dooms us all to everlasting hell on earth, as monotheistic Christians, Jews, and Muslims force everyone to choke on the toxic fallout of their ancient god-spat. The world simply cannot survive any one religion that does not embrace all others—we have too many people, in too small a space, armed with too terrible of weapons to endure even one more generation of chronic, monotheistic crusading.

Though it comes wrapped in righteous pronouncements and would-be moral absolutes, monotheism springs from a deep-seated fear and loathing of other people. Rather than resolve such dark emotions within oneself, the monotheist, puffed up with the smiling certainty of one doing the Lord's work, strives to mend the evil in others by bringing them to the one true God. Most monotheists have little awareness of the profound disrespect they show to the opinions and ways of other cultures, nor of the inevitable conflict sown when one religion condescendingly invalidates another (especially when that other is also monotheistic). The dangerous logic of monotheism—God himself commands me to do whatever necessary to convert you—ever spawns the very evil that the sincerely religious have spent millennia trying to eradicate.

The time has come to move beyond the commandments of second-hand revelations and go straight to the heart of the religious impulse: peace on earth, goodwill to all. It will no longer do to just show tolerance of other faiths; we must welcome, enjoy, and even celebrate a wide diversity of views and practices. The creative logic of multi-faith societies means that peace will come easier and goodwill extend further, that a primary source of human conflict will finally dissipate, and that our ancient fear of an avenging God will transform into an abiding, healing love for all others.

Differently Equal

Belief in a shared future requires rejecting the radical fundamentalist claim to possess the whole truth in favor of the belief that life is a journey in search of the truth and that we all have something to contribute. That leads us to the core of what we value in the integrated global community: Our differences are important, but our common humanity matters more.

—**Bill Clinton**[7]

During the "gays in the military" flap at the beginning of the Clinton administration a poll was taken to gauge American attitudes toward homosexuality. A series of questions asked, in different ways, whether the respondent considered homosexuals right or wrong and whether they deserved the same civil rights, protections, and considerations as heterosexuals. The country was roughly split down the middle, with much depending on the specific question and the way it was framed. One question, however, had strikingly unambiguous results: when people were asked, "Do you know any homosexuals?" those who had spoken in defense of homosexual issues nearly all answered yes, while those who had spoken against nearly all answered no.

The simple message from that little slice of life points to a clear, if humbling, resolution to the dangerous logic of xenophobia. For whenever we fear those others—fags, cunts, ragheads, kikes, spics, wops, krauts, japs, chinks, niggers, injuns—we really fear not them but their foreignness. We fear that which we do not know; more precisely, we fear our own lack of knowledge. We fear *from* our own sorry ignorance. When we fear them enough to wish them terror, hate them enough to lash out in anger, loathe them enough to countenance the most shameful massacres and genocides, we do so out of the misguided conviction that their differences make them threatening to us and thus deserving of abuse.

The xenophobe glimpses the grand sweep of human diversity—our different bodies, religions, races, philosophies, languages, histories, and customs—and reactively fears it all, turns it all into reason for hostile distrust given to aggressive behavior. "Different than us" becomes "less than us," and "less than us" becomes "less than human." A group of well-armed, xenophobic dominists can eradicate a village, a race, or a whole civilization with nary an afterthought once they've branded the victims with inferior status; it simply does not matter what one does to those "less thans," those primitive creatures, those strange, inscrutable foreigners.

George W. Bush surely ranks among the most xenophobic of American presidents. Despite the opportunities afforded by having a father who was ambassador to China, a globe-trotting vice president for eight years, and then president for four more years, young George rarely travelled outside of America, nor applied himself to any serious study of other cultures. As president, he followed the xenophobe's path to a stubborn unilateralism, a strutting superiority, and a crotchety incuriosity regarding other lands and peoples. Midway through his term of office, international polling found that while most people still admired America, they hated its leadership, and especially its president. One suspects that Bush took perverse pride in such reports, as did many of his fellow Americans.

The world desperately needs the anti-Bush, now, at all levels of society. We need leaders who thrive on international engagement, who look forward to the slow talking things through and "getting to know you" of regular summit meetings, who show genuine interest in the customs of foreign lands, who believe in the necessity of learning from other nations. We need "ping-pong diplomacy," cultural exchange students, a revitalized Peace Corps, and increasing foreign aid for peaceful purposes. We need a strong, more-relevant-than-ever United Nations.

We need all the expanding connectedness of globalism, coupled with a passionate respect for and interest in local cultures and values. We need for people everywhere to get out of their parochial shells, to travel more, to taste strange foods, to learn new languages, to visit different churches, to live abroad, to mix and share and experience the fullness of "life with other."

We especially need to reconcile the founding principles of America—that all people are created equal and are equally endowed with the rights to life, liberty and the pursuit of happiness—with a principle tenet of biology—that the healthiest systems display the greatest diversity. The world's great strength and ultimate future lies in the near infinite spectrum of human differences, giving rise to emerging potentials, positive change, and progressive development. We must turn toward each "other" with curiosity, excitement, and a hunger to know more, rather than recoil in infantile fear. We have nothing to lose but our walled-in, terror-stricken little lives.

Dominists will reactively pooh-pooh all this "getting to know you" diversity talk as a bunch of touchy-feely hooey or, even worse, as dangerously naïve advice for this all-too-dangerous world. What of places like Bosnia and Rwanda where neighbors turned against neighbors with vicious, sadistic zeal? What of all the domestic violence in the world, where people abuse those who they have "gotten to know" the best? We don't need to get to know all those alien others better, warns the dominist; we just need to insulate ourselves from their likely evils.

So runs the dangerous logic of xenophobia: the more we fear our fellow humans, the more insular our lives, the less we know of other worlds, and the easier it becomes to rationalize all forms dominist aggression and abuse. We do not resolve this conundrum by becoming even more fearful, more insular, and more other-ignorant, but by embracing the creative logic of differently equal: yes, people come in different bodies, of different races, worshipping different gods, speaking different languages, with different histories, and living in different societies; and yes, we all equally deserve the same life and liberty and we all pursue the same simple human happiness and love. Our differences make us neither better than nor less than; rather, our differences strengthen, clarify, and adorn our essential oneness and deep wells of common goodness, all so very worth knowing, and such a sure path to peace.

Gender Peace

But I want to tell you something. This pattern, this "system" that the white man created... has done the American white man more harm than an invading army would do to him.

—**Malcolm X**[8]

The traditional construct of man as hard, unfeeling, aggressive and conceptualizing, and woman as soft, yielding, nurturing and intuitive, insults male as well as female.

—**George Leonard**[9]

The 1991 Clarence Thomas confirmation hearings for the U.S. Supreme Court opened a bleak and seamy view into the sexist heart of American culture. The sight of a solitary Anita Hill, stoically bearing the vicious scrutiny of a panel of old, white, wealthy men, will forever hang in the American consciousness as a damning portrait of dominist reality. By the time it had all played out we had learned volumes on the abuses of power, and had borne collective witness to the unyielding strengths and self-oppressing habits of the status quo, as well as the slimier nature of sexual politics in action.

Of course, in the end the old boys prevailed; Thomas won his position and has since gone on to serve as the far-right, anti-feminist reactionary that Hill and others warned against. Though the following year was proclaimed as "the Year of the Woman" in American politics, women still made up just 12% of the US Congress, and a full decade later had added but a few more seats. A number of other feminist indicators showed a similar lack of progress. Women's wages remained stuck below that of men's for comparable work. Public and domestic violence against women continued to run rampant. Unmarried women and their children made up disproportional numbers of the poor, the unemployed, and the homeless. With Bush packing the courts for years to come, women's reproductive rights and the legal control of their bodies seemed doomed to death by a thousand blows.

All of which reveals a critical lesson: We will never resolve the sort of sexual conflict that Thomas and Hill represented through our courts and legal systems. Men and women cannot hope to litigate their way out of the dominist tensions of the past several thousand years.

This does not mean that the various legal gains of the women's movement should go unappreciated. It certainly helps to have the vote, to have access to better education and employment, and to experience some protection, however tenuous, from systemic harassment. But only a self-serving dominist could claim that women now count for as much as men in our political systems, or receive equal treatment in most businesses, or experience genuine freedom from the foul climate sexual harassment. The changing of a law merely urges us toward, but hardly assures, the changing of deep-seated human habit.

Moreover, as veteran feminists, civil rights workers, and environmentalists will all attest, the dominists never really give up their power, despite occasional legal setbacks. For every legal gain in the struggle against dominism, we can expect a backlash of even greater proportions. The verdict of Roe v. Wade brought us Operation Rescue and women's health clinic bombings and a staunchly conservative Supreme Court. The passage of the Civil Rights Act brought us regressive quarrels over quota bills, affirmative action, and the dangers of multiculturalism. Passing the Endangered Species Act brought us James Watt, the property rights movement, and clearcut forests as far as the eyes can see. The most sincere and well-reasoned attempts to weaken overclass power only give rise to new strategies and weapons on the part of the dominist elites.

The collapse of communism throughout the Soviet bloc provides another case in point. Despite its many faults, most of the communist world managed a fair equality between the sexes and various ethnic groups if only because quasi-egalitarianism was enforced as law. As each communist government was overturned and the people became "free," ethnic and religious hostilities exploded, and women's numbers in government quickly declined. Without the constraints of the totalitarian state, ancient patterns of dominist oppression abruptly backlashed into new expression.

Though we should not cease our revolutions against oppressive masters or our struggles against oppressive laws, ultimately any such struggling that fails to fundamentally alter dominist reality, only feeds it. We cannot let the dominists have their way, yet we cannot fight them with their own methods and truly should not *fight* them at all. This applies most obviously to violent assaults and overthrows—for viral dominism thrives in aggressive relationships—but proves true also in many legal/democratic processes. The laws that govern any dominist system, along with the prescribed methods for changing those laws, serve as critical determinants of the system. Thus, our most conscientious legal efforts from within the system, if only directed toward incremental corrections, rarely result in genuine, meaningful change. We will find it forever difficult to do direct battle with dominist reality without giving substance to the spreading contagion of viral dominism.

None of this will come as a surprise to the early feminists who first experienced and then proclaimed, "The personal is political." The woman who spends her days striving for a larger role and better pay in the workplace and then goes home to second-class status in her marriage; the activist who looks on with alarm as peace demonstrations turn hateful, ugly, and violent; the environmentalist who drives a gas-guzzling, fume-spewing car;

the person of color who catches herself racially profiling others; the do-gooder, progressive-minded author who seethes with rage toward the ruling elite: those who commit themselves to a whatever-it-takes struggle against systemic political dominism must ultimately confront the dominist realities within their personal lives.

We need look no further than our daily interactions for both cause and cure to the dominism in our world. The sexism that we see in society perfectly mirrors the sexist realities within our families and most intimate relationships. Each derives from and feeds into the other: the sexual dysfunctions and gender tensions of society create the ideal conditions for fundamentally sexist families, which naturally condition boys and girls to grow into the sexually-challenged and gender-tense men and women of sexist societies. Any path to a just, equitable, and peaceful society will necessarily pass through our primary relationships, especially those with members of the opposite sex. Only as we resolve sexism at the personal level can we even hope for a resolution of the political.

This calls us then to more of that subjective, interpersonal, psycho-emotional self-exploration and growing that makes dominists so uncomfortable. Even among the more progressively inclined it can seem much easier, and far preferable, to organize grand social movements, to march on behalf of this cause and that, to work tirelessly for legal and political change, to foment revolution, even to storm the ramparts—to do anything rather than sit down face to face with one's most intimate other, to tell the whole truth and nothing but, to think differently and communicate openly and to allow oneself to feel the full panorama of human emotion. Yet only through such uncompromising self-work can we hope to untangle the socio-sexual knots, aberrant behaviors, and perpetual gender warring that so defines modern culture.

Sexism persists as an especially virulent strain of xenophobia. The opposite gender looms like a dark continent filled with exotic, unfathomable creatures of alien origins, who urgently attract—yet ominously threaten—an always mysterious source of wonder laced with doubt, of passion mixed with dread, and excitement mingled with fear. To the extent that we cannot understand them, we tend to fear them; because we fear them, we ever mistreat them. The eternal battling of the sexes springs not from basic human nature or genetics or God's own plan or original sin, but from a fundamental failure to understand, our original miscommunication. No amount of changing laws and fiddling with customs will get to the real work of resolution; for that, more and more people must undergo emotional retraining and personal transformation until the world teems with those who can understand, who no longer fear one another, and who find living and working together peacefully the most normal and natural of outcomes. Wherever two or more have learned to come together as differently equal partners, we all have moved a little closer to living peace.

For the Common Good

We can either have a situation where we have a small number of people with a huge amount of wealth or we can have a democracy. But we can't have both.

—**Bill Gates, Sr.**[10]

[There] is looming up a new and dark power... the enterprises of the country are aggregating vast corporate combinations of unexampled capital, boldly marching, not for economical conquests only, but for political power.... The question will arise and arise in your day, though perhaps not fully in mine, which shall rule—wealth or man; which shall lead—money or intellect; who shall fill public stations—educated and patriotic freemen, or the feudal serfs of corporate capital....

—**Justice Edward G. Ryan, 1873**[11]

The National Security Strategy[12] released by the Bush administration in the summer of 2002 claimed that America would only experience real security when the rest of the world had been transformed into its likeness. The strategy declared that with the major totalitarian states of the 20th century defeated, "America is now threatened less by conquering states than we are by failing ones. We are menaced less by fleets and armies than by catastrophic technologies in the hands of the embittered few." While providing justification for invasions of those "embittered few" deemed as most threatening to global security, the real thrust of the document went to U.S. responsibilities, obligations, and opportunities to export and widely promote the two great pillars of American society: democracy and free market capitalism.

Democracy and capitalism, free people and free markets, go to the heart of America's greatness, its exceptionalism, and its promise in the evolution of human culture. In a wanna-be Christian nation that regularly contradicts the teachings of Jesus, the establishment and protection of these freedoms has become the one true religion and Holy Grail. Good Americans turn all teary-eyed on the subject of freedom and have come to accept without question the continuity between individual freedoms and the freedoms of the marketplace: neither can exist without the other, and any infringements on one represent an infringement of both. To the extent that such freedom-loving Americans care about the rest of the world, they ardently profess that American-styled democracy and capitalism can solve all problems, better all peoples, and improve all nations.

The proselytes of this viral Americanism blithely discount the terrible difficulties that have befallen so many newly "free" nations: the haphazard break-up of the Soviet Union, the wrenching, horrible tragedy of Yugoslavia, and such freed but failing economies as Chile, Argentina, and Brazil, to name a few. "Mere growing pains," the Americanizers proclaim. Just as America has had its own problems fully manifesting a free society, including a cataclysmic civil war well into its growing process, so should developing nations expect some hard work and rough times on the road to freedom. As long as they open their markets (especially to America) and hold some reasonably free elections, then any suffering, dislocation, and civil strife such countries undergo warrant little more than a condescending shrug from their American superiors, as if to say, "There, there, now, take your medicine like a man." Should a nation such as China, cautioned by the chaos in the former Soviet states, move too slowly toward democratization or opening markets, it can expect an ahistorical blast of self-righteousness from US politicians and pundits.

Even worse, these evangelizing Americans first ignore then outright attack any democratic systems or market economies that do not absolutely toe the American Way. America presumably has nothing to learn from history or from the experiences of its peers (since it has none). Rare discussions of European-style democracy or Canadian-style healthcare or Japanese-style pension systems get quickly derailed with dire warnings of creeping socialism and the futility of State-run economies. Even to suggest that America needs improvement or that there may exist some more optimal systems for organizing a government or an economy lays one open to charges of America-bashing and incipient treason. Not surprisingly, the dissemination of American-style democracy and capitalism has come to take on all the form and trappings of an Old Testament religion: there exists one and only one true way and those who do not follow deserve their suffering, while heaven awaits those who help spread the good news.

Aside from the arrogance of thinking that any one way will work best for everyone, we really must question just how well democracy and free market capitalism have worked together in America. After more than two hundred years of free and open elections, American democracy has some glaring faults, including low voter turnout, ugly, mean-spirited campaigns, near total control of the legislative processes by big money interests, and, as the 2000 election proved, serious problems at nearly every stage of the electoral process, from the slapdash design of ballots and voting machines to the antiquated rules that cashiered Al Gore. America's capitalism, likewise more than two hundred years in development, still produces as many scandals as success stories, leaves unconscionable numbers of citizens unemployed and without access to essential goods and services, runs roughshod over the environment, behaves imperialistically toward other nations, and channels so much money into the political process as to render the overclass fairly immune to community oversight.

Though Americans naturally think of democracy and capitalism as working in concert, each justifying and supporting the other, these two profoundly differing viewpoints have clashed and conflicted throughout America's history. For while democracy aims to distribute power more equitably among all, capitalism promises that only the worthy few will achieve great wealth. Democracy follows the concerns of *demos*, the People, while capitalism follows the bottom-line materialism of stuff and money. Democracy, at its best, brings people together to decide vital matters of common concern. Capitalism splits the People into fields of separate actors, each looking after his and her own interests, with little regard for those of others. Democracy epitomizes the group, public and cooperative, while capitalism stands for the individual, private and competitive.

Which brings us to the heart of the matter: the more free and unencumbered America's market economy, the less effective its democracy and less free its people. Capitalism undermines democracy. To the extent that America achieves the capitalist goals of reducing taxes, removing government regulations, and privatizing public enterprises and institutions, the nation turns undemocratic. The American people have managed to overlook or reluctantly accept the gradual slide from democracy to domocracy because it has been predicated as but an unfortunate side effect—soon to be remedied—on the way to perfect capitalism. The dominists have so successfully conflated democracy and capitalism as to make the trampling of underclass freedoms and the abridgments of civil rights seem natural, inevitable, and unimportant, so long as the overclass elites can go on buying, selling, and profiting with impunity.

Consider America's tortured attempts at campaign finance reform. Everybody knows that electoral victory nearly always goes to the candidate who spends the most money, that incumbents use the power of their office to raise funds and thereby retain position and power, and that the wealthy use their campaign contributions to influence politicians and the electoral process. America has truly, sadly, become "the best democracy that money can buy." Yet efforts to move toward public financing, or to place limits on campaign spending, or to lessen the influence of large donations fade before the rhetoric of free market capitalism, as if the process of choosing our leaders should steadfastly follow the same guiding principles as that of choosing a new detergent. Dominists define campaign contributions as a type of public discourse and then frame any attempts to limit such contributions as interferences with the freedom of speech. In America, the freedom of the wealthy to decide public policy shall not be abridged by the common ideals of a genuine, working democracy.

Or consider the constant tension between government regulations and the rights of businesses and corporations to freely pursue their profits. With dominism-driven capitalism on the ascendant, attempts to in any way regulate the marketplace—for product and worker safety, to protect the environment, to create opportunities among underclass citizens, to provide a social safety net for all—invoke howls of disdain from the rich and powerful. Most politicians, eager to join said rich and powerful, have come to adopt a more or less anti-government ideology, with the standard industry-blessed platform of reducing taxes, shrinking government, and eliminating bothersome regulations. Few politicians can even make a good case for *having* a government, much less articulate the necessity of enlightened—yes, liberal—governance in the common lives of the People. Really, who needs government when the wisdom of the marketplace—capitalism's "invisible hand"—will see to it that only safe, well-designed, fairly-priced, and socially-beneficial goods and services ever succeed? Never mind all the crooks, manipulators, and avaricious fools who forever distort the market with their dishonesty—if we all just exercise our freedom to not do business with such people then they will swiftly and surely change their ways, and without all the inconvenient nagging of government regulators. Or so the free marketers promise, even as the invisible hand picks our pockets.

Ultimately, the prophets of triumphant capitalism aim for the virtual elimination of government. We see this in the first demands that the international financiers place on all newly "free" nations: that they privatize most of the activities of their governments, putting the banks, land, crops, extractive resources, pension systems, healthcare, and security services into the control of private individuals and international corporations. That such "reforms" invariably lead to a widening in the gap between the haves and have-nots, with increasing misery for those in the underclass, never slows the march to global privatization. In America, the privateers have set their sights on public education, Medicare, Head Start, the postal system, the public financing of various media and the arts, and, the jewel in the crown, Social Security. They would have us believe that private, unregulated enterprises could do all of these things better than government—that men and women motivated by personal profit will always outperform those motivated by civic responsibility, by the desire to serve others, by spiritual principles, or by an impassioned patriotism.

Dominists derive power from the self-fulfilling logic of their wrong-headed and stone-hearted manifesto. The more America commits to capitalism, competition, and bottom-line materialism, the less democratic its institutions become, and the more likely the people are to turn against government in favor of the siren promises of dominism. In the totally privatized America that the dominists envision, power devolves from the federal government to the states, from the states to local public organizations, and from public organizations to private, well-armed fiefdoms in perpetual competition for scarce resources. Democracy has no place or function in such a world, as the power of private needs—that is, profit needs—ever overwhelms the concerns of the People.

If America really wants to bring freedom and democracy to the rest of the world—a worthy goal, and the surest counter to global terrorism—then it must first resolve this long-running conflict between free markets and free people. Despite the assurances of neoconservative theorists, personal freedom without the regulating force of community oversight, as expressed through laws, rules, licences, and customs, leads inevitably to conflict, strife, and ultimate rule by dominist elites. While the government that governs least may indeed govern best, in the total absence of governance we see people at their worst. For all the genuine evils of totalitarian over-governance, we do no better sliding into the oligarchic controls of under-governance.

America could really use a few new myths, indeed, a whole new story. Paeans to the rugged individualist recklessly braving the cutthroat competitions of life must give way to tales of groups, organizations, and governing bodies selflessly cooperating for the greater good. Celebrations of national independence should evolve into global celebrations of interdependence. The prevailing notion of personal profit as a fair and effective motivator in human endeavors needs the tempering influences of empathy, compassion, service, community, and a bottom-line concern for the most disadvantaged in society. Money can no longer serve as the prime measure of a person's value or of the worthiness or lack thereof of social policies; instead, we need to view individuals and their governments through a universal prism of transcendent, ethical, and spiritual values. Nor can dominist force—power to the strongest, richest, and most capable of violence—continue as the primary way of making decisions and resolving conflicts. America needs to manifest nothing less than a genuine working democracy, where power resides in the voice of the common people.

Humanature

To survive, our minds must taste

redwood and agate, octopi,

bat, and in

the bat's mouth, insect. It's hard

to think like a planet.

We've got to try.

—**James Bertolino**

In Australia, parents now restrict the amount of outdoor play for their children, and when boys and girls do go out, they must wear wide-brimmed hats and scarves around their necks, especially during summer. They do this to protect themselves from the sun. The hole in the ozone layer, never more than a bothersome theory to most Americans, has become an indisputable and life-altering catastrophe to Australians.

A few statistics frame the issue: 75% of Australians past the age of sixty have had some form of skin cancer, Australian deaths due to skin cancer have been rising since the 1960s, and, though recent attempts to mitigate the problem have proven somewhat successful, scientists still expect that two out of three Australians will develop skin cancer at some point during their lives. Since excessive ultraviolet radiation has been proven to cause such cancers; since the depletion of ultraviolet-shielding ozone has only been a problem for some forty years; and since older, cancer-stricken Australians were not even exposed until they were adults—it should not take an environmental extremist to sound the alarm for Australia's children. An entire generation faces serious risks—toxic sunlight—the likes of which humans have never encountered before and have barely begun to address.

Toxic sunlight. We read those words and think of children everywhere, and think of our own childhoods, of long summers playing under the sun, of skin tanned dark by late August, of normally brown hair bleached blond. Now we must say to children: "only so many hours a day," and "only if you put your sunscreen on," and "don't forget to wear your hat." In just forty years, human industry has corrupted our fundamental relationship with the sun.

Though questions remain as to the causes and long-term effects of ozone depletion, few dispute that in Australia (and other parts of the world overexposed to ultraviolet radiation) plant, animal, and human biological functions have already undergone serious changes. Even if we imagine that changes in our planet's biosphere could cause positive changes for humans (for we are adaptable creatures), we hardly can know for certain. Whatever the long-term effects of ozone depletion, they have been necessitated by a series of entirely mutable human choices. Ozone depletion *does not have to happen*. Industry can easily replace every ozone-depleting chemical in current use with something better. Though this may mean added costs for specific goods and services, when we consider the big picture—the continuing evolution of human society in relation to all life on Earth—such expenses pale in significance.

Too many Americans never consider the big picture, or any concerns outside of their own personal or, at best, tribal needs. We behave as if our actions have no long-term consequences whatsoever. Our corporate and government leaders have difficulty thinking beyond the next public opinion poll or quarterly financial statement, much less intelligently planning ten, twenty, thirty years and more into the future. We buy into the false choice of "economy versus ecology" and then shrug with hopeless resignation as our world degenerates due to short-term, private economic demands. We continue to trumpet the magic of free markets, despite countless examples of purely selfish market decisions that have led to monumental eco-abuse.

Even worse, we seem unaware of our contributions to our own evolutionary process. We quarrel over various ecological problems as if the only question were how much more damage the planet can sustain. (The planet will go on adapting to our most foolish excesses long after we're gone.) Some questions we should be asking: Who will we become as a result of environmental degradation? What changes in human nature will likely result from sudden, massive, inhospitable changes in the environment? Is this the evolution we want?

Do we want children who grow up afraid of the sun? Do we want children who grow up breathing smog and eating lead and drinking DDT from their mother's breasts? Do we want children who never swim in oceans long ago polluted and never hike in forests long ago razed? Have we given any thought at all to the developing psyches of such children and to who they will "naturally" become as adults? We've gone beyond just tinkering with their environment to blindly altering their DNA, brain cells, and body chemistry. We have badly skewed their view of the world, their whole sense of human nature, and their primary patterns of relationship. As such children mature, they will people a rather different world, for they will have become rather different people.

The time has come that we accept responsibility for the evolution of our world. Evolution means "adaptation to the prevailing environment;" human actions can powerfully affect the prevailing environment and thereby positively or negatively influence evolution. It is past time for people everywhere to get this and to begin making sound choices in favor of a benign and balanced environment that will inspire the best of human nature.

Though environmentalists have been pressing this case on multiple fronts since the 1960s, attempts at genuinely changing the anti-environmentalism of dominist culture have been sporadic at best, especially in America. Americans still seem light years away from sane and sustainable policies dealing with energy, pollution, renewable resources, forestry, genetically modified agriculture, ozone depletion, climate change, and industrial development. Debates on these topics rarely get past private economic concerns. The acquired need for gas-guzzling SUVs outweighs any thoughts as to the effects of such vehicles on future generations. Corporate concern over the next quarter's bottom line renders environmentalist worries over a bunch of future unknowns irrelevant. The need to keep the nation's economy motoring on, however foolishly, undermines the most conscientious and business-friendly efforts to fine-tune the engines. The bottom-line logic of dominist culture always consigns environmental issues to the bottom of priority lists.

A frustrating case in point has been the slow death of the Kyoto Protocol. Reached during an international conference in 1997, the Protocol laid out a series of steps to dramatically reduce the industrial emissions that have been implicated in global climate change. Though President Clinton signed the Protocol in 1998, the Republican Congress vowed that they would never ratify it, and three years later President Bush declared it dead. It mattered little that the world community had come together to work on a serious threat of global dimensions, that it had negotiated through some thorny conflicts on the way to a fairly balanced working document, and that everybody agreed there was still work to do, still more to learn, still issues to talk through. To Bush America it appeared to threaten certain American industries, and we could never allow mere environmental concerns to interfere with corporate cash flow.

But Bush did more than just kill a promising if incomplete treaty. He also spurned and seriously set back what had been a good attempt at multilateral cooperation. In so doing, he stymied a critical movement toward international partnership and pushed the world instead down the road of disconnection and alienation.

Concern for the environment ultimately brings a recognition of our connectedness—how we connect to one another, how humans connect with the natural world, how actions in one sector of an environment connect to other sectors. A healthy ecosystem comprises a complex, dynamically-balanced interrelationship of diverse yet equal members—a living partnership. If we want to further develop in this world without wreaking irreversible damage we can only do so as willing and able partners connected with all other species and—the more difficult task—with people of all other races, religions, ethnic groups, nations, and political/economic philosophies.

From the all-encompassing global problems of ozone depletion and climate change to more local concerns with recycling, water quality and waste disposal, our search for environmentally sustainable solutions will always lead us through the same basic insights: all people are essentially connected; all people must have equal access to the necessities of life; and all local/personal actions ripple out to effect the whole world even as global/political events continuously influence each individual. We are all in this together and we will only achieve genuine success by learning to act as partners. The Kyoto Protocol marked a bold, if belated, movement toward truly global partnership.

Conversely, the Bush administration stood for one small but enormously wealthy group of Americans in defiant isolation from everyone else. Dominism first causes, then thrives in, a world of disconnection. Since any sincere attempt to address environmental problems will compel people toward connection, cooperation, partnership, and peace, dominists must take offensive positions against anything perceived as pro-environment.

Dominism forces people to approach environmental issues as separate and disconnected tribes (as indigenous peoples, as special interest groups, as corporations, as nation-states, or as regional, political, and economic blocs) primarily concerned with the real or imagined demands of their own tribal survival. As any one tribe pursues its own needs with blatant disregard to the needs of others ("I'm not going to let a bunch of environmental extremists take away one American job!" whined a petulant president), the worst of environmental excesses become non-negotiable "rights," such as the right to continue producing the petrochemicals of global climate change, the right to clear-cut forests, or the right to go on causing mass species extinction.

Moreover, as long as any tribe chooses a "my needs are all that matter" approach to the environment, all tribes descend to the same low level of interaction. The most tragic failing of Bush America was that instead of using its world-leader position to forge the way toward a truly new world order of international cooperation, it fostered an atmosphere of distrust, disconnection, and mean-spirited competition. Instead of turning America's great material wealth and advantage toward positive global evolution, the president, head stuck deep in oil-rich sand, angrily defended and advocated for continuing with business-as-usual.

We cannot continue with business-as-usual. Just 10% of the world's population, Americans consume some 40% of its resources while producing nearly 50% of its wastes. Such figures do not begin to reflect the ecological impacts of America's chronic financial commitment to sustaining the world-wide arms race or of its interference in the affairs of less-developed nations. Yet even more frightening, given the dangerous logic of dominism, most of the world emulates America's development, however irrational, globally-unviable, and ultimately suicidal such emulation may be. Should we ever succeed in bringing American-style free market capitalism to people everywhere, the planet would suffer a collapse of Malthusian dimensions.

A central law of the Iroquois Nation—that leaders take no action without first considering its impact for seven generations into the future—carries the truth of our connectedness to a final, critical level. "Seven generations" places our short-term needs in a greater and more intelligent context. Asking "Is this really necessary?" from the perspective of one's great-great-grandchildren's grandchildren provides a wise and discerning guide for all of our actions. It works as a powerful light of awareness, bringing the true costs of any abuse of the environment, other humans, or ourselves into sharp focus.

"I sense those beings of future times hovering," writes Joanna Macy, "like a cloud of witnesses . . . . The imagined presence of these future ones comes to me like grace and works on my life."[13] What if these beings of the future were given a seat at every corporate board meeting, were consulted with before any tree was cut, were listened to before the production of a single ounce of forever-poisonous atomic waste? What if "a cloud of witnesses" oversaw our choices, commented on the consequences, and offered the most heartfelt encouragement for the challenges ahead? For those times when we may have difficulty answering, "Is this really necessary?" we need only ask them. Even if we hear no answer, that we asked, listened, and sincerely wanted to know invokes awareness enough to guide our actions.

All living things connect—people to people, species to species, ancient ancestors to future descendants—and environmental conditions ebb and flow over time and space as measures of the quality of our connectedness. No country has an environmental problem that does not ultimately affect all countries. Though we continue to act like independent, "me-first!" fiefdoms, the world's nations in fact comprise one green planet at common and collective risk. We can, as connected beings, take responsibility for the environment we all share and address challenges and problems as if they were our own. Only when we feel the threat to Australia's children, or children anywhere, as a threat to *our* children, will take enlightened steps toward positive evolution.

Though we have all become somewhat immune to the dire warnings of environmental experts, in Australia, and other hotspots around the globe, we must now face the truth. The time for meaningful action has arrived. Wake up and get to it. Don't forget to wear your hat.

Eight

Making Peace

Nonviolence demands that the means we use must be as pure as the ends we seek.

—Martin Luther King Jr.[1]

We are the ones who have the most profound task in human history—the task of deciding whether we grow or die. This will involve helping cultures and organizations to move from dominance by one economic culture or group to circular investedness, sharing and partnership.... It will involve a stride of soul that will challenge the very canons of our human condition. It will require that we become evolutionary partners with each other.

—Jean Houston[2]

In the months leading up to the 2003 invasion of Iraq, there arose an unprecedented international peace movement. Demonstrations took place throughout America, ranging from small groups holding regular street-corner vigils to hundreds of thousands that gathered for major events in New York, San Francisco, Washington, and other cities. Millions more took to the streets internationally, with huge antiwar turnouts throughout Europe and Asia. Though the mainstream US media served up mostly military propaganda, the Internet came into its prime as an activist tool and communication forum, spawned thousands of peace-related sites, spread relevant and inspiring documents worldwide, and initiated letter, email, and fax campaigns, including a "call-in" protest that overwhelmed government switchboards for a day.

While President Bush claimed to be unaffected by the protesters—"it [would be] like deciding...policy based upon a focus group"—they clearly slowed the rush to war. Even after the US Congress, still deep in its post-9/11 war-trance, gave unconditional accordance to whatever Bush decided to do, the fact that worldwide public opinion ran upwards to 90% against American plans for a preemptive invasion forced first Bush and then Secretary of State Colin Powell to go before the United Nations to make the case for war. When the UN Security Council, unimpressed by what turned out to be mostly fraudulent evidence, decided on another round of weapons inspections, it effectively delayed the war by several months. And, when Bush finally had his invasion, the intense international antiwar scrutiny had a tempering effect on US military tactics and strategies.

Yet even before the bombing began, conventional wisdom proclaimed the peace movement a failure. Pundits drew comparisons to the antiwar movement of the '60s, a silly exercise since those demonstrations did not begin until thousands of American draftees had already died in Viet Nam. As that war grew more deadly, with embittered survivors returning home from Southeast Asia with terrible tales, it still took years of constant antiwar activism to shift public opinion and influence official policy. Moreover, while the demonstrators of the time were vehemently against that particular war, most knew little about thinking, living, or making peace.

So while today's peace movement could not stop an invasion that, we now know, many in the Bush administration were intent on perpetrating from the outset of his presidency, it did succeed in awakening the idea of peace within the collective consciousness. As Dr. Robert Muller, former assistant secretary general of the U.N., stated, "Never before in the history of the world has there been a global, visible, public, viable, open dialogue and conversation about the very legitimacy of war."[3] Never before had people everywhere engaged in the transformational practice of thinking peace. And never before had the fundamental principles and practices of dominism been brought so thoroughly into the light of awareness.

If we-the-peaceful can stay awake and avoid slipping back into denial, and if the Internet continues to grow as a relatively free medium of mass connection and communication, than this peace movement will not only have moderated the first major war of the 21st century, it will alter the nature of human conflict for generations to come. We have now encompassed our world with an instantaneous informational net, making the age-old lies of dominism ever more difficult to sustain. The electrovibrational pulse of human communications racing at ever-increasing speeds about the globe heralds a world rousing into radical wakefulness, with people everywhere beginning to think of peace as the first, last, and only resort. We will no longer march in lockstep off to supposed good wars, even wars against evil terrorists and despicable tyrants, because war can no longer happen in the dark shadows of human deceit and denial.

The Cycle of Fear

We cannot have world peace without peace in our own lives. We cannot attack our planet by the way we live, and then go off to a peace rally and hope to set right all the imbalance we have caused. Peace is first a private matter. It cannot grow except from there.

—**Doris "Granny D" Haddock**[4]

The dogmas of the quiet past, are inadequate to the stormy present. . . . As our case is new, so we must think anew, and act anew. We must disenthrall ourselves, and then we shall save our country.

—**Abraham Lincoln**[5]

Two years after the terrorist attacks of 9/11, George W. Bush remained a popular president and formidable candidate for reelection. Despite the facts that he and other members of his administration had lied about Iraqi weapons of mass destruction and about Saddam Hussein's connections to al-Qaeda terrorism; that the post-war realities in Iraq and Afghanistan badly contradicted US pledges to bring peace and democracy to those troubled lands; that the Israeli-Palestinian conflict was worsening daily; that horrific terrorist attacks continued around the world; that states, cities, and various key agencies were all crying out about the lack of federal funding for essential Homeland Security needs; and that the administration continued to stonewall any serious investigation into, and avoided learning from, the intelligence mistakes and executive errors that preceded 9/11, the American people remained solidly behind their President. Indeed, he received his highest praise from the public for his leadership in the war against terrorism.

It certainly helped Bush that Americans were so media-misled and denial-dumb that, in various polls, nearly half said that most of the 9/11 hijackers were Iraqi (none were), 59% thought Saddam Hussein was largely responsible for 9/11 (was not), a third thought that US forces discovered weapons of mass destruction in the first month after the Iraq War ended (never did), and 20% thought that Iraq had actually used such weapons during the war (sigh). To the frustration of those opposing Bush, every new argument or fresh piece of evidence of Bush's calumny only served to strengthen his support. Not even the most compelling recitation of the facts could undercut the stubborn insistence of Bush America: in these terrible, fearsome times, we face a multitude of terrors and threats, and all good Americans should rally behind their leaders, who surely know what's best, and who would only mislead for the greater good.

Such solidarity at times of war has been the case throughout human history. Practically speaking, it makes great sense that people come and stick together to battle common foes. Yet a deeper, far more powerful force drives people during wars and other great cataclysms: the emotion of fear. To the extent that people feel frightened, they will tenaciously—desperately, foolishly—adhere to the status quo. Since the status quo forever trends toward increasing dominism, it follows that the more fearful a population, the more dominist its leadership and institutions.

Fear breeds dominism and dominism feeds fear. This simple equation impels the ancient and unending cycle of violence, the chronic impulse toward power-over aggression and force, and the pandemic of viral dominism. Obviously, the victims of aggression—the attacked, invaded, and abused, the underclass losers, the poor and oppressed—live in states of persistent fear, forever dreading the next violent act, worrying over the loss of what little they possess, and pathetically clinging to the sorry status quo that defines their lives. Yet even the winners in dominist culture lead lives marked and driven by chronic fears:

- The militarist fears the enemy, of course, the sneak attacks and sudden invasions, the unknown weapons, the undercover strategies and death-dealing tactics, the lethal threats to home and family, the unthinkable possibilities of destruction and defeat. Without a sufficiently fear-inspiring enemy, the whole rationale and purpose of militarism, along with flag-waving civilian support and bomb-building budgets, fades in relevance. America's fifty-year fear of Communism spawned the largest military in human history, at incalculable costs. As currently framed, America's fear of Islamic terrorism figures to last longer and cost much more.

- The unilateralist fears the loss of control that comes from connecting to and sharing power with others. Unilateralism casts a pall of dread and suspicion on the most innocent interactions and rejects the whole notion of trust. In a dominist world, each party seeks to elevate its own prospects while tearing down or impeding everyone else's. Rather than working at consensual processes that can resolve conflicts for the common good, the unilateralist forever promulgates, and thus reasonably fears, hidden agendas, underhanded maneuvers, and backstabbing deals.

- The monotheist fears damnation and punishment from the angry and jealous Father God. "You will have no others," He sternly proclaims, with eternal hellfire for those who disobey His commandments or misread His scriptures. Monotheism stresses the fear of God as a fundamental of faith. "You will fear," He commands, with the only respite to come in the afterlife, and only for those who have most earnestly feared God while alive.

- Sexism teaches us to fear any real or imagined encroachments upon or straying from culturally sanctioned gender roles. We fear men who seem too womanly and women who seem too manly. We fear the individual man or woman who gravitates toward activities or responsibilities that we deem "wrong" for his or her gender. We especially fear our own perceived shortcomings—the physical, mental, and emotional ways that we fail to measure up to the gender expectations of our culture.

- Xenophobes fear strangers, foreigners, and outsiders. Since their fear extends to any actions or behaviors that seem in any way strange, foreign, or outside status quo norms, xenophobes effectively fear everybody, including friends and family.

- The bottom-line materialist fears poverty and views choices, interactions, and events as either moving one toward or away from personal profit and increasing wealth. Any loss of money, for even the noblest reasons, triggers feelings of anxiety and fear.

- Competitors fear losing. The more competitive a culture, the more that everything gets turned into a contest with clear winners and losers, and the more that everybody fears possible failure. Even the most mundane and common issues—who has the biggest car, or the most expensive dress, or the cutest, smartest, strongest, or most talented child—become compelling reasons for chronic worry.

• The secretive fear getting caught, being found out, feeling exposed. Their lives turn in tightening spirals of deceptive tactics, leading to fears of exposure, leading to further deceptions and cover-ups, leading to increasing fears of exposure.

• Anti-environmentalists fear Nature, the whole wild and unbounded, feral and chaotic, messy and untamed realm of the non-human, the alien species, the ultimate Other. Moreover, they fear their essential connection to the natural world, a connection that begins with one's own body. The fear of Nature cloaks a deep, unconscious fear of Self, and spawns an array of anti-environmental actions—razing, poisoning, cutting, shooting, damming, demolishing, burning, flooding, caging, killing—which all turn out to be profoundly anti-human.

The dangerous logic of dominism presumes that all of these fears stem from inalterable aspects of the human condition. The whole world looms as a dark and threatening place, filled with nasty critters and even nastier people, all intent on causing harm. We deal with threats as a constant in our lives and only the strongest, the toughest, the most capable of fighting and most willing to win will survive. Attack or be attacked, kill or be killed, dominate or be dominated.

The creative logic of thinking peace agrees that life presents an unending series of threats and challenges and that we cannot avoid the difficult feelings of fear. We can, however, avoid the conditioned, habitual, unthinking reactions of the dominist. We can learn to experience fear as an awakening, as an opportunity to see things anew, to try something different, to take off in fresh directions. Fear can inflict a tightening knot of stress and tension or it can serve as the rushing energy of intelligent and capable response. Fear can drive us into nightmare realities of threats cascading into greater fears or it can open us into more creative power than we ever dreamed possible.

Throughout history, we have had three choices when facing fearful circumstances: to fight back against the source of the fear, to run from it, or to surrender to it. As we have seen, each of these options has had the identical outcome of spreading dominism and thus, in the long run, of spreading fear. In the opening years of this new millennium, a fourth choice has become viable: in the moment that we perceive threatening circumstances and feel the disturbing emotional energies of fear, we can awaken to the idea of acting peacefully, and then open to non-dominist answers to the problems at hand. First, we stop the reactive, fear-driven, war-think "solutions" of chronic dominism from taking over, then we peace-think our way to real solutions.

President Peacethink's response to 9/11 would have begun with an acknowledgement of the horrible injustice that had been inflicted upon innocent people and a pledge to bring the guilty parties to justice while working to make America safer from future attacks. Since virtually every nation stood by America in its grief, ready to act with America in its struggle against terrorism, the president would then have formed a genuine, multilateral, U.N.–sanctioned and –directed coalition of the willing. This coalition could have taken a nuanced, multidimensional, and internationally sensitive approach toward addressing the root causes of terrorist acts. A peace-think response to 9/11 could have ushered in a whole new era of international relations, could have birthed a true community of nations that celebrated their interdependence, that reveled in their diverse ways, and that worked together to resolve all conflicts for the greater good. It still can.

Connect and Conquer

The whole world is now having this critical and historic dialogue—listening to all kinds of points of view and positions about going to war or not going to war. In a huge global public conversation the world is asking: "Is war legitimate? Is it illegitimate? Is there enough evidence to warrant an attack?"

—Dr. Robert Muller[6]

With the advent of the Internet, modern peacemakers have been blessed with a most potent force for waging peace. I've already discussed its promise as a communications and organizational tool. The ability to spread news, information, and calls to action instantaneously to unlimited numbers of people worldwide has vastly improved the once-plodding process of group organization. Cyber-groups pulled together via online discussions and conversations have proven surprisingly strong, innovative, and resourceful. The democratic and decentralized structure of Web discourse and commerce, combined with its relative low cost, has (so far) kept it from being taken over and controlled by dominist elites.

Most profoundly, the Internet as a medium of connection. Though we may still harbor some doubts about the reality, viability, or wisdom of cyber-communities, Web-life should eventually be seen not as a threat to our more intimate, flesh-and-blood relationships, but as the perfect complement. The Internet connects people through their minds—thinker to thinker—regardless of distances in space or differences in nationality, race, religion, gender, or age. As access to the Internet spreads globally, like-thinking people can link up, communicate, share ideas, and work toward common goals. Age-old divisions fade in relevance for those who experience tangible, effective connection.

Scientists in a range of disciplines have been making this point for years: everything connects. Ecologists and biologists have shown that within any ecosystem every living thing connects to every other living thing and that altering or removing one part of such a system impacts the whole. Environmental medicine demonstrates that individual health intrinsically relates to the social and environmental conditions one lives in. Physicists talk about the connections between the observer and the observed, between subjective and objective realities, and between any two related objects, no matter how far removed. According to most economists, we should no longer think of separate nations with their insular economies, but of one global economy that ties all nations together. Climatologists similarly speak of a global climate that people everywhere affect through their choices and actions, an idea that resonates with chaos theorists who imagine that the flutter of a butterfly's wings can cause high winds halfway round the world.

In the 20th century, this notion that everything connects came concretely into form through a series of technological advances. Invisible radio waves beamed out across entire continents, bringing sounds and voices simultaneously into millions of homes, linking huge populations through shared experiences. The visuals of television made the links even stronger, and allowed for the first media-mediated events, such as the funeral of John F. Kennedy, or the Watergate hearings, when whole nations sat down together, to watch and feel and think in common. Telecommunications have made it possible for people to easily connect from most any two spots on the planet, while modern transportation systems easily and rapidly enable us to come together physically.

Everything connects, and as we accept, understand, and embody that message, our experience of connectedness grows stronger and more vital, and our lives improve in myriad ways. The "power-with" that comes from people acting in concert not only feels better than the "power-over" of dominist reality, it works better. When we commit time, money, and energy to creating rather than destroying, to celebrating rather than resenting differences, to cooperating rather than competing, to sharing openly rather than hoarding in privacy, to practicing love rather spreading fear, then we tap into heretofore unsuspected resources and our whole world turns in positive directions.

For most of human history it has been difficult to overcome the divisiveness of dominism in any meaningful, lasting way. True, as our oldest and most-remembered songs and stories attest, individual men and women have always had the experience of discovering love and of joining the ancient dance of sexual communion, thus tasting the joy of connection and spreading it through their immediate and extended families. Yet, as the songs and stories also attest, love often ends badly, sex can cause more trouble than pleasure, and families typically spread more dominist angst than loving connection. For as long as dominism has been on the ascendant, the creative power of human connection has been fragile, fleeting, and painfully, paradoxically private.

In the opening years of the new millennium, the peace-thinking forces of connection have been graced with new tools and charged with a visceral sense of urgency. If we do not overcome the divisive war-think of dominist culture, then we can expect to reap the terrible winds of global war and environmental apocalypse. The military-industrial engines of destruction have grown too massive, too lethal, and too brutally efficient to abide any longer. We can come together as one people—bound by common threats and united by common responses, challenged by common problems and committed toward common solutions—or we can perish separately, divided, alone, and afraid.

Every conflict we encounter in life challenges us with the same set of choices: will we contract fearfully into ourselves, casting Others as cutthroat competitors and evil ones, or will we reach out through our imagined boundaries, connecting and cooperating and practicing love? Do we struggle on as separate entities, never strong enough, secure enough, or rich enough, or do we discover the strength, security, and wealth that grow in genuine partnerships? Do we continue on with the ancient conflict-exacerbating strategy of "divide and conquer" or do we come onto common ground, affirm our common interests, and insist on resolving all conflicts for the common good?

Talking Peace

To suggest that war can prevent war is a base play on words and a despicable form of warmongering. The objective of any who sincerely believe in peace clearly must be to exhaust every honorable recourse in the effort to save the peace. The world has had ample evidence that war begets only conditions that beget further war.

—**Ralph Bunche**[7]

We're interconnected. We're interdependent. If they're miserable, unhappy, jealous, misguided, they're going to hurt you. So you go and you change that. And you do it with money and investment and understanding. Is it expensive? Of course it is! But not as expensive as a war.

—**Mario Cuomo**[8]

While we can never stop people from having conflicts, we can learn to resolve all difficulties, from the personal to the political, with nonviolent, respectful, empathetic, compassionate communication. Even the Internet, for all its linking and connecting, does little good if it only spreads flaming attacks and spamming hatred. The manner of our communication—the words we use, the ideas conveyed, and the feelings expressed—determines the positive or negative direction of any outcome. When two or more parties cannot sustain meaningful communication in the midst of conflict they have no hope for peaceful resolution. To the contrary, the failure to communicate guarantees worsening relationships and intensifying conflicts.

To the dominist mindset, the mere suggestion of effective nonviolent communication can seem but a weak and irresponsible fantasy. Nonetheless, the desire for peaceful conflict resolution runs deep in the human spirit, as does the ability to communicate without aggression or force. At all levels of society and in a wide range of professions we find certain individuals who have a knack for gently guiding people through difficult physical, mental, and emotional problems. The art of peaceful conflict resolution flows from a set of long-practiced and refined communication skills easily learned by those ready and willing to leave the war-think of dominist culture behind. Ultimately, it all comes down to four key elements: careful listening, respectful speech, empathy, and compassion.

****

Good communication rests on a foundation of careful, conscientious listening. We will never understand others unless we have paid close attention to their words, listening without prejudging, without thoughtless reaction, and without rehearsing our replies while they continue speaking. In order for real communication to happen, we must stay open to whatever others say while they likewise remain open to our message.

Yet "staying open" does not mean being inert, disinterested, or passively receptive. Good listening requires an active intention to connect, to hear the feelings coming through the words, and to get all the way to the heart of the matter—the unaddressed needs that drive any conflict. We have to purposefully work at careful listening, even with our most intimate friends and family, and all the more so with enemies and adversaries.

So much of what we think of as communication fails the careful listening test. While one person speaks, the other carries on an internal monologue, thoughts spinning busily away, disagreeing with this and criticizing that, practicing rejoinders and replies, never actually hearing what's being said. When both parties carry on a conversation in this way, little information ever gets conveyed. We may think we have talked things through, when in fact we have only spewed noise at one another, strengthening our pre-existing opinions in the process.

Really listening to someone, or to an opposing viewpoint, requires that we suspend our own thoughts and opinions long enough to hear another's voice. We cultivate an inner quiet so that we can receive and, hopefully, understand the thoughts and opinions of others. Only when all parties listen in this way can the genuine communication of nonviolent conflict resolution happen.

****

Yet, careful listening will accomplish little if one only hears a litany of insults, complaints, and accusations. All parties in a conflict must agree on a baseline of common, mutual respect and must strive to sustain and express such respect throughout their communications. Despite whatever bad blood, terrible history, and awful incriminations may fester in a relationship, if we truly want peace, we must commit to treating our adversaries with real respect.

Negotiations that begin with disrespectful name-calling go nowhere. George Bush publicly branded entire nations as evil, called Saddam Hussein a despicable tyrant and Kim Il Jung a pygmy who starved his own people, and declared anyone who disagreed with Bush-think a traitor, a terrorist, or worse. Bush seemed most animated and, to his followers, most presidential when pronouncing his lack of respect for some other nation and its leadership, pronouncements always peppered with chest-thumping braggadocio about America's superiority in all things. Despite his claims to be "a uniter, not a divider," his propensity for disrespectful language drove wedges between peoples and caused every conflict he intervened in to worsen.

By contrast, in his years as a global peacemaker Jimmy Carter has demonstrated time and again that the opening stage of any negotiation entails pronouncements and displays of respect. When he traveled to North Korea on behalf of the Clinton administration, Carter showed an easy acceptance of Kim Il Sung's sobriquet of "Great Leader" and made clear to Sung and the North Korean people that this was a high state meeting of major significance. Though Carter's diplomacy incensed dominists and led to the usual accusations of weakness and appeasement, it in fact requires formidable inner strength and courage to extend respect to your adversaries, while nothing could be easier, and weaker, than flinging barroom insults and schoolyard taunts. In the end, Carter's approach led to the Agreed Framework of 1994, a working if imperfect resolution that had North and South Korea moving toward rapprochement, until Bush came into office.

With practice, we find that it costs us nothing to withhold disrespectful language when dealing with adversarial relationships. We can still make clear behavioral boundaries—"If you do this, then, respectfully, I will have to do that." We can still, indeed should, express our disagreements with past actions, as well as share our concerns about gathering threats, while avoiding any I-don't-care-what-you-think ultimatums. Respectful speech should not dither or evade or come across as cowed, vague, inscrutable, or overly nuanced. On the contrary, we show the utmost respect by striving to express ourselves directly, honestly, and forthrightly, yet without rancor, bile, insolence, insult, hate, aggression, or force.

If we will simply apply the Golden Rule to communication—speak to others as you would be spoken to—then all of our relationships, however conflicted or estranged they've become, can turn in more positive directions. Like the passing of a peace pipe, or the exchanging of gifts, respectful speech brings people closer, fosters connections, and engenders a spirit of peaceful reconciliation. We can talk anything through if we commit ourselves to careful listening and respectful speaking.

****

The dictionary defines "empathy" as "the action of understanding, being aware of, being sensitive to, and vicariously experiencing the feelings, thoughts, and experience of another of either the past or present without having the feelings, thoughts, and experience fully communicated in an objectively explicit manner." To have empathy for another, then, means that we comprehend intimate information through a subtle, nonverbal, unwritten manner of communication. We are empathic when we can sense another's thoughts and feelings with enough clarity to obtain an understanding of their actions, needs, and desires.

Our capacity for empathy naturally manifests as a function of our connectedness. From the technological connections of the Internet and telecommunications to such softer connections as sharing common interests, living together, talking, touching, dancing, and having sex, the experience of feeling connected leads directly to an enhancement of empathy. The closer and more connected we feel to others, the more means and opportunities we have for exchanging critical information, and the more empathic we become.

When we lose the experience of connectedness, our capacity for empathy declines. To the extent that disconnection prevails throughout both the personal and political spheres of American culture, we have become a tragically antipathetic people. From a widespread lack of empathy comes much of the disrespect that riddles our daily communications, and the inability to appreciate the special needs and difficulties of the underclass and various outgroups. It fosters the tortured rationales of the militarist, the unilateralist, the xenophobe, the monotheist, and the sexist, as well as the flailing incompetence of our international relations. When people have no feeling for what's going on in the lives of others—worse, when people do not even want such feelings—they consign themselves to private little hells of failed relationship.

In reaction to the outrages of 9/11, most Americans felt fully justified in the invasions of Afghanistan, Iraq, and any other country that might harbor terrorists. Many condoned the imprisonment, torture, or assassination of anyone with possible links to Islamic terrorism and agreed with the governement's insistence that the whole world support us in such actions. Even those who lived thousands of miles away from ground zero and knew none of the people killed in the terrorist attacks still felt righteously compelled to answer violence with even greater violence and treated all pleas for nonviolent reconciliation as unpatriotic and anti-American. We had been grievously injured and, though some innocents would surely suffer, we had to answer with more grievous injury.

Their utter lack of empathy caused most Americans to miss the simple fact: the perpetrators of 9/11 had lived through experiences every bit as terrible and terrorizing as those they inflicted on America. Their countries had been invaded, their homelands bombed, their relations murdered, their people humiliated, and they felt justified in their rage, aggression, and violent force, even if innocents had to die. Their cause was every bit as just as our cause. More importantly, every bomb we unleashed in our war against terror would have precisely the same effect on those we bombed as did the exploding airplanes of 9/11.

Feeling empathy for others does not necessarily mean that we agree with their actions, that we like what they have done, or that we must in any way change ourselves in response to their demands. Feeling empathy *does* help us to understand why others act the way they do and to see that, all things being equal, we may have acted in much the same way. From this simple recognition of common ground and common humanity comes a greatly enhanced capacity for effective communication.

****

"Why do they hate us so?" It was the question everyone asked in the wake of terror. How could those Islamic radicals, those foreign devils, those wretched others hate us so much? Bush America answered: They hate us because of our freedom. They covet our success, our wealth; they envy our power and greatness. They hate us enough to lash out in the most horrific ways, destroying thousands of innocent lives, because we stand as the global paragon of the good, so wonderfully good that we bestir their vile, incipient evil.

Well. It was an answer that ignored history, denied geopolitical issues and forces, and neatly elided any responsibility for prior American actions. Bush America flatly avoided all notions of cause and effect—it was simply unthinkable that the terrorists may have inflicted suffering on us because we inflicted suffering on them, that their hatred for us only mirrored the undisguised loathing too many Americans, and especially those in power, had for the people of the Middle East and the religion of Islam. Most Americans never grasped the most obvious answer: they hate us because so many of us hate them.

A much better question to have asked on September 12, 2001 would have been: What were the unaddressed needs of the terrorists? What injuries and privations had they experienced, so dire and so long ignored, that could drive them to such deplorable depths? Not, why did they treat us so demonically, but, what inner demons, born in desperation and need, caused them to act as they did?

I can already hear the objections: What pansy questions! Who cares what such miscreants were thinking or feeling? Who gives a fig about their decrepit little lives? Evil is as evil does, and the evildoers of 9/11 need to be stamped out, not understood, but destroyed with an unambiguous ferocity that will dissuade any wanna-be terrorists before they ever get started on their evil ways.

This defines the moment of truth in all our conflicts, personal and political, petty and profound: either we feel a pressing concern for the unmet needs that motivate all parties in a conflict or we reject any concerns whatsoever for the feelings and opinions of others. We either care, with urgent persistence, or we could not care less. We either feel compassion for everyone caught up in the pain and suffering of human conflict, or we restrict any such feelings to ourselves and our own, if indeed we feel at all.

Compassion combines a sympathetic awareness of others' distress with a compelling desire to provide aid and assistance. We feel another's pain and we feel obliged to help alleviate it. When we approach a conflict in the spirit of compassion, we look especially for the unanswered needs that underlie and propel human aggression, force, and violence. We realize that people in desperate need invariably resort to desperate measures, that all of the dominist aggression, force, and violence in our world stems from desperation born out of prior injustices left unresolved. Compassion lays bare the dangerous logic of dominism in all its many guises—we see the twisted motivations of the militarist, the unilateralist, the monotheist, we feel the aching needs of the sexist, the xenophobe, the bottom-line materialist, we sense the unresolved complaints driving our cutthroat competitions, our secrecy mongering, and our assaults on the environment.

Compassion opens us to a more positive and inspiring human story. To the extent that we nurture our innate capacity for compassion, we look to and mostly see the basic good in all people. Compassion reveals others at their best, while rendering their lesser qualities and worst behaviors both understandable and transformable. Compassion lifts us from the hurt-hurt, lose-lose damnable logic of war-think into the win-win, conflict-resolving blessing of peace-think.

When even one individual chooses to listen carefully, to speak respectfully, to reach out empathically, and to extend the olive branch of compassionate concern to the "enemy," then the potent seeds of a profound planetary shift have been planted. Each of us, in every moment of our lives, and especially in times of conflict, faces the same choice: to tighten and contract into the militant, distrustful, denial-dumb apartheid of dominism or to open ourselves to an omnipotent compassion that can truly heal all wounds, resolve all conflicts, and end all wars.

The Parable Resolved

We see the future in our mind's heart and we take the small next step that will enable us to get there together. This is the activity of radical hope.

—Deena Metzger[9]

Imagine a group of tribes living within reach of one another. If all choose the way of peace, then all may live in peace. But what if all but one chooses peace...?

For most of human history the answer to this conundrum has been written in blood and gore, in battle upon battle and war after war, in unrelenting violence that has spread like the most god-awful plague, invading the unprotected, murdering the innocent, and forcing survivors to become violent themselves and to pass the ways of violence, aggression, and force on to their young. Early on it became clear that continuing to choose peace in such circumstances was a recipe for certain disaster, heartache and failure, dissolution and death. And so it happened that viral dominism overcame humanity, propagating from each act of violence, person to person, culture to culture, until all had been touched, changed, conditioned to dominist thoughts, beliefs, and misperceptions, the dangerous logic of dominism insinuating so deeply into the marrow of men and women as to become human nature.

For all the advances of civilization, the 20th century only intensified the terrorizing grip of viral dominism. Militarism ran rampant, merciless and unremitting, with hundreds of millions killed in war without end, while the weapons and tactics of mass slaughter grew ever more deadly. As the Parable predicts, this pandemic of expanding terror only brought more power and influence to dominist elites and their war-think ways—every bullet fired, landmine planted, bomb exploded, and rocket launched made the military-corporate-security-state that much stronger, wealthier, and politically entrenched. Moreover, modern culture continued the millennia-old glorification of dominist elites, of conquering kings and duty-bound soldiers, of those who have the most money and land, of men who have had the most women, of religions that have the most followers, of nations that have the most deadly weapons.

Naturally, advocates for peace have fared poorly in such a world. Though Jesus sang "blessed are the peacemakers," he himself was murdered young, and the history of peacemaking has been a tale of frustration and futility and too many martyrs, their hope-filled lives crushed beneath dominist wars on everything. If remembered at all, their messages get perverted toward dominist ends—think of all the battles fought in Jesus' name—or we treat them with condescending pity, scorn them for their weakness and appeasement.

During the run-up to Bush's invasion of Iraq many religious leaders spoke out against what they perceived—rightly—as an unnecessary and unjust war. They pleaded for peace in the Lord's name, quoted scripture and appealed to goodness, reason, and compassion, all to no avail. Bush America turned a deaf ear to any thoughts of nonviolent reconciliation, along with any worries over the spiritual ramifications of slaughtered innocents. When pressed to square the coming war with Christian values, they'd stubbornly invoke "an eye for an eye," with little recognition of the Old Testament origins of that blood-soaked maxim, or that Jesus had staked his life on a radical turning from all such war-think ways.

Still, despite the depressing history of human violence, the continuing horrors of the moment, and the threats of terror yet to come, I see more cause for hope than despair. In the past three chapters, I have listed reasons: the wide-spread realization of the obsolescence and futility of militarism, as evidenced in the near-universal revulsion toward the invasion of Iraq and its ugly aftermath; our growing understanding of the power of conscious awareness and the whole process of "waking up," as individuals and as institutions; the ascent of the Internet as an independent, inexpensive, democratic, anti-corporate media; the myriad ways in which people can now experience meaningful connection; and the continuing refinement of the basic tools of compassionate communication and nonviolent conflict resolution. Woven together, these changes point to a much fabled transformation.

Yet, one essential step remains: the most powerfully dominant must willingly share power with those they have dominated. This shift, this ultimate shaking off of our habits of chronic dominism, cannot come about through any threats or acts of violence. For all the inspiration gained when the oppressed force open the prison gates, cast aside their chains, and overthrow overclass tyrants, to the extent that such revolutions resort to coercive force and violence, they sadly perpetuate dominism. We only avoid the contagion of viral dominism by pursuing change in purely non-dominist ways. Thus, the definitive transformation of the most powerfully dominant in any relationship—the final revolution—must come from within the individuals and institutions themselves.

Just as Jesus counseled that we "turn the other cheek," so the peacemaker must remain resolute in the ways of nonviolent reconciliation until the dominist chooses peace over violence. Just as Gandhi taught, "we must be the change we want to see in the world," so the peacemaker must commit to thinking, living, and keeping the peace until others become peaceful of their own accord. Much as we might feel compelled to, we must not aggressively coerce or violently force even the most egregious thugs to give up their dominist ways. We cannot fight dominism with dominism, counter oppression with oppression, or eliminate violence through violent means.

We *can* speak truth to power—loud, clear, sane, ineluctable, and incessant truth—we can calmly recite it before parliaments and legislatures, preach it in churches, synagogues, and mosques, and say it in newspapers and magazines, and again in Internet blogs, forums, and chatrooms, and on the television, and on the radio, and again in coffeehouses, meeting halls, and public squares. We can become beacons of honest relationship and fair dealings. We can commit ourselves to peaceful living: laying down our weapons, seeking partnership, building consensus, celebrating diversity, sharing the wealth, cooperating for the greater good, and coming into meaningful connection with Nature.

And what if all but one chooses peace? As long as the world remains a dangerous place, we can learn from early

America: together we stand, divided we fall. We can link ourselves, individuals and nations, arm and arm, and armory with armory, a positive front against all bullies, rogues, and malcontents. We will build, eventually, a world so just and fair as to produce no more terrorists, nor tyrants, nor invading tribes. On our way to such a world, we can stop violent aggressors with major, multilateral peacemaking armies using the minimal force of a rational defense, thereby mitigating the potential contagion of viral dominism. Similarly, at the local level, we can sustain community-based, people-friendly policing, strong enough to stop violent crimes in progress, wise enough to prevent most such crimes from ever happening.

As we commit to this work of active, robust, heroic peacemaking, a seismic shift will occur throughout dominist culture. Five-star generals will take up the cause of disarmament and international peacekeeping. Unilateralists will seek out vital alliances based on consensual decision-making. Monotheists will open to the possibility of other gods, and other ways. Men and women will declare gender peace and discover the joys of living in balanced partnership. Ancient habits of racism, nationalism, homophobia, and ethnic hate will dissolve before the irresistible pulse of human differences merging, blending, and synergizing. The wealthy will understand the wisdom of investing in communities that amply and fairly meet everyone's basic needs. Cooperation will supplant competition as the national ethos and core economic precept. The cult of secrecy will give way to a culture based on openness and trust. Humans will at last become true stewards of the Earth, affirming vital connection with all creatures, engaging in healthy, sustainable development, and making loving care of the environment—humanaturalism—the organizing principle of the 21st century.

As the most dominant nation in history and the most dominant force in current affairs, America now has the power to make all of this happen. When the political and corporate leaders of American society choose—freely, willingly, gladly—to forswear dominist principles and practices, giving up their private gains and pyrrhic victories in favor of inclusive, win-win, compassionate values, then the whole nation will rise out of the prisoner's sleep, shake off the shackles of denial and deceit, and gratefully take up the suddenly simple task of living, connected, in peace.

When America models *that* to the rest of world—offers active peacemaking as the final blossom of the American century, the core value of America's exceptionalism, and the universally-shared destiny America would manifest—then the nation fulfills its awesome promise and ushers in a world where all are treated as equals, where life and liberty flourish, and peace is the common currency of all our relations.

Notes

Chapter One

1. Howard Zinn, *The Future of Nonviolence* (2002, Boston: Beacon Press), p. 126.
2. Helen Knode, *The School for Violence*, LA Weekly, (October 9, 2001).
3. Andrew Bard Schmookler, *The Parable of the Tribes* (1984, Berkeley: U of Cal press), p. 21.
4. ibid, 20.
5. ibid, 21.
6. ibid, 22.
7. ibid, 266.
8. Robert Wright, *A Real War on Terrorism* (Sept. 13, 2002), Slate, http://www.slate.com/id/2070210/
9. John Robbins, Terror, *Love and The State of the World*, (November 1, 01), Common Dreams, http://www.commondreams.org/views01/1101-01.htm

Chapter Two

1. Donald Rumsfeld, from a press conference, (September 18, 2001), Badger Herald, http://badgerherald.com/news/2001/09/18/bush_thanks_american.php
2. Lee Griffith, *The War on Terrorism and the Terror of God*, (2002, Eerdmans: Grand Rapids), p. 7.
3. Wendell Berry, *The Failure of War*, (December 8, 2001), Common Dreams, http://www.commondreams.org/views01/1207-01.htm
4. Noam Chomsky, *American Terrorism and the Role of Intellectuals*, (January 16, 2002), Salon, http://www.chomsky.info/interviews/20020116.htm
5. Ann Coulter, *This Is War*, (September 12, 2001), anncoulter.org, http://www.anncoulter.org/columns/2001/091301.html
6. Sonia Johnson, *Wildfire*, (1989, Albuquerque, NM: Wildfire Books), p. 18.
7. Sam Keen, *Faces of the Enemy*, New Age Journal, (March 1991), p. 47.
8. Bill Moyers, *Which America Will We Be Now?*, (November 19, 2001), The Nation, http://www.thenation.com/doc/20011119/moyers
9. Alan Greenspan, testimony before the Committee on Financial Services, U.S. House of Representatives, on July 17, 2002, http://www.federalreserve.gov/boarddocs/hh/2002/july/testimony.htm
10. George Orwell, *Such, Such Were the Joys*, (May 1947), Netcharles, http://www.netcharles.com/orwell/essays/suchwerethejoys.htm
11. Bertrand Russell, *The Conquest of Happiness*, (1958, Bantam Books: NY), p.53.
12. Jules Henry, *Culture Against Man*, (1965, Mcgraw-Hill: Texas).

13. For a comprehensive compilation of research documenting the issues with competition, see: Alfie Kohn, *No Contest: The Case Against Competition*, (1986, Boston: Houghton Mifflin).

14. James Madison, speech, Virginia Convention, 1788.

15. Daniel Ellsberg, *The Salon Interview: Daniel Ellsberg*, (Nov. 19, 2002), Salon, http://dir.salon.com/story/news/feature/2002/11/19/ellsberg/index.html

16. Rachel Carson, *Silent Spring*, quoted in Theodore Roszak, *Person/Planet* (1979, New York: Anchor Books), p. 317.

17. David C. Korten, *When Corporations Rule the World*, (1995, Berrett-Koehler Publishers), p. 261.

Chapter Three

1. Wendell Berry, *The Failure of War*, (Winter 2001/2002), YES! Magazine, http://www.commondreams.org/views01/1207-01.htm

2. George Leonard, *The Transformation*, (1972, Los Angeles: J.P. Tarcher), p. 158.

3. See: *The Power of Emotion*, (2002, Rochester: Bear & Co.); *Breathing*, (1990, Santa Fe:Bear & Co.), and *Dancing With the Fire* (1989, Santa Fe: Bear & Co.).

4. William Irwin Thompson, *The Time Falling Bodies Take to Light*, (1981, New York: St. Martin's Press), p. 155.

5. Dorothy Dinnerstein, *The Mermaid and the Minotaur*, (1977, NY: Harper & Row), p. 160.

6. Alice Miller, *For Your Own Good*, (1984, Toronto: Collins Publishers), p. 58.

7. ibid, p. 17.

8. ibid, p. 7.

9. ibid, p. 16.

10. ibid, *Mein Kampf*, quoted in Miller, p. 243.

11. ibid, p. 284.

12. Carol Lee Flinders, *The Values of Belonging*, (2002, San Francisco: Harper), p. 80.

Chapter Four

1. Two German citizens reflect on the rise if Nazism. "*The Holocaust*," a Series on *The History Channel*.

2. Dan Rather, *CBS News*, (September 18, 2001).

3. Paul Krugman, *In media res*, New York Times, (November 29, 2002).

4. John Bradshaw, *The Family*, (1988, HCI), p. 78.

5. Paul Krugman, *The Bully's Pulpit*, New York Times, (November 6, 2002).

6. Alice Miller, p 16.

7. Brian Swimme, "*How to Heal a Lobotomy*", from *Reweaving the World*, ed

Irene Diamond and Gloria Orenstein, (1990, Sierra Club Books), p. 15.

8. Geov Parrish, *War and Health*, Working For Change, (January 10, 2003), http://www.workingforchange.com/article.cfm?ItemID=14344

9. Upton Sinclair, *I, Candidate for Governor: And How I Got Licked*, (1994, University of California Press, New Ed).

Chapter Five

1. J. William Fulbright, *The Arrogance of Power*, (1967, Random House).

2. Maureen Dowd, *Coup De Crawford*, New York Times, (August 21, 2002).

3. *The National Security Strategy of the United States of America*, The White House, (September 17, 2002), http://www.whitehouse.gov/nsc/nss.html

4. Howard Zinn, *Failure to Quit: Reflections of an Optimistic Historian*, (2002, Boston: South End Press; New edition), p. 45.

5. Geov Parrish, *Operation Enduring Republicans*, Working For Change, (November 8, 2002), http://www.workingforchange.com/article.cfm?itemid=14045&CFID=3501545&CFTOKEN=2273005

6. Alexis de Tocqueville, *Democracy in America*, I, Chapter XVI, (1961, New York: Knopf-Vintage).

7. U.S. President Abraham Lincoln, (letter to Col. William F. Elkins), (November 21, 1864), Ref: *The Lincoln Encyclopedia*, Archer H. Shaw, (1950, NY: Macmillan), http://www.ratical.org/corporations/Lincoln.txt

Chapter Six

1. Jeanne d'Orleans, *Politics and Poetry*, Body and Soul, (June 03, 2004), http://bodyandsoul.typepad.com/blog/2004/06/politics_and_po.html

2. Robert Alberti, *Fight Terrorism With Relentless Doses of Hope and Compassion*, Minneapolis Star Tribune, (September 29, 2001), http://www.commondreams.org/views01/0929-05.htm

3. Susan Sontag, *Real battles and empty metaphors*, New York Times, (September 10, 2002).

4. Larry Dossey, *Space, Time & Medicine* (1982, Boulder: Shambhala), p. 222.

5. For a thorough deconstruction of cancer war statistics, see: Samuel S. Epstein, M.D., Cancer-Gate: *How to Win the Losing Cancer War*, (2005, Baywood Publishing Company); Guy B. Faguet, *The War on Cancer: An Anatomy of Failure, a Blueprint for the Future*, (2006, Springer); and, Ralph W. Moss, *The Cancer Industry*, (1996, Equinox Press).

6. Alberti.

7. Christopher Fry, *A Sleep of Prisoners*, 1951.

8. Niro Markoff Asistent, *Why I Survive AIDS*, (1991, New York: Simon and Shuster), p. 75.

9. Ibid, p. 5.

10. Ibid, p. 24.
11. Two current resources for the issues of longterm AIDS survivors: http://www.thebody.com/cdc/news_updates_archive/mar20_02/psychology_aids.html and http://www.healtoronto.com/survivors.html
12. Todd Gitlin, *From Put-Down to Catch-Up*, The American Prospect vol. 14 no. 3, (March 1, 2003).
13. Thomas Jefferson, Letter to James Madison, (December 20, 1787). *The Writings of Thomas Jefferson*. Ed. H.A. Washington. Vol. II., (1853, Washington, DC: Taylor & Maury), p. 327-333.

Chapter Seven

1. Thom Hartmann, *Blood, Oil, and Tears*, CommonDreams, (September 4, 2003), http://www.commondreams.org/views03/0904-11.htm
2. Bill Clinton, *Clinton Blasts US Approach to International Affairs*, Agence France Presse, (April 16, 2003), http://www.commondreams.org/headlines03/0416-01.htm
3. Marion Winik, *A Sorrowful Certainty That The Worst Is Yet To Come*, Philadelphia Inquirer, (October 8, 2001).
4. Tom Paine, *Common Sense*, (1776, Philadelphia: W. & T. Bradford).
5. Deena Metzer, *Becoming Peacemakers*, CounterPunch, (December 31, 2002), http://www.counterpunch.org/metzger1231.html
6. Sean Driscoll, *Letters*, Salon, (November 28, 2002), http://archive.salon.com/news/letters/2002/11/28/sullivanletters/print.html
7. Bill Clinton, *The path to peace*, Salon, (September 10, 2002), http://dir.salon.com/story/news/feature/2002/09/10/clinton/index.html
8. Malcolm X, as quoted in Wendell Berry, *The Hidden Wound*, (1989, San Francisco: North Point Press) p. 1.
9. George Leonard, *The Transformation*, (1972, Los Angeles: J.P. Tarcher), p. 197.
10. Bill Gates, Sr., *Now with Bill Moyers*, (January 17, 2003), http://www.pbs.org/now/transcript/transcript_inheritance.html
11. Alfons J. Beitzinger, Edward G. Ryan: *Lion Of The Law*, (1960, Madison: The State Historical Society of Wisconsin), p. 115-116. From an 1873 address to the graduating class of the University of Wisconsin Law School.
12. *The National Security Strategy of the United States of America*, The White House, (September 17, 2002), http://www.whitehouse.gov/nsc/nss.html
13. Joanna Macy, *World As Lover, World As Self*, (1991, Berkeley: Parallax Press), p. 220-221.

Chapter Eight

1. Martin Luther King, *Letter from Birmingham Jail*, (April 16, 1963), http://www.nobelprizes.com/nobel/peace/MLK-jail.html
2. Jean Houston, from a mass email, (September 18th 2001), JeanHouston.org

3. Dr. Robert Muller, *The Vital Role of the UN in Preserving Planet Earth*, from a speech before the United Nations Association of San Francisco, (February 5, 2003). Dr Muller's words were transcribed in her own words by Lynne Twist. http://www.ratical.org/co-globalize/MullerInSF.txt

4. Doris "Granny D" Haddock, *Will We Represent Love in the World?*, (January 25, 2003), from her 93rd birthday speech, http://www.grannyd.com/speeches.php?id=16&action=list

5. Abraham Lincoln, from the Annual Message to Congress, *The Collected Works of Abraham Lincoln*, ed. by Roy P. Basler, (1953, Abraham Lincoln Association).

6. Dr. Robert Muller.

7. Ralph Bunche, *Some Reflections on Peace in Our Time*, upon receiving the Nobel Peace Prize, (December 11, 1950), http://nobelprize.org/nobel_prizes/peace/laureates/1950/bunche-lecture.html

8. Mario Cuomo, *Three questions on Iraq*, Salon, (February 10, 2003), http://dir.salon.com/story/news/feature/2003/02/10/cuomo/?pn=2

9. Deena Metzer, *Becoming Peacemakers*, CounterPunch, (December 31, 2002), http://www.counterpunch.org/metzger1231.html

About the Author

Michael Sky is the author of *Breathing* (Bear & Co, 1990) and *The Power of Emotion* (Bear & Co, 2002), two books that offer practical, proven methods for becoming more peaceful individuals. His first book, *Dancing With the Fire* (Bear & Co, 1989), is an in-depth exploration of the practice of firewalking.

Michael is also a computer consultant and web designer and is the creator and editor of **thinkingpeace.com**, **breathinglessons.net** and **macworks.info**.

He lives with his wife and daughter on a small green island in the Pacific Northwest.

He can be reached at sky@thinkingpeace.com